THE
SELF-SUFFICIENCY
BIBLE

In 2000 Simon Dawson and his wife, Debbie, took a major risk – they sold their flat in London and moved with a horse and Great Dane to the heart of the countryside. Scraping together every penny, they bought 8 hectares (20 acres) of land on Exmoor and built a smallholding, where they now enjoy a self-sustaining, virtually self-sufficient life, growing their own fruit and vegetables. They have an extended family of 50 pigs, almost 100 chickens, a dozen sheep and lambs and a handful of ducks, geese and turkeys.

Simon Dawson is a blogger and regular contributor to regional press and radio, including a weekly column in *The North Devon Journal*. He has cooked on the Good Food Channel for celebrity chefs Gary Rhodes and Michael Caines, and in 2008 he and Debbie became champions for the South West in Gary Rhodes' 'Local Food Hero' campaign. They have also appeared on BBC One's *Countryfile*. Simon and Debbie teach courses on self-sufficiency, smallholding and basic butchery.

THE
SELF-SUFFICIENCY
BIBLE

From Window Boxes to Smallholdings —
Hundreds of Ways to Become Self-Sufficient

SIMON DAWSON

WATKINS
Sharing Wisdom Since 1893

This edition published in the UK 2013 by
Watkins, an imprint of Watkins Media Limited
Unit 11, Shepperton House,
83-89 Shepperton Road
London N1 3DF

enquiries@watkinspublishing.com

3 5 7 9 10 8 6 4

Designed and typeset by Paul Saunders

Printed in Great Britain by T J International Ltd

A CIP record for this book is available from the British Library

ISBN: 978-1-78028-541-2

www.watkinspublishing.com

MIX
Paper from
responsible sources
FSC® C013056

This book creates the same feeling that we all enjoy when our first course arrives at the table. Page after page, as course after course, new flavours are experienced, excitement grows and a true enthusiasm and dedication develops. The book captures Simon and Debbie's passion for food, and the land it comes from, so by the last page I feel hungrier than ever!

Gary Rhodes, OBE

Simon's quest for self-sufficiency might not save the planet, but in a world obsessed by innovation and technology, he's discovered that our path to salvation is rooted in the simplicity of the past.

David Kennard, author of *A Shepherd's Watch* and Channel 4's *Mist: Sheepdog Tales* series

I've watched Simon and Debbie's progress with great interest over the past few years and through my involvement with Local Food Heroes. I just love the philosophy which they bring to Hidden Valley Pigs and now through this wonderful book, which is all about great, local food and its relationship with the land. Artisan food producers really do create wonderful foods for all to cook with and enjoy. Within this book you will find stories of such producers here in North Devon.

Michael Caines, MBE, two-star Michelin chef

The proof is in the pudding, and I can testify that Simon's bacon is delicious. Therefore he is clearly doing something right!

Tom Hodgkinson, *Sunday Telegraph*

A treasure-trove of brilliant ideas and easy-to-follow step-by-step instructions.

Adam Henson, BBC One's *Countryfile*

Self-sufficiency is all about having a go and creating whatever you need from whatever you have to hand, be that a homemade smoker to smoke the perfect salmon, or a polytunnel in which to grow the perfect tomato. It's clear Simon has actually 'been there and done that' so this book is essential reading if you are planning your idyllic future or actually living it now.

Dick Strawbridge, author of *It's Not Easy Being Green* and *Self Sufficiency for the 21st Century*

To Debbie

Contents

List of Illustrations

Acknowledgements

A book such as this cannot be written alone, and lots of people helped along the way with ideas and advice. The most important is my wife, Debbie, without whom this book would never have been possible. Thanks also need to go Paula Bishenden, Eileen Bowen, Alison Homer and Robert Crocumbe for all things bovine, and to Derek and Debs Jones for advice on fishing and gluten-free foods. A tower of thanks goes to my agent Jane Graham Maw www.grahammawchristie.com, and to Michael Mann and everyone at Watkins Publishing, who have been brilliant. Finally, and possibly most important of all, heartfelt thanks go to my friends the animals: Darcy and Dex, my dogs; Kylie, the matriarch sow; The General Lee, our boar; the pigs, geese, ducks, chickens, turkeys, sheep, horses and all the rest of the gang, on whom we practised our craft and learnt so much.

Foreword

It was New Year's Eve, and we had been invited to a party in a pub in Devon. We were packed shoulder to shoulder with farmers and outdoor types, the carpet sticky with spilt beer and crunchy with peanuts. Next to me Debbie, my wife, said something I didn't catch. 'Sorry?' I said. There was a jazz band playing loudly in the corner with a singer who looked so old I wondered if the rest of the band had borrowed her from a local nursing home to make up the numbers. 'I said, I want to give up work in London and move down here to Devon,' Debbie said, as I found out later. She was probably shouting, but I still couldn't hear her. Some of the farmers around us were waltzing, some jiving, some doing the twist. They were happy.

I was nearly at the end of my Reinbeer, and tilted the glass, smiling. It was pointless trying to speak, and I didn't want to spend the evening saying 'sorry' to everything she said, so I smiled and nodded, hoping she had said something about the need for more alcohol. Her chin dropped, and she mouthed the word, 'Really?' It was New Year's Eve, my glass was empty and I wanted another. I nodded enthusiastically, mouthing back, 'Yes, really,' delighted at her reaction over my intention to drink the bar dry. She got up and flung her arms around my neck, kissing me wildly and shouting, 'I love you, I love you, I love you,' directly into my ear. Then she picked up my glass and rushed for the bar, darting between the dancers. The band was still playing, although not necessarily all the same tune and I was happy to see the singer still on her feet. I'm sure at one point I heard her shout into the microphone, 'Do you know how old I am?' I settled back into my seat, Debbie at the bar collecting our drinks, content that I was a relationship god.

Honestly, that's how it happened. Without my really knowing it, I'd agreed to change my life for ever. Three months later, we had quit our jobs, sold our London flat and moved to Exmoor. In the beginning I knew nothing. I knew a thorn bush on account of the, er, thorns, and I knew a stinging nettle when I touched one, but that was as far as my outside knowledge went. Then, for Christmas, Debbie bought me Kylie. 'She's your own pig,' she said. (I could see that, I just wasn't aware I needed one.) 'I thought we could breed from her.' The following year I bought her four ducklings as my Valentine love token – and they say romance is dead.

All we could afford was 20 acres of scruffy but beautiful woods and fields next to a stream on Exmoor. Nothing had been touched on it for several generations, and there wasn't a gate that didn't disintegrate

when you opened it, or a row of fencing that stood upright. It needed work and investment, but more than that it needed someone who knew what they were doing. Sadly, it got me.

Looking back, the fact that I was forced to take on the project was the best thing that could have happened. I had to discover for myself what everything was, what it did, what it tasted like, how it worked and how best to use it. I listened to the old-time farmers and mixed in a little modern technology of my own. Soon, our self-sufficient smallholding was born, and as soon as it was, the television cameras arrived.

Through the kitchen window I could see Debbie on the phone, waving frantically at me. It was three years after we had first walked our land, and the place was looking good. The fencing was up and so were the gates. There were chickens ranging free, pigs running in the woods, Kylie was the proud mum of eight little bruisers and we even had a handful of sheep. Life was busy, and it was about to get a whole lot more hectic. As I reached Debbie she stopped waving and started scribbling on the back of an old envelope, speaking into the telephone as she did so. I read over Debbie's shoulder as she wrote: 'A TV company want to come and film us!!!!' The celebrity chef Gary Rhodes had heard of what we were doing and wanted to include our smallholding in his search for a local food hero on UKTV Food (now Good Food Channel). I polished the pigs and combed the grass and they came. As a result, Hidden Valley Pigs were South West finalists in Local Food Hero 2007 and, in 2008, we went one better and became local food champions across the region.

More pigs followed. Currently there are seven breeding sows and one extremely handsome dude, The General Lee, who is the piggy-husband to them all, and daddy to all the piglets. We also have laying chickens and table birds, ducks, killer geese, lucky-turkey-leaky who has seen two Christmases more than most, a one-eyed sheepdog called Dex, several very pretty sheep and a head-butting ram. There is a vegetable plot so big it takes me all summer to weed it and an ancient orchard. All in all, it's a foodie's self-sufficient paradise.

I'd learnt so much it seemed churlish not to pass it on. I started running courses on butchery, livestock management and growing your own food; I write about self-sufficiency for various magazines, and here I am now writing this book. I'm not expecting everyone to up sticks and get themselves a smallholding in the rural middle of nowhere, but I do get the sense that most of us would like to be a bit more self-reliant than we are.

So what I have written aims to be a practical guide that will show you how to approach a self-sufficient lifestyle, how to forage and eat for free, how to feel healthier with a greater sense of pride in how you live your life, how to involve children in the concept of self-sustainability, what to do with animals and how to treat them kindly, and how to help the environment.

There are 12 chapters to this book, each one focusing on a particular area with the aim of making self-sufficiency come alive for everybody. It shows you how the kids can grow lettuce, strawberries or peas; how you can make butter and cheese and keep chickens for fresh eggs. It shows you how to make your own wine and beer, forage for nuts and berries or wild herbs, how to dye material and clothes using plants, as well as how to turn to nature for useful medicinal soothers. Each chapter explains how to use the information depending on your experience, resources, equipment and how far you want to go on the scale of self-sufficiency. This means that the kitchen garden chapter, for example, will have something for you whether you have a window box, an urban back garden or a more substantial area of land.

This is a modern approach to self-sufficiency, an attempt to update centuries' worth of old wives' tales, rural truisms, herblore and folklore by looking for the points at which they connect with the way we live our lives today. By doing that, by taking those old life skills and bringing them into the present, the first thing you will realize is how cutting-edge it all feels. Far from feeling fuddy-duddy, it feels fashion-able to learn how to turn to nature for solutions to everyday problems. Walk up and down the aisles of any supermarket and count how many times you see the word 'natural'. It's everywhere, on food, cosmetics, household cleaners and medicines. The modern-day appetite for natural ingredients is insatiable, and yet many people fear picking herbs and flowers to use in anything other than food, and sometimes they're afraid even to use them in cooking. But, really, I think it's not fear; it's something else. Really, they would love to do it, but they've just forgotten how. In the following pages, I've provided the key to regaining those skills.

Simon Dawson

Introduction

Self-sufficiency seldom makes headline news, but it never seems to be very far away as a topic of conversation. Rather like the weather, or the housing market, it is one of those subjects that people enjoy discussing endlessly – perhaps because it offers the chance of making exciting changes to one's lifestyle. But what does self-sufficiency really mean?

Strictly defined, self-sufficiency is a way of living in which no support or aid of any kind is required from external sources: complete personal independence from the outside world. Yet self-sufficiency as it is understood today has a broader and more forgiving meaning. It is about becoming more independent and resourceful, about being able to do things for ourselves – not everything, but as much as we feel comfortable with. It is a means of taking responsibility for ourselves and taking control of our lives, doing things the way we want them done, and determining the end result. It is a way of securing our future, putting food on the table and looking after ourselves and our families, even when the budget is tight. It is about life skills, about achieving self-reliance and acquiring self-esteem.

Self-sufficiency embraces the concept of sustainable living, and at its heart lies an understanding of and a respect for the rhythms and pulses of the natural world. The closer we live in harmony with the environment, the better it is both for us and for the world around us. As human beings we are all dependent on one another to varying degrees, yet this dependency is not always welcomed because of the loss of freedom that it sometimes entails – we can start to feel that we have no control over our own lives. The more we depend on others, the less control we feel we have. It's a difficult balance, and a very personal one. Self-sufficiency can be the lever with which to adjust this balance between doing things for ourselves and depending on other people to do them for us.

However, this book is not intended as a definitive guide to self-sufficiency. I have based it on my own ideas and the experience I have gained as I have worked out a lifestyle that suits me. Everyone's idea of what they want to achieve from self-sufficiency will be different, and so it should be. The intention here is simply to show what self-sufficiency involves, top to bottom, so that anyone can find aspects of it that will complement their own lifestyle or enable them to live in the way they would like to, whether they live in a city apartment, a house with a garden, or a rural smallholding. Along with the other important aspects of sustainable living I take a look at renewable energy, but this is a topic that is so huge that here I am really only able to scratch the surface. A list of further reading and links to some of the myriad helpful and informative sites on the Internet are provided at the back of the book.

Probably the biggest cause of people's falling by the wayside in their search for a self-sufficient life is taking on too much too soon. There can be an overwhelming temptation to go hell for leather and try everything at once. This can lead to frustration and disillusionment, and the small successes you should be enjoying become rapidly over-shadowed by what seem to be huge, dark failures. Before you know it you have scrapped the whole idea and moved on, with little to show for it but a bad taste in your mouth and a motley collection of plant pots and animal housing. The trick is to take it slowly, bit by bit.

For that reason, it is not a bad idea to start off in one area, and then build on that. There are natural offshoots to every part of self-sufficiency: for example, you might move from baking bread into making butter, and from keeping chickens for eggs into hatching some of those eggs and raising the chicks. As your confidence grows, the pace will naturally pick up and soon self-sufficiency becomes second nature. To begin with, look for a format that will complement your current life. I started with a list like this:

- Set out to make one loaf of bread and one tub of butter a week.

- With the buttermilk make a soft curd cheese (simpler and faster to make than hard cheese).

- Buy a whole chicken and joint it yourself, making up your mind to use every bit of it.

- Start off some indoor herbs on the kitchen windowsill, such as basil, coriander, thyme, chives, dill or even chervil.

- Buy a whole fresh fish from the wet fish stall and fillet it yourself.

Try that or a similar formula over the course of a month and see how it feels and how it fits in with your life. There will be some parts you'll enjoy more than others, some aspects your family will prefer, but the important thing is that you have set yourself reasonable, achievable targets and you have made it fun. Once the month has passed and you feel the foundations have been successfully laid, then you can start being a bit bolder, a little more adventurous. After all, in self-sufficiency, as in any other lifestyle, the more you put in, the more you get out of it. And for the time and effort you do invest, the rewards are tenfold.

Part of being self-sufficient, to however small an extent, is trying to avoid waste. The simple fact is, the more we spend, the more we waste. Recent surveys have estimated that in the UK we throw away on average between a quarter and a third of the food we buy. That's a staggering amount. Try an experiment. For one month, jot down every food item your family buys. Then next to each item, put a tick if you use it, a cross if you don't. Now tot up the cost of all the crosses. That's how much you can instantly save without even thinking about it. And it's not just food. If you look at lightbulbs left on in empty rooms, televisions left on standby, mobile phones left on recharge, washing you dry in the dryer rather than out on the line, you'll probably find you can reduce your electricity consumption – and bills – substantially.

Finding the right level in any new lifestyle is all about feeling your way, and self-sufficiency is no different. It's about learning to recognize what feels right and building on the positives. If you enjoyed baking a loaf of bread, try grinding your own flour. Make jam, and if the jam goes well, spend an autumn afternoon foraging for wild berries to make the next batch. If the berrying goes well, go mushrooming, and so on. Self-sufficiency is the ultimate bolt-on lifestyle, allowing you to do as little or as much as you like. And so you begin to get a sense of momentum, with one thing leading naturally to another.

With a little know-how, a few tricks and some smart ideas, your world takes on a whole new feel. Food is fresher, tastier and healthier. Children have an outlet for their creative urges and at the same time equip themselves with basic life skills. Men and women can rediscover their inner 'hunter-gatherer' and become more resourceful, and families cut back their food and utility bills. And although the idea of never setting foot inside a shop or supermarket again might be very appealing, in practice it's unlikely to happen, because to make jam you need to buy sugar, to make bread you need yeast, to make butter you need cream… Of course, there are ways round this (sourdough bread; a house cow), but you'd need to run a full-time smallholding to get anywhere near achieving it.

It does not matter whether you have virtually unlimited resources or are unemployed, whether your home is a rambling old house in the country or a small apartment in a tower block, or whether you are new to self-sufficiency or an old hand – the feeling of satisfaction at being able to do things for yourself is wonderful, and with even the first few steps into self-sufficiency the benefits are tangible; you will:

- save money;

- become healthier;

- feel a sense of pride in how you live your life;

- involve children in the concept of sustainability;

- help the environment;

- produce less waste;

- enjoy better-tasting, homemade food.

Self-sufficiency satisfies on so many levels. It is frugal living without missing out. It is a form of existence that has evolved over thousands of years, and is still evolving now to embrace new technologies (even the Internet), and this is partly what makes it feel so current and so appealing. In modern as in ancient times, self-sufficiency enables us to live a life that is natural, healthy and economical.

This book guides you on how to achieve that lifestyle by working smarter, not harder. Time is often more precious than gold. That is why planning is essential. For this reason every chapter will run through the resources and equipment needed to tackle the project, and will help you to formulate a plan before you begin and to assess what you do and don't want to do.

Anyone, whether they have access to a window box, a garden, an allotment or land enough to rear all their own meat year round, will find something exciting and useful in the pages that follow. There are old ideas with a fresh twist and crisp new ones just waiting to be investigated. This is a guide, but it is also a place to come and have fun – a place that inspires with workable, practical and achievable ideas that will make you sit up and think, *I can do that.*

CHAPTER ONE

The Kitchen Garden

Coaxing a tiny seed to develop into a crop of plump, juicy tomatoes, or seedlings into a delicious year-round harvest ready to be taken straight from the garden into the kitchen, takes time and patience, a little knowledge and a lot of enthusiasm. Even the most accomplished gardeners lavish love and attention on their plants. And lest you sit there shaking your head, let me warn you that it's catching. In the time it has taken me to write this book, tucked away in an upstairs bedroom, my closest friends have become two chilli plants on the windowsill in front of me. I've stopped short of naming them, but our conversations have been long and involved. They are quite simply the best chilli plants I have ever grown, with the most vibrant and healthy looking chillies just begging to be cooked.

Growing vegetables is *almost* that simple. The clever bits are in the details. And the details contained in this chapter are intended to support the gardener without intruding on that simplicity: there are tips to make tasks easier and less time-consuming; advice on how to increase your chances of success or to enrich the successes you may already have had; enough background information to help broaden your knowledge without it becoming tiresome; and some inventive ideas on self-sufficiency to spark your imagination.

PLANNING YOUR GARDEN

There is a tremendous sense of excitement and anticipation involved in planning your kitchen garden. Among the first considerations are your friends and family and each person's likes and dislikes – from the vegetables and salads they enjoy to the everyday meals, the dinners and barbecues as well as the special occasions you will share with them. Think not only about what your family eats but also how much of it is actually consumed. If only one of you likes spinach, then don't plan an entire row as it will inevitably end up being wasted. The choice of which plants to grow is, of course, enormous. But whether you opt for exotic, rare and expensive varieties or everyday vegetables, such as carrots and peas, or even a combination of all of these, one thing is certain: your home-grown versions will taste so much fresher and crisper than their often bland and wilting shop-bought counter-parts. Whatever your final decisions, planning your vegetable patch – whether it is in an allotment, a small plot in the garden or even a simple window box – is one of the most enriching experiences. And part of the pleasure lies in the knowledge that your garden will be unique.

When weighing up your options, another consideration, especially if your vegetable plot is close to the house, is to try and make your garden attractive. A serviceable plot might be good for the palate, but it's unlikely to be good for the soul. Think about including some climbers – runner beans and cucumbers, for example – and growing them into a backdrop of uneven shapes around supports such as wigwams, trellises and arches (see page 15). Try and avoid planting in dead straight rows and break it up with different compositions here and there. Add colour and texture by mixing fruit, herbs, flowers and vegetables in the same area. But, above all, be inventive. The more you put into your garden, the more fun it is to create and the happier you will be with the result. However, if the plot is not near your house (if it's an allotment some distance away, for example) and aesthetics is not a consideration, then obviously a more practical approach may be preferable, planting in straight lines to maximize the available space and get the most out of your land.

Every locality has its quirks. In some areas one plant will flourish while another will fall dismally short of expectation. Such peculiarities may be due to location, altitude, the amount of sunlight, the soil, any number of things. So it's always advisable to walk through your neighbourhood to see what other gardeners are favouring – it's no different from sitting in a restaurant and watching what the waiter brings out to the other diners before you pick from the menu yourself.

EQUIPMENT

If you have a garden, the chances are you will already have the basic gardening equipment, but there may be some additional hardware and software that you'll want to consider acquiring. Some suggestions follow.

At least one spade

A four-tined garden fork to dig over the earth

A rake to level the soil

String to mark your lines

A trowel to plant

A hoe to keep the weeds at bay

A watering can or hosepipe to keep the plants moist

A sharp knife to cut and harvest

A basket to load with produce

Lengths of bamboo or long sticks for the climbers

Seeds from your favourite varieties of herbs and vegetables

Pre-germinated plants ready to go outside

Fruit canes

Using your own resources

Finally, a major planning consideration for any self-sufficient gardener lies in deciding what you can make or build yourself. Not only is it far cheaper to do this but watching your plants thrive in something you have created with your own hands is deeply satisfying. Also think about how you can reassign and recycle bits and pieces that might otherwise not find a home – anything from plastic bottles, containers and barrels to old car tyres, shower doors and discarded pieces of furniture can be put to good use in the kitchen garden. Old pallets with the wood stripped off them are particularly useful and can be made into anything from cold frames and raised beds to doors.

When using wood to build for the garden, buy water-based paint or preservative to protect the wood, as anything else may leach chemicals into your soil and could contaminate your vegetables. It always pays to read the label, which should state whether the product is appropriate for use around the vegetable plot.

SITING YOUR PLOT

You cannot place too much importance on choosing the right spot in your garden or allotment for planting. Plants need plenty of sunlight but they also need protection from the wind, which can be a problem as you'll need an area that's both sheltered and exposed at the same time! This conundrum is worth spending some time thinking through as research shows that vegetables that are grown in a sunny, sheltered spot will increase in yield by nearly 30 per cent. Hedges and banks are good for protection as long as they are not too tall and cast shadows. Avoid planting at the bottom of a sharp slope as cold air will drop down it and could turn the area into a frost trap. If you are planning a window box, place it in a south-facing window or as close to one as possible. An alternative is to have moveable pots outside so that you can position them to follow the sun and hug a fence or bush for protection, without the worry of your plants spending half their lives draped in shadow.

PREPARING THE GROUND

The secret to growing healthy plants lies in the soil, which is composed of varying amounts of minerals and organic matter. When soil is good, only half of it is solid. The rest is made up of the air and water that moves through a honeycomb of chambers, known as soil pores, which allow the ground to effectively breathe in and out. If there is too much moisture or excessive compacting in the soil and these pores clog up, the air is unable to get through and the plant roots suffocate; if it is too lose and airy, water drains away without stopping around long enough to be used productively.

Most of the solid part of the soil is made up of minerals. These minerals fall into three main groups: sand, silt and clay. The texture of the soil will depend on the minerals that are dominant in your area. Soil is the most tactile substance in the world. Whether you're planning a vegetable patch in the garden, in an allotment, in a window box or a tub on the front doorstep, get some of the earth and run it through your fingers. How does it feel? To get an idea what you are looking for, imagine the soil in your fingers is made up from small, medium and large grains. The larger the grain, the looser the earth will feel. A sandy soil with large grains will crumble and feel gritty and light whereas a clay soil full of tiny grains all clumped together feels cloying, heavy and almost certainly damp. Becoming familiar with your soil in this way by touching it and rubbing it will help you to understand what needs to be done to it in order to transform your garden into a fertile, thriving plot that will produce delicious fruit and vegetables all year round.

What you're looking for in a good growing soil is a well-balanced mix, composed predominantly of sand to let the air in and out, but with a rich organic matter, such as compost, running through it that will be full of lovely nutrients and will help hold the moisture without clogging the pores. This type of soil is known as a loam. Remember that in order to develop and thrive, plants need the following six essential ingredients: good soil, sunlight, air, water, warmth and nutrients.

Nutrients

Although a good soil structure is essential, without the right nutrients for the plant to feed, growth will be poor and the yield disappointing. Fertilizers, compost and manure are all amendments to the soil that are rich in the three primary nutrients (phosphorus, nitrogen and potassium) and the three sub-primary nutrients (calcium, sulphur and magnesium). Mixing in a good compost or manure will feed and enliven the soil into a rich, nutritious, fertile ground in which your plants will flourish.

If you have access to farmyard manure (from cows, pigs, chickens or horses, for example), allow it to rot down for at least six months before spreading it over the cleared bed as mulch (see page 26). This should be done in late winter, or you can dig it through in early spring. (Poultry manure is highly acidic and should not be used unless it is at least a year old, and even then only on soil with an alkaline pH.) Discarded straw bedding is highly prized by gardeners because it contains nitrogen-rich urine. If you are able to sort through the muck-heap yourself, always go for urine-soaked bedding – the more of this in your manure mix the better.

The alternative to farmyard manure is compost. This is a favourite topic of conversation for gardeners, and opinion on the best materials and production methods will differ almost as widely as on the subject of what plants to grow and how best to cook them. Compost is essentially a homemade mix of vegetable waste, garden waste (avoid using anything that may contain seeds) and paper that has been left to rot. Over the course of about a year the heap will produce bacteria and decompose naturally until it becomes crumbly and dark in colour and is a far cry from its original state.

Materials for use in compost (partial list)

Coffee grounds and tea leaves

Feathers

Grass cuttings, hedge trimmings, any trailing or climbing plant

Hay and straw

Leaves, pine needles, weeds and seaweed, peat and moss

Newspapers

Sawdust and wood ash

Vegetarian kitchen scraps and peelings

Materials to avoid in compost (partial list)

Cat and dog droppings and the contents of animal 'litter trays'

Coal ash, charcoal and barbecue waste

Diseased or treated plants

Potato plants

Rhubarb leaves

Scraps of meat

Seeds and pips

Much of the nutrition for your plants will come from farmyard fertilizer or homemade compost – so be generous!

RAISED BEDS

Raised beds are purpose-built growing areas that are elevated from the ground. Neat, tidy, easy to maintain and attractive, this system has a lot to offer. It is perfect for gardens with poor soil or bad drainage because by creating a new growing area you can more readily add anything you like to it in order to overcome any shortcomings in the soil. Although it is possible to do this on ground level, the big advantage of raised beds is that they are confined, so everything you do to improve the soil is contained within its walls. They also intensify your efforts and make the garden, and you, more productive. If you have the space to set up three or four raised beds, crop rotation (see page 21) will be easier to introduce.

Building a raised bed

Raised beds need not be huge – anything between 15–45cm/6–18in high is fine (this height makes them easy to work). Railway sleepers, stout planks of wood or scaffold boards set two high in a square make excellent beds. To secure them together, either screw or nail a baton to the end of the plank, railway sleeper or scaffold board (whatever you are using) to form the inner corner – in other words, attach the planks to batons rather than to each other. If necessary, these types of raised beds can easily be dismantled at the end of the growing season. But if you are able to lavish more care and attention on the project, then a beautifully constructed square or circular permanent raised bed made from bricks and cement certainly takes some beating and will look really attractive in the garden.

If either of the options described above is too expensive or too much work, then to make a moveable raised bed, pick up a 205-litre/45gal. plastic drum (recycling centres often have a stack of them to give away) and cut it in half around its middle with an electric jigsaw. Cut both ends off so that you are left with two stumpy, open tubes. Sink the drums a little way into the ground and fill them with composted soil. You can decorate them, paint them dark green or black, or site them in the flower garden where they'll be surrounded by colour and hidden. Another option is to grow bushy plants around them, but be sure to allow for an access area.

VEGETABLES, HERBS AND SALAD

Looking at vegetables in their botanical groups will assist you in the organization and planning of your garden. In particular it will help you to decide what to include in your annual vegetable plot and your crop rotation for the following year. The table overleaf divides some of the most common and popular vegetables into their family groups.

Like every family, the vegetables within each group have similarities and there are therefore often standard procedures or rules to follow for planting and care. But for every rule there is usually an exception. Because each group is so diverse, it may well be that the varieties within each family have very different needs. For example, the cauliflower and radish are both members of the brassica family, but cauliflowers like to be started under cover around January to March whereas radishes

VEGETABLE FAMILIES

Family	Vegetables
Alliums	Chives, garlic, leeks, onions, spring onions
Brassicas	Broccoli, Brussels sprouts, cabbages, cauliflowers, radishes, swedes, turnips
Cucurbits	Cucumbers, melons, squashes
Leaves and greens	Chard, lettuces, spinach, swiss chard
Legumes	Broad beans, French beans, peas, runner beans
Roots	Beetroots, carrots, parsnips
Solanaceae	Aubergine, chillies, peppers, potatoes, tomatoes

should be sown direct (i.e. directly into the soil) any time between March and September. The golden rule is, therefore, always seek additional information for planting and care: read the seed packet, ask at a garden centre or, better still, join an online gardening forum.

Alliums

The onion family includes some 250 edible varieties worldwide. They are fairly robust plants and generally quite resistant to disease, which makes them strong candidates for any plot. Onions can be grown from seeds, transplants or sets (small bulbs pre-started into growth). They like cool temperatures, so you can start planting around the time of the last frosts (this will vary according to the region in which you live). However, the growth of onions is most influenced by the amount of sunlight the plants receive and they are therefore divided into three categories: long-day (14 hours of sunlight), intermediate (12 hours) and short-day (10–11 hours). It is therefore advisable to select the appropriate variety for your area, otherwise the crop may be disappointing.

Spring onions should be sown direct. If you plant a handful of them every week or so throughout the spring they will give you constant summer and autumn crops. Also in this group is garlic. Can anyone ever have too much of this wonderful vegetable in their garden? Garlic should be planted in late autumn or early spring for a summer harvest. The more sun they get, the better the harvest will be. But beware the flowers – if too much of the garlic's energy is concentrated on producing the flower, the size of the bulb is disappointing. The trick is to simply nip the flower off.

Leeks should be treated like a younger brother: be gentle, caring and understanding with them. Start them inside and transplant them out around June or July. When the white part of the leek shows about 5cm/2in above the ground, earth them up by giving them a little extra soil around the base – this will block out the light and produce a longer white shank.

Brassicas

The wonderful brassica family is diverse, colourful, unexpected and slightly quirky, with some very odd likes and dislikes. According to recent studies they are also incredibly good for you, with high levels of vitamins A and C as well as some very important cancer-preventing properties. But because brassicas are such a diverse group it is difficult to generalize about them, so always seek reputable advice if in any doubt about the planting or care of specific vegetables in the family.

Although they are biannual plants, brassicas are often cultivated as annuals as this gives them a certain amount of resilience during any cold snaps and also means they will grow quickly. They like to be outside and are quite comfortable in cool conditions, but they need to be started under cover. Brassicas enjoy plenty of water but prefer a well-drained soil. The soil should be neutral – that is, neither acid nor alkaline (around pH7). If your soil is acidic, sprinkle some lime or wood ash on the surface to reduce the acidity. These plants dislike unexpected company, so weeds have to be kept down by hoeing once a week. Although they look tough, pests upset them and disease can wipe them out. Clubroot is a particular enemy and mainly infests beds that have not been rotated (avoid planting brassicas in the same spot for at least two years). If your ground suffers from clubroot, start the brassicas off in a large pot until they are well established with strong, healthy leaves, before transplanting them out. Slugs, snails, cabbage fly and flea beetle are among the bugs to look out for. If possible, check them once a day when you water them to make sure they are not under attack, and pick off any freeloaders.

Cucurbits

Compared with the brassicas, cucurbits (also known as gourds) are normal, well-adjusted and easy to grow. Their likes are simply met with lots of sunshine and plenty of water and for this they will reward you with a crop that can, if they're really happy, go beyond bountiful and verge ludicrously close to plot domination. The trick is to harvest them while they are young and sweet in summer.

Leaves and greens

From winter greens to summer salads, this family is the chief supplier of low-calorie, quick-growing, healthy, edible leaves. But best of all, your home-grown plants won't be washed in chlorine, like most of the leaves on supermarket shelves. Wait until the weather is warm, sow the seeds direct, keep them well watered and they will love you for it. Harvest young and carefully and they will love you all over again with a second crop. Kale is great to grow – not only is it near-indestructible but it's also high in iron, which means it's incredibly good for you.

Vegetable lasagne

This Italian favourite made with your home-grown vegetables is ideal served with a fruity or wild leaf salad (see the Forager's wild leaf salad on page 267 for inspiration). Adding eggs to the cheese sauce means that the sauce will rise and set slightly, allowing for easy cutting and serving.

1 recipe-quantity Ratatouille (see page 18)
450g/1lb spinach, blanched, drained and chopped
9 no-pre-cook lasagne sheets

FOR THE CHEESE SAUCE
50g/2oz butter
2 tbsp plain flour
570ml/1 pint milk
50g/2oz mature hard cheese, grated
2 eggs, beaten
2 tsp Dijon mustard.
sea salt and freshly ground black pepper

To make the cheese sauce, melt the butter in a heavy-based saucepan over a low heat, then stir in the flour and mix to a paste. Cook for 1–2 minutes. Remove the pan from the heat and gradually pour in the milk, stirring continually to prevent lumps forming. Once all the milk has been incorporated, return the pan to the heat and bring slowly to the boil, still stirring, until the sauce is smooth and has thickened, then reduce the heat and simmer for 5 minutes, stirring occasionally. Season. Finally, beat in the cheese, eggs and mustard. Preheat the oven to 180°C/350°F/gas 4. Lightly oil an ovenproof dish measuring 25 × 16 × 7.5cm/10 × 6½ × 3in and spread one-third of the ratatouille in the bottom. Top this with one-third of the spinach, then three of the lasagne sheets.

Repeat the layers twice, ending with the remaining lasagne sheets. Pour the cheese sauce over the top and bake in the preheated oven for about 40 minutes until bubbling and brown.

Legumes

Legumes, which include peas, beans and pulses, are packed with protein. For thousands of years before meat became a staple in our diet, they were an essential alternative means of supplying protein. After grains, beans were, and probably still are, the most important food source in the world. Perhaps surprisingly, even the humble pea pod is packed with nutrients and makes a great addition to the diet (it can also be used to feed livestock). The benefits of legumes for the self-sufficient gardener do not stop short at their nutritional value and outstanding flavour (there is nothing quite like the taste of fresh runner beans – if they're not a favourite of yours, the recipe for runner-bean chutney on page 234 may help you change your mind). They are also nitrogen fixers and are therefore good to include in your rotation plan to follow heavy feeders, such as potatoes, to breathe a little life back into the soil.

Any climbing plant can and should be grown against a support (runner beans, borlotti beans and some types of climbing tomatoes are obvious examples). For best results, start your beans in root-training containers (rather than buying them you can use the inside of a toilet roll) and plant them out when four leaves have formed. Set each plant close to a support – it should naturally curl itself around the support as it grows, although you may need to give it a helping hand by simply leaning the tendril against the support (see illustrations on page 15).

Supports for climbing plants

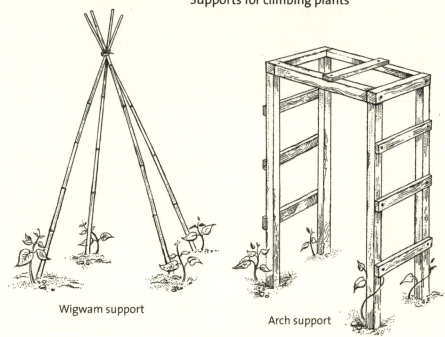

Wigwam support

Arch support

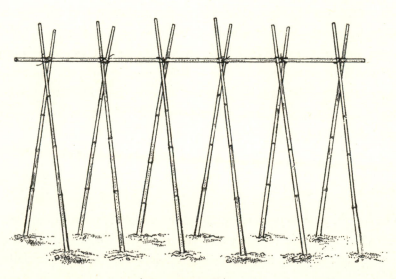

Long row support

Peas à la français

This classic French recipe makes an ideal accompaniment to many meat and vegetarian dishes. You may not need all of the butter and flour paste, but any remaining can be kept in an airtight container in the fridge for weeks and can be used to thicken any sauce or gravy that you want.

> 75g/3oz butter
> 5 spring onions, chopped
> 2 Little Gem lettuces
> 450g/1lb fresh garden peas
> 75g/3oz plain flour
> sea salt and freshly ground black pepper

Melt 25g/1oz of the butter in a large saucepan over a low heat and fry the spring onions until softened. Quarter the Little Gem lettuces lengthways through the root so that you have little 'boats' of lettuce heart that stay together, then add to the saucepan and stir together with the onions for 1–2 minutes. Add the peas and 100ml/3½fl oz water and bring to the boil, then reduce the heat, cover and simmer for about 10 minutes until the peas are tender. Mix the remaining butter and the flour together to form a paste, then add lumps of it to the liquid, a few at a time, stirring gently until the sauce has thickened. Season to taste.

Roots

The humble root vegetable will not only feed you and your family but also your livestock. Sheep, cattle and pigs will thrive on any of the roots, especially swedes and turnips (always cook potatoes before feeding to pigs as they cannot absorb the nutrition from raw potatoes).

Horses adore carrots and chickens will browse away happily at any of the leaves, though avoid potato leaves as they are poisonous. If you have livestock, it's well worth setting aside a corner (or more) of a field and filling it edge to edge with root vegetables. Even if you haven't any livestock, roots are the kitchen gardener's friend because they are quick to grow, durable (carrots will live happily in the frost) and can be eaten whole or made into a root purée to add a deliciously different texture on the side of a roast dinner. (Radishes are good substitutes for turnips; they cook faster and can be harvested three weeks after planting.) Dig a little wood ash (to help guard against root maggot) into good draining soil and sow direct. For the smaller vegetables, clump them fairly close together in irregular intervals about your plot. Larger vegetables require a little bit more room to stretch. Water well and try not to let them dry out.

Carrot cookies for pooches

115g/4oz carrots
2 garlic cloves
1 egg
225g/8oz plain flour
115g/4oz rolled oats
25g/1oz wheatgerm

Preheat the oven to 200°C/400°F/gas 6 and grease two baking sheets. Put the carrots in a saucepan with some water and boil until tender. Tip the carrots into a blender, add the garlic, and blend to a purée. Tip the purée into a bowl, add the egg, flour, rolled oats and wheat germ and mix together. Shape the mixture into biscuits and place half of them on the baking sheets. (The rest will be cooked as a second batch.) Bake in the preheated oven for 30–40 minutes until golden brown. Remove from the oven and transfer to a wire rack to cool while you cook the next batch.

Solanaceae

With the exception of potato and sweet potato, this is an indoor family. Solanaceae like to be on a warm windowsill looking out – if you grow them outside, they're likely to disappoint you. Because this group tends to grow quite tall and produce large, heavy fruit (such as the tomato and the pepper), it needs lots of water and a good strong cane for support. The odd one out in the family (there's always one) is the potato. Chit potatoes undercover by gathering egg boxes, or egg trays if you can get them, and put a single potato in each segment where the egg would normally sit. After a few weeks they should begin to germ-inate and shoots will appear. Plant them in a trench with the shoot up, cover over and lay a line of compost or manure over the top. If you live in an area where sacks of potatoes can be bought cheaply at the market or garden centre, concentrate on growing an unusual variety, such as pink fur apple potatoes.

Ratatouille

This is a great way to get a meal from the garden. Serve immediately in a bowl with crusty bread to dip into the juices, or pour it over cooked pasta (ideally homemade – see page 72). This recipe can be varied by using mushrooms in place of the aubergine, courgettes and peppers.

900g/2lb mixed red and yellow tomatoes (a mix of cherry and large
    tomatoes is fine)
2 plump garlic cloves, chopped
2–3 tbsp olive oil
1 aubergine, chopped
1 red onion, chopped
2 courgettes, chopped
1 red and 1 yellow pepper, halved, deseeded and cut into strips
handful of basil leaves, torn
sea salt and freshly ground black pepper

Preheat the oven to 200°C/400°F/gas 6. Put the tomatoes and garlic
in a shallow ovenproof dish, drizzle with 1 tablespoon of the olive oil
and sprinkle with some salt. Roast in the preheated oven for about 40
minutes until the tomatoes have softened and are starting to shrivel
slightly. Meanwhile, in a frying pan, heat another tablespoon of the
oil and sauté the aubergine over a moderate heat until softened and
golden. Remove with a slotted spoon and transfer to a large saucepan. Repeat with the remaining vegetables, cooking one type at a
time and adding more oil as necessary, until all the vegetables are in the
saucepan. Remove the tomatoes from the oven and add to the
saucepan, then cook the mixture over a high heat, stirring, to reduce
slightly. Remove from the heat, season to taste and add the basil before
serving.

Seeds

Most vegetables are grown from seed and the varieties available are
outstanding, although you may find supermarkets and garden centres
limit their stock to the most popular few. For a wider variety try
mail-order seed catalogues or, even better, though possibly not for a
beginner, think about joining an online seed exchange at one of the

many online gardening forums. Gardeners who intend to gather their own seeds need to ensure that the plants are not F1 hybrid variety, as the seeds gathered from these are infertile. (An F1 hybrid is the off-spring that is produced by crossing two different varieties of the same plant species; the hybrid is bred to eliminate the bad characteristics and enhance the good characteristics of the parent plants.)

When planting a seed it is important to establish where your plant would like to be started. There are three choices: *in situ*, in a nursery seedbed or under cover. *In situ* is when the seed is planted straight into the plot, where it will remain undisturbed until harvesting. Roots should be planted *in situ* as they don't take kindly to transplanting. A nursery seedbed is a safe, well-protected area where seeds can ger-minate into seedlings. Many of the brassicas benefit from starting in a seedbed. The downside to the seedbed lies in the temptation to pack it too tight in the knowledge that the seedlings will be trans-planted as soon as they are strong enough, and so it can be quite high-maintenance, with lots of fiddling to ensure overcrowding does not become a problem.

The other option is to start the seeds under cover in a greenhouse, polytunnel, conservatory or on the kitchen windowsill. By starting them inside, you're essentially extending the growing season for the more tender and delicate plants, giving them a chance to germinate in a controlled environment without the risk of a cold snap killing them off. If you own a wine-making kit, a good tip for the self-sufficient gardener is to borrow the heat-pad from your kit and use it to keep a constant temperature going under a seed propagator. A heated seed propagator is a container (sometimes self-watering) that is heated from underneath and enables you to control humidity and thereby encourage germination.

CROP ROTATION AND GOOD GARDEN-MANAGEMENT

Crop rotation involves planting vegetables in their botanical families and moving them around to different parts of the plot every year in an organized sequence. This system enhances soil fertility and soil structure, prevents soil depletion and disease, reduces soil erosion and pest build-up, and controls pests and weeds.

Put a plant in the ground, allow it to grow and it will inevitably attract insects and probably some sort of soil disease. With luck, the infestation will take a while to become large enough to be a problem, by which time the plant will already have been harvested. With good management and a keen eye, the nasties won't even have their feet under the table. However, once they've arrived they won't leave – they hibernate, hide and wait for next year. Plant the same plant in the same place the following spring and the insect or disease is sitting pretty, with last year's head-start giving it ample opportunity to really get a grip and ruin your crop. The solution to this problem, and one that has been practised for centuries, is to rotate the different vegetable families around the plot, never planting the same crop in the same place two years on the trot, and thus cutting the pest's lifecycle. This will also help to keep the ground fertile and the weeds down.

A standard four-year rotation plan is displayed in the table below.

EXAMPLE FOUR-YEAR CROP ROTATION

	Year 1	Year 2	Year 3	Year 4
Plot A	Legumes	Brassicas	Roots	Potatoes
Plot B	Brassicas	Roots	Potatoes	Legumes
Plot C	Roots	Potatoes	Legumes	Brassicas
Plot D	Potatoes	Legumes	Brassicas	Roots

Although this plan is ideal because it gives a good, four-year gap between each family, it is only effective in a fair-sized plot (around 15m/50ft). If you have a small plot, a four-year plan may be impractical and ineffectual – the pests you have confused by planting runner beans in the spot where potatoes used to be will only be bewildered long enough to figure out that all they need to do is trundle a short distance to where the spuds are now. But if you do have a small plot and it's not possible to rotate, then don't stress about it: be as flexible as you can, try not to follow one vegetable with another of the same family and keep an extra-wary eye out for trouble. If a problem flairs up with one particular family then consider not growing it for a couple of years – check back to the rotation plan to see what would be good to grow in its place.

COMPANION PLANTING

Companion planting involves growing different crops close together so that they help each other in pollination, the absorption of essential nutrients and pest control. So companions are plants that grow well together and offer some form of protection, either by attracting the good bug or deterring the bad bug. Examples include growing garlic among carrots to deter root fly, or dill and sweetpeas among climbers – dill to encourage aphid-eating hoverflies and sweetpeas to enhance pollination (their strong scent attracts bees).

Alliums: The onion family has a wonderfully deterring scent and should be planted with brassicas or potatoes. Favourite companions are carrots and cabbage – the combined scent of these plants grown together confuses the pests that are common to each (the carrot fly, cabbage fly and onion fly). Alliums do not like legumes.

Brassicas: This motley crew is aided enormously by alliums, nasturtiums, geraniums, rosemary and by other strong-smelling herbs and flowers, which help to deter the cabbage-white butterfly. Favourite companions are nasturtiums and cabbages. Brassicas do not like Solanaceae.

Cucurbits: This group is friendly with legumes and many of the salads, such as radish and lettuce. Avoid planting with alliums and strong-scented herbs as they can take on the smell. Cucurbits love nasturtiums as they attract bees, which help enormously with pollination and therefore with crop yield.

Leaves and greens: This group gets on well with most, but in particular they like legumes and many of the same companions as brassicas. Favourite companions are spinach with cauliflower.

Legumes: Known collectively as green manure for their nitrogen-giving properties, these are great companions for most, but can overpower many of the Solanaceae. Spinach loves cauliflower; sweetpeas among the climbers will attract higher pollination. Avoid growing legumes with alliums.

Roots: Living underground, roots are reasonably happy on their own, although carrots seem to thrive in the company of sage. Avoid planting too close to alliums – even though alliums will deter carrot-root fly, they will contaminate the flavour. When harvesting, sprinkle chopped chives or onion skins on the ground to deter carrot-root fly as the blighters can smell a freshly dug carrot from miles away.

Solanaceae: Always start with a positive … they get on well with alliums! Other than that, Solanaceae are pretty moody and with a few exceptions, it's best to grow them (in the UK at least) on their own, inside or in containers or grow bags. Among the exceptions are potatoes, which, once chitted, should be planted outside into slightly acidic soil (never attempt to reduce the acidity in the ground for potatoes). Chitting is a method used to start off a potato by exposing it to daylight and allowing the little nodules, which will later become the shoots, to develop on the outer skin. If you keep your crop of potatoes together in one spot, they don't seem to mind company they can see, as long as they don't have to touch.

GROWING IN A SMALL SPACE

Lack of space has to be the biggest complaint among gardeners. If you have a salad box on the windowsill, you'll need two. If you have a vegetable plot 3m/10ft wide in the garden, it could do with being twice the size. And allotments – who can possibly struggle by with just one? Yet when you put your mind to it, you'll be amazed what you can grow, where you can grow it and just how much you can produce.

First of all, think about what's local. If a lot of people in your area are growing potatoes, then don't grow them yourself – utilize your precious space for something more interesting that your family loves and is not so easy to get fresh. Salad is the prime example. Freshly picked salad tastes unlike anything you empty out of a bag from the shops, so grow a micro salad in a window box. The 'cut and come again' varieties are perfect and are ready to be picked again in a little over three weeks. If properly cared for they should give three crops. If you have two boxes and sow them in succession you will never be without salad. To jazz up a dull salad box, add peas (and pick them as shoots), beet, perpetual spinach and rocket to the boxes. Among the other plants that thrive and look colourful and pretty on a windowsill are herbs and chillies (which also dry and preserve well).

Children love the patio garden because so much of what they plant is ready to see and pick so quickly. It's a great way to spark their interest and teach them the first steps in self-sufficiency and grow-your-own. If you have a courtyard or patio, no matter how small (as long as it gets some sun), fit a couple of hanging baskets, which are ideal for strawberries and tumbling cherry tomatoes. An apple tree can be trained to grow against a wall and will look stunning. Blueberries grow well in patio containers, as do runner or climbing beans when planted up canes in a wigwam arrangement (see page 15). Carrots also thrive in deep patio containers, which is the method used by most prize-winning carrot growers. Each champion grower will have his or her own favourite mediums to produce the best carrots but a sandy soil that has not been recently fertilized seems to be particularly good.

Tyres are good for growing potatoes and provide a microclimate in which the plants can thrive. Not only are they wonderfully space-saving, they are also easily available and generally free (and therefore ideal for the self-sufficient gardener). Sit a couple of car tyres one on top of the other and fill them with a good, rich composted soil. Press four chitted potato plants about 10cm/4in or so into the soil and water after planting. When the green shoots reach 10–13cm/4–5in, add another tyre and fill it with soil. You can continue this process with as many as four or five tyres, adding more soil each time. With more than five or six tyres, however, it is a struggle to keep the plants well watered. When you want to harvest the potatoes, take off the tyres one by one and you should be rewarded with a bountiful crop in each section. An alternative to this procedure is to buy organic potato grow bags.

THE ONE-HOUR-A-WEEK GARDENER

The concepts of 'do-nothing farming' and the 'no-work garden' were introduced by a Japanese farmer, Masanobu Fukuoka, in the late 1930s. His methods were based, among other things, on the belief that plants take 95 per cent of their nutrition from the air and only 5 per cent from the ground. According to him it therefore seemed pointless cultivating the ground prior to planting. Fukuoka's argument was compelling and many people have championed his cause over the years, kicking back in an armchair to watch telly and do absolutely nothing in the garden (although of course we now have a far greater understanding of what a plant requires for healthy growth – nutrients, correct soil pH, and so on). The downside to this back-to-nature approach is that your plot ends up looking incredibly ugly. So if a 'no-work garden' isn't really practical, you could opt to become a 'one-hour-a-week' gardener, which requires no fuss and minimum effort.

Preventing weeds

One obvious way to avoid the task of constant weeding is to tend towards planting crops such as carrots and onions that don't like excessive weeding and prefer to be left undisturbed. But as most of the work in the garden involves weeding, the more you can do to prevent weeds growing in the first place, the less you will need to do to keep them down – and the most effective way to do this is by mulching.

Mulching

Mulch is a thick layer of compost, well-rotted manure, bark, grass clippings, straw or gravel (for a path) that is spread across the surface of weeded soil (mulch may prevent weeds, but it won't kill them off if they're already established). This layer (which should be between 5–15cm/2–6in deep) forms a barrier that stops weeds from accessing sunlight and oxygen and therefore prevents their growth, which does somewhat shore up Mr Fukuoka's claim that 95 per cent of nutrients are taken from the air. You can cover the whole of a plot in mulch at the end of the growing season. Use an organic mulch: the worms will work it into the soil and it will be perfect come next spring, when all you will need to do is re-mulch around your plants to prevent further weeds.

Wooden boards

Another labour-saving idea to prevent weed growth is to lay wooden boards between your rows of plants – scaffold boards work particularly well. Avoid using treated wood as this could cause soil contamination.

Homemade irrigation systems

One of the great time wasters in the garden is the nightly marathon of watering the plants. You can minimize labour and save water by setting up your own simple hosepipe irrigation system. Before planting your crops, drill some small holes in a hosepipe and bury it beneath the ground (not too deep – the water from the pipe needs to target the roots of your plants. The hosepipe should snake back and forth below your plot. Plug one end of the pipe and fix the other end to your rainwater butt. Set the tap to a slow drip so that the plants will receive a gentle yet steady supply of water. (A more temporary measure is simply to lay the hosepipe on the surface of the soil.) You can take this idea a step further by filling a hessian sack with manure and suspending it in your water butt so that the garden is watered and fertilized at the same time.

PROTECTING YOUR PLANTS

We've all been there – peering through the living-room window out into the garden and watching the rain hammer down on to our vulnerable seedlings or, worse still, seeing a white blanket of frost creeping across the garden as though someone is laying out a freshly laundered sheet. And while you stand by and witness all your hard work slowly dying before your eyes, your one and only thought is that nobody had predicted this weather! Well, if it's the weather's job to be unpredictable, then it's the gardener's job to be prepared. So what follows is all about protection and creating an artificial climate for your plants.

Greenhouses

Greenhouses are an absolute delight in the garden, not least because they iron out a lot of the wrinkles in a beginner's knowledge and allow anyone to grow for the table virtually year-round. They offer plants light and warmth and can also be heated. The best greenhouses are anchored on to a concrete floor, which eliminates the temptation to grow directly in the floor (which is essentially the earth in your garden). Growing plants in the same place on the floor of your greenhouse for a couple of years running will cause the ground to become 'sick' – that is, infested with pests and disease, over-worked and no longer productive. A concrete floor avoids this danger and forces you to plant in pots or grow bags.

Seeds in a greenhouse come on a treat as early as February or March, which means that your growing season is extended and your plants are ready to go outside when it starts to warm up. However, there is a caveat in moving plants from a nice warm greenhouse out into the elements, and you will need to acclimatize them over a period of a week to ten days (see step 5, below).

Steps to growing seeds in a greenhouse

1. *Germinating*: Plant seeds in a seed tray or seed propagator – be sure to read the label on the seed packet to determine the best potting medium for the type of seed. Keep them warm, well-watered and in as much sunlight as possible (never site your greenhouse in the shade).

2. *Pricking out*: Once the seedlings have pushed up through the surface and developed some nice green leaves, then it's time to move them into larger growing quarters. The usual route is from the propagator or seed tray to a 10cm/4in pot, then to a 20cm/8in pot and from there to a grow bag or garden plot.

3. *Potting*: When it comes to potting, the gardener's maxim is 'large plant, small pot'. Growing a large plant in a small pot encourages

the development of a good root ball because the roots are more contained, which then makes it easier to pot on. When transferring your plants, take care never to move a dry plant. Always water well, leave for an hour or so and then move the plant.

4. *Hardening off*: This term relates to acclimatization. Imagine you've just returned from a holiday in the sun: you step off the plane, walk through customs and into arrivals with your t-shirt barely covering your tan. Almost immediately every hair follicle on your body stands to attention screaming, 'It's freezing!' Whip a plant out from the warmth of the greenhouse and the shock is much the same, only it doesn't fumble through the suitcase for a fleece, it shrivels up and dies. The trick is to let it get used to the new environment over a period of a week to ten days by moving it to a halfway house, such as a cold frame or cloche (see pages 33, 35). Some plants can be taken out during the day and brought back into the greenhouse at night for a week to ten days to harden off.

Once the seeds are out, your greenhouse becomes home to all the delicate vegetables, such as tomatoes, cucumbers, peppers, salad, chillies, strawberries and aubergines. When these are done, it's the turn of the winter crops, such as winter salad plants and cut-and-come-again seedlings to be started off in the greenhouse. Although something of a luxury, if your goal is to become self-sufficient in salad and vegetables through most of the year (preserving the excess for the inevitable months when nothing is ready), then a greenhouse is ideal.

Polytunnels

A cheaper alternative to a greenhouse is a portable polytunnel. One of its advantages is that it's moveable, so you can plant straight into the soil – in other words, the soil won't become 'sick' as it can be rested and left open to the elements. Half the battle with polytunnels lies in siting them correctly. In the summer they can become like bake-houses, with stifling humidity; unlike greenhouses, they do not have the luxury of windows for ventilation. If you can buy or build a polytunnel with a door at either end, so much the better (see below). If so, site the tunnel so that the air will flow right through the structure, in one door and out the other – although make sure it is well secured to the ground as a gentle airflow can soon turn into a vicious wind and pluck up your tunnel like a kite. Also bear in mind that if the length of the tunnel is placed east to west, direct sunlight will beat down on the south-facing side throughout the day. In the height of summer this can be a problem, so think about positioning it north to south.

In winter a polytunnel can be transformed into a poultry house and is therefore a tremendous asset to the self-sufficient gardener. This can be achieved quite simply by edging the inside with straw bales. However, the structure is not fox proof, so be sure to construct a compound around it. The polytunnel should be moved to a different place the following spring as poultry manure is highly acidic and should not be used to fertilize the ground unless it's at least a year, preferably 18 months old.

Building a fixed polytunnel

Building your own polytunnel takes a little time and effort, but the investment will allow you to reap rewards in years to come. Before erecting any permanent or semi-permanent structure, always check with your local council whether planning permission is required.

1. Decide how large you would like your structure to be. The smallest effective polytunnel is 2.5m/8ft feet long by 1.8m/6ft wide, but they can be as large as 12m/40ft, or even 18m/60ft in length.

2. Clear and level the ground.

3. Using string and wooden stakes, mark out the length and width of your polytunnel (in other words, determine its 'footprint'). Use the 'Pythagoras 3:4:5' rule to create a 90° angle for the corners of your structure (this is the standard rule for ensuring neat, right-angled corners – references to it can be sourced online). To do this, start from one of the corners, measure 1m/3ft along the width and mark it. Return to the same corner and measure 1.2m/4ft along the length and mark it. You now need to create a diagonal measurement of 1.5m/5ft between these two marked points in order to achieve an angle of exactly 90°. You may need to adjust your two markers several times (moving them slightly in or out) before achieving the diagonal. When you've done this, measure along the length of your tunnel in multiples of 1.2m or 1.5m/4ft or 5ft, marking each interval. These divisions will create the spacing for the frame. Now measure your desired width. As long as the corner you have measured is exactly 90° and both lengths and both widths have been measured accurately, then you will have achieved a perfect oblong for your polytunnel.

4. Then take a length of scaffold tubing, begged from a local building site or scaffolding company. It's fine to use bent or damaged tubing and companies are often glad to be rid of it. Cut the tubing into 60cm/24in lengths. Using a heavy hammer and a wood block to protect the top of the tubes, drive the tubes about 45cm/18in into the ground (with about 15cm/6in protruding) at the marked intervals of 1.2m or 1.5m/4ft or 5ft along each of the long sides. Ensure that the tubes are sticking up as straight as possible out of the ground.

5. Next fit the hoops. Metal hoops tend to heat up excessively on hot summer days causing the plastic covering around them to sag and melt. Another disadvantage is that metal is expensive. An alternative is to use plastic mains water piping, which won't melt the covering and is cheaper and easier to work with. Cut it into

identical lengths so that when it's bent around the centre to form the arc of the tunnel, the highest point is approximately 2m/7ft above ground level. The number of hoops you need will correspond to the length of the tunnel and to the number of scaffold tubes at your marked points along one of the lengths. Fit the piping over the scaffold tubes in the ground (see 4, above) to form arches from one side of the tunnel to the other. Drill a hole through both the water pipe and the scaffold tube and run a screw through them to ensure that they are fastened firmly together. Secure all the hoops to the pipes in the same way.

6. Now for a spot of carpentry. To construct the doorframe: at either end of the tunnel, fit two wooden uprights, roughly the length and width of a standard door, from the ground to the top of the tunnel. Secure a wooden strut across the top of the uprights (attach with nails, wire or string – whatever works best). Then take two lengths of wood underneath the hoops from one end of the tunnel to the other and fix them with nails or screws to the top of each of your door uprights. Starting at the bottom of the door uprights, run skirting boards all the way around either the inside or the outside of the polytunnel (either way is fine).

7. The polythene for the cover comes in huge rolls (approximately 6m/20ft wide) and can be sourced online or from stockists such as building suppliers. (Cheaper sources include building sites and anyone building an extension – builders use it to keep structures watertight before the walls and roof are in place, and later discard it on a skip. Don't worry about any small tears or rips in the polythene as these can be taped up.) Cover the entire frame of the tunnel with polythene. Fix the polythene to the frame (the skirting, the sides and the top of the tunnel) using flat-top nails, pins or even drawing pins. Ensure that the tunnel is well secured to the floor so that it won't get lifted up by a strong wind.

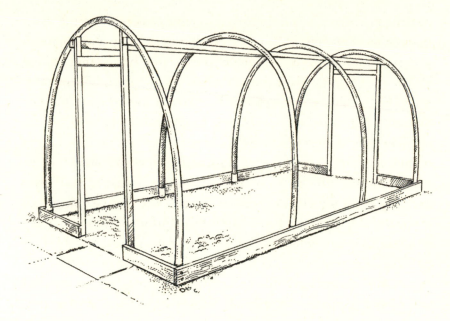

The completed frame of a polytunnel (without polythene cover)

8. To make the door: design a simple door with two panels – the bottom panel should be made with polythene and the top panel with gauze, to provide ventilation. Attach the panels to the door-frame with whatever fasteners seem to work best with the materials you are using. The polythene at either side of the doors at each end of the tunnel should be folded around the supporting structure and then pinned securely in place.

Cloches

Also known as a hot cap, a cloche (from the French for 'bell') is a small cover or house for individual plants that have been bedded out in the plot. Designed to protect the plant and give it a head start, it can be used for any young seedlings that you feel may be vulnerable. In particular, it is excellent for spring-planted brassicas and salad leaves through most seasons of the year. By using a cloche on a newly transplanted plant that has been brought outside after having been started inside, you give the plant time to adjust to its new home and surroundings. A cloche is therefore a bit like a halfway house, but one that you can remove once the plant is happy and stable.

When deciding at what stage to move your plants outside, bear in mind that if you wait until after blossoming (when the plant is older, hardier and the growing season is likely to have moved on and it will therefore be warmer) the chances are that the yield may be quite small; if you are able to move your plant outside prior to blossoming and give it an environment in which it can acclimatize, the crop is likely to be more substantial. The benefits of cloches are that they offer good ventilation (always leave the top open), protection from many bugs and nasties, insulation from harsh weather conditions, such as frost wind and rain, and you can buy them cheaply or make your own.

Cloches can be used to protect different plants throughout the year, for example:

Winter: Oriental greens such as pak choi and leaf radish, cut-and-come-again winter salad and, towards the end of winter, peas.

Spring: Seedbed sowings such as beans and most of the brassicas.

Summer: Peppers, tomatoes, Mediterranean salad leaves and sweet corn.

Autumn: Hardy salads, beets and lettuce.

Making a cloche

There are several simple ways to make a cloche by re-using old bottles and containers. One option is to remove the lid from a large plastic drinking bottle and lower it, base first, over the plant, making sure all the leaves are tucked safely inside. But in my experience the best method is to cut the bottom off an old glass demijohn. Glass cloches not only look better but offer far more protection than plastic ones.

To remove the bottom from a glass demijohn, fill the sink with approximately 5cm/2in of very cold water and sit the demijohn in the middle of it. Allow it to stand in the cold water for a while so that the glass will cool. Then pour boiling water direct from the kettle into the demijohn all the way up to the line of cold water. When the hot water from the inside meets the line of cold water on the outside, a neat seam will split all the way around the glass and the bottom should drop out. If it doesn't work for any reason (atmospheric conditions, the thickness of the glass or perhaps the temperature of the water), allow the demijohn to cool naturally back to room temperature and try again. You can 'cut' a demijohn at any height simply by adjusting the amount of cold water in the sink and filling the demijohn with boiling water to the same level.

Cold frames

Cold frames are small, sloping enclosures made from wood but with a glass lid. They make ingenious use of the sun's solar energy: the frames are positioned to face the south, the sun warms the air and the soil within the frame, and the glass prevents the heat from escaping. Because cold frames can get quite hot, it is a good idea to invest in a thermometer so that you can regulate the temperature by sometimes propping up the lid to allow a little cool air in. The cold frame is somewhere between a greenhouse and a cloche and is used for hardening off plants coming out of the greenhouse, bringing on seedlings in seed trays for later transplanting, helping hardy salads through the winter, bringing on early spring seedlings, keeping a winter supply of fresh herbs and even for even planting *in situ*. Although cold frames can be purchased, many gardeners opt to build their own.

Building a cold frame

If you have a fence or wall against which you can affix your cold frame this is ideal as it will provide a rigid back for stability and will also mean you have only three sides to build. However, the frame must face the south in order to receive the best of the sun. Salvaged window frames or shower doors make excellent lids or you can use polythene on top of chicken wire (the wire prevents the polythene from sagging in the rain). It is always best to build the frame to match the size of your lid. If you don't have a south-facing wall or fence and are building a frame with four sides, the frame should be three planks of wood high at the back but only two planks high at the front so that it will slope forwards. First, measure your lid and cut the planks of wood to match the size of the lid (the following instructions assume an oblong shape). When assembled, the frame should be very slightly smaller than the lid so that the lid overlaps the frame. Cut five planks for the sides and five planks for the front and back sections. Then assemble the frame in three stages:

1. *Bottom section*: Take four planks, position them into an oblong and screw them together using corner posts or batons. (The corner posts, like the frame itself, should be two planks high at the front and three planks high at the back.) This will give you your base.

2. *Middle section*: Take four more planks and screw them into the corner posts (as 1, above) so that your cold frame is now an oblong of four planks high.

3. *Top section*: Now take a side plank and cut it in half diagonally so that you are left with two angled planks that will slope down from the back to the front of the frame. Screw them to the front and back planks via the corner posts. Fit the back length and screw it in place, along with the 'T'-hinges for the lid. Finally, secure two wooden pivots to the inside of the side panels towards the front of

the frame so that the lid can be propped open to let air in and regulate the temperature. The pivots should be able to swing up and down so that the lid can be closed (see illustration).

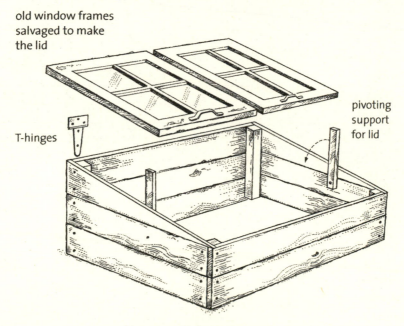

old window frames
salvaged to make
the lid

T-hinges

pivoting
support
for lid

A basic cold frame design

PICKING AND EATING THROUGH THE SEASONS

Although you can preserve salad, fruit and vegetables in many wonderful ways (see pages 226, 241, 247–255), there is nothing quite like picking and eating fresh produce. Part of the skill involved in self-sufficiency lies in finding ways to do this through as many months of the year as possible. Greenhouses, polytunnels, cloches and cold frames are all aids for the kitchen gardener, but so is the kitchen itself with its

Vegetables Through the Year

	January	February	March	April	May
Beans					
Broad (early)					✓
Broad (late)					
Runner					
Beetroot					
Broccoli					
Purple sprouting		✓	✓	✓	✓
Brussels sprouts	✓	✓	✓		
Cabbage					
Spring				✓	✓
Summer					
Winter	✓	✓	✓	✓	
Carrots					
Early					✓
Main					
Cauliflower					
Spring					
Summer					
Winter				✓	✓
Courgettes					
Cucumber					
Garlic					
Leeks	✓	✓	✓	✓	✓
Lettuce					
Onions					
Parsnips	✓	✓	✓	✓	
Peas					
Potatoes					
Early					
Main					
Radish				✓	✓
Rocket	✓	✓	✓	✓	✓
Spinach (perpetual)	✓	✓	✓	✓	✓
Swede					
Sweet corn					
Swiss chard	✓	✓	✓	✓	✓
Tomatoes					

June	July	August	September	October	November	December
✓	✓					
✓	✓	✓				
	✓	✓	✓	✓		
✓	✓	✓	✓	✓		
✓	✓	✓	✓	✓	✓	
			✓	✓	✓	✓
✓	✓	✓				
	✓	✓	✓			
			✓	✓	✓	✓
✓	✓	✓	✓	✓		
	✓	✓	✓	✓		
✓	✓	✓	✓			
			✓	✓		
✓						
✓	✓	✓	✓	✓		
	✓	✓	✓			
	✓	✓				
			✓	✓	✓	✓
	✓	✓	✓	✓		
	✓	✓	✓	✓		
			✓	✓	✓	✓
✓	✓	✓	✓	✓		
✓	✓					
	✓	✓	✓	✓	✓	
✓	✓	✓	✓	✓	✓	
✓	✓	✓	✓	✓	✓	✓
✓	✓	✓	✓	✓	✓	✓
				✓	✓	✓
		✓	✓	✓		
✓	✓	✓	✓	✓	✓	✓
	✓	✓	✓			

warm windowsill. In fact, with a little planning and forethought, it is quite possible to have something fresh on your family's plate every single week of the year.

Storing fruit and vegetables

With proper storage some fruits and vegetables can be kept fresh for quite long periods. Some examples follow.

Apples: Wrap them individually in brown paper and store in the dark – it is important that they do not touch each other.

Onions and garlic: Lift them and allow them to dry until their skins go papery. Then plait or string them together in the traditional manner and hang up. (Information on plaiting and stringing can be obtained online or from a garden centre.)

Potatoes: Lift them and allow to dry for a day or two before storing. On no account should they be washed. Any potatoes that are free from blemish can be stored in a paper sack and kept in a cool place throughout the winter. However, they must be protected from frost as this will ruin their texture – an old blanket or garden fleece tucked round the filled sacks will suffice.

Swedes: Brush them clean and, when dry, store in a net.

NATURAL PEST CONTROL

Attempting to keep pests and unwanted animals away from your prized vegetables long enough for them to grow can sometimes feel like you're fighting a losing battle. Slugs and snails slither their filmy trails of destruction across your leaves and seedlings, leaving nothing but sad-looking lines of empty stalks sticking out of the ground.

Cabbage-white caterpillars will lay their eggs and decimate your brassicas as fast as look at them. Foxes, moles and squirrels can cause devastation by digging, using the garden as a toilet and eating the vegetables and seedlings. But effective pest control can be achieved by introducing a combination of companion gardening (see page 22), nightly slug patrols and organic and other deterrents.

Beer and citrus traps

Slugs and snails adore beer (though not lager; it's the smell of the yeast that lures them) and the thought of a drink will entice them anywhere. Simply dig a hole in the soil near your plants, fill a small container with beer and place it into the ground so that the lip of the container is level with the ground. If all goes according to plan, the slug will be attracted by the beer, fall in and drown! Proprietary traps are also available online or from garden centres. Traps should be checked and replenished every day. If the thought of giving away good beer fills you with horror, an alternative is to use upturned citrus shells from halved and squeezed grapefruits or oranges. For some reason the slugs crawl under the shell and you can then pick them up and dispose of them (although I have never found this as effective as the beer trap).

Brassica collars

Brassica collars are disks placed around the neck of vulnerable plants to stop cabbage-root fly. They resemble the pleated collars that were worn around the necks of well-to-do ladies and gentlemen in the 16th and 17th centuries. Collars for plants can either be purchased or made quite easily by cutting circles in old carpet or lino of about 10cm/4in in diameter, with one radius snip from edge to centre so that it will fit on the plant. Slip the collar around the base of the plant and press firmly into the soil. They are more effective than you might think.

Broken eggshells

Back to the dear old slugs. These molluscs are responsible for more wholesale destruction in the vegetable plot than just about all the other blighters put together, so the more you can do to halt their progress the better. Next time you make an omelette or anything with eggs in it, put the shells aside to dry. When you have a dozen or so, crush them in a pestle and mortar until they're in bits (but not powdery). Sprinkle the crushed shells around the base of tender plants to deter the slugs from slithering across them.

Male urine

Male urine is a great deterrent for foxes. (The hormones in female urine prevent it from being effective, which is probably good news for the girls.) Use this method sparingly and avoid making the outside of your chicken house or vegetable garden smell like a public urinal!

Mole traps and repellers

Mole traps typically take the form of tunnels that are placed into the mole's burrow – they either flip closed when the mole runs through them or have a scissor mechanism that grabs hold of the animal's body. Traps should be checked daily. Moles have a very canny sense of smell, so a newly bought trap or one that has been excessively handled should be buried in the ground for a couple of weeks before use. Mole repellers are a humane way of preventing the burrowing beasties from tearing up your garden – they emit sound waves that the moles find discomforting.

Rhubarb leaves

The vibrant pink to green stalks of the rhubarb may be delicious in jams and desserts (see page 253) but the wide leaves that fan out at the top of the stalks are poisonous. Normally discarded (never on to the compost heap), the leaves are of no use to man or beast – or, as it turns out, to aphids. Take a couple of the leaves and tear them into a bucket of water. Let the mixture stand for a day or two, then strain and spray it directly on to the affected leaves. The leaves of the stinging nettle are also effective if used in the same way. When harvesting leaves that have been treated in this way, take extra care to wash them thoroughly before eating.

Squirrel traps

You can trap squirrels in cages set with bait or you can shoot them with an air rifle. In Britain, if you decide on either of these options, you should target only the grey squirrel, never the native red, which is a protected species. If you do kill a grey squirrel, then use it. Cure the tail and the skin (see page 149) and eat the meat by dry frying – it tastes a little like a gamey rabbit.

Tin foil

The danger when planting out your peas is that you turn your back for two minutes and every bird from a mile around has descended for dinner. If this happens, run a line of string (or bailer twine) from end to end above your row of peas and tie on to it semi-scrunched tin foil that twinkles in the sunlight and flaps in the breeze to scare the birds away. Old CDs also work well. But if you feel this might upset the natural look of your garden and transform it into something resembling a seventies glam-rock disco, then consider using hazel sticks stuck into the ground so that they tower over your tender seedlings like sentinels.

CHAPTER TWO

The Home Baker

Baking is as much about the smell as it is the taste: that gorgeous aroma of hot bread that makes your tummy roll over and plead emptiness, that come-hither smell of a chocolate cake cooling on a rack and that yeasty, sugary smell of hot-cross buns just waiting to be split and buttered. Supermarkets know all about this, which is why they make sure that the smell of their shop-baked bread is wafted over their customers as they walk past. Beautiful warm loaves are then scooped up and given pride of place in the trolley, so that they don't get squashed, and young children are placated with a torn-off corner of warm crust to chew on when they grizzle in the checkout queue. Such is the power of the smell of hot, freshly baked bread.

Home baking can be undertaken at various different levels: some people might make the occasional loaf of bread or a cake, others will indulge in some baking whenever the opportunity arises, whilst others still will take it to a different dimension: grinding their own flour and baking everything the family needs. Whichever type of baker you think you are, this chapter is for you. Simple, fun and with a self-sufficient twist wherever possible (hence the grinding of your own flour), this chapter also allows for the fact that life can be hectic and not everyone has the time or the inclination to mill their own wheat. For that reason, you will find speedy versions of some recipes, such as the 5-minute chocolate cake cooked in a mug in the microwave, which is currently to be found, in various forms, on over 9 million websites, which shows that, for many people, an almost instant chocolate cake is very appealing!

The recipes in this chapter are designed to be mixed and matched depending on how comfortable you feel with self-sufficiency, and how much time you have available. Whether you are cooking for dinner parties or everyday meals, and whether you are an experienced baker or have never been near bread dough in your life, this chapter will show you how to turn out delicious homemade baking with a smell that will rumble every tummy and a taste that makes you smile, and might even allow you to walk right by the hot-bread section in the supermarket without a second glance.

WHEAT

Bread, cakes and biscuits, pastry and pies, pasta and batter – the common ingredient to all of these is flour, and flour is wheat. Despite the fact that wheat is the third most-cultivated grain (after corn and rice), our knowledge of it hardly expands beyond the packet of flour sitting in our kitchen cupboards. But from a wheat point of view, that's only a third of the story, because each wheat kernel has three parts to it:

- the **bran** forms the outer layer and contains fibre, B vitamins and trace minerals

- the **endosperm** forms the largest part of the centre and contains carbohydrates, gluten and protein

- the **germ** forms a tiny part of the centre, yet it contains antioxidants, vitamin E, B vitamins, unsaturated fat and protein, making it the healthiest part of the kernel

Yet the only part that is used to make white flour is the endosperm, which is the part full of starch and gluten. The other two-thirds – all that goodness, all those vitamins and minerals and roughage – never make it into the bags of flour on the shop shelves, except for those of wholemeal flour.

Certainly baking your own bread, cakes and biscuits is far better for you than buying them off the shelf, but if you really want to be getting all the goodness that wheat has to offer, then milling your own wheat is the way to go. A grain mill is a small, neat machine that looks a little like a hand-cranked coffee grinder, and will grind enough flour for a family-size loaf of bread in under 2 minutes. And don't let the cost of the machine put you off either, as the average family would spend more on bread alone in just 6 months. Whether you are dedicated to a self-sufficient lifestyle or simply looking for quick and easy ideas to enrich your family's life and health, get a home grain mill. On the grounds of taste, cost, health, speed and fun, you won't regret it.

YEAST

Used in everything from beer to cheese and yoghurt to bread, yeast is the vital ingredient that makes dough rise.

Yeast can be bought in packets as dried yeast or fast-action yeast for bread machines, and it is also (but less widely) available as fresh yeast, which makes the most wonderfully light bread. (Next time you are by the hot-bread section of the supermarket, smile very nicely at the baker behind the counter and ask for a little of their fresh yeast.)

Then there are natural yeasts, such as beer. In times gone by, women would knock on the doors of the breweries begging for a little beer from which they could make bread. In reality, the idea of beer bread is often a lot better than the bread itself, because just flour, beer and water tend to make a loaf you could knock nails in with, unless you give the yeast a little help by using either self-raising flour or by adding a little baking powder and sugar. But it still needs a long prove, preferably overnight, and when done has a slightly sour-dough finish. Different beers produce different flavours, as you would imagine, so a heavy, dark beer produces a heavy, dark loaf. Experimenting with different beer-bread recipes is great fun and you're sure to find one you like.

MAKING BREAD

Anyone can make bread. You don't even need a kitchen – you could make some just sitting around an open fire in the woods. Neolithic man did it this way for millennia and the descendants of this early bread are still enjoyed today as tortillas, chapattis, naans, pittas, oatcakes and johnnycakes. But give a person a kitchen, some flour, water, yeast, a glug of oil, a little salt, and little sugar or honey, and the result will be a really good loaf of bread.

Using a bread machine

If you have a bread machine, you don't even need to stand there kneading the dough, because it does it all for you. But bread machines, although fantastic devices, can have the tendency to turn out uniform bricks – tasty bricks, but bricks nonetheless. For a superior homemade taste, the trick is to get the bread machine to do all the hard work for you, and at the proving stage turn out the dough and shape it yourself into a country loaf (loose on the tray and dusted with flour), a flat tear-and-share bread or nice round rolls. Cooking the bread in the oven like this will improve both the flavour and the texture and give it much more of a homemade feel.

Basic bread-machine bread

> 1 tbsp oil
> 650g/1lb 7oz strong white flour (or home-ground flour), plus extra
>   for dusting
> 1 tsp sea salt
> 2 tsp sugar or honey
> 7g/¼oz sachet fast-action yeast

Pour 400ml/14fl oz warm water and the oil into the bread-machine pan, then add all the dry ingredients. Set it to 'dough' mode. As soon as the dough has been mixed and kneaded, but before it starts to prove, turn the machine off. Remove the pan and turn the dough out on to a floured work surface, then shape as required. Prove and cook in a preheated oven set at 200°C/400°F/gas 6, allowing 20–30 minutes for a standard loaf and 12–15 minutes for rolls. If you want a crusty loaf, place a dish of hot water in the bottom of the oven when baking.

Variations

For an Italian-style loaf or pizza base add tomato purée and herbs to the dough. For a French-style loaf, simply omit the oil.

For a sweet bread, replace 150g/5½oz of the white flour with wholemeal flour, and add 1 tbsp cinnamon and 150g/5½oz sultanas as well as an additional 1 tbsp sugar. Cook as a loaf or shape the dough into rolls and bake, then brush over a sugar glaze for the best sticky buns ever.

Handmade bread

Whilst the bread machine is a great time and energy saver, nothing quite beats the love and the passion involved in making bread the traditional way; love, passion, and something of a violent side, because making bread by hand is incredibly physical and involves hitting, slapping, punching and squeezing, as well as the more sensual side of kneading and caressing. Kneading involves stretching the dough by pushing it away from you using the heel of your hands, then folding it back towards you with your fingers, repeating over and over and over again, rotating the ball of dough as you do so, for at least 10 minutes until the dough is springy and elastic and doesn't stick to your hands or the surface. (You will know when it's done because your arms will feel as though they are about to fall off.) It's a great workout, a great stress reliever, and, of course, the more effort you put into it, the more calories you burn, and so the less guilty you will feel when you rip off a huge hot hunk when it's done and smother it in something horrendously fattening and eat the lot.

The first major difference between the bread machine and hand-making is in the yeast. The ready yeast that's ideal for the machine doesn't transfer very well away from it, and for this reason it's best to use a dried yeast, which you will need to activate by mixing it with hand-hot water (run the water over your wrist until it feels pleasantly warm, not boiling and not tepid). Alternatively, if you can find it, use fresh yeast.

Basic handmade bread

1½ tsp dried or fresh yeast

1½ tsp honey or sugar

1 tbsp oil

1 tsp sea salt

650g/1lb 7oz strong white flour (or home-ground flour), plus extra
for dusting

Put the yeast and honey in a cup containing 5 tbsp hand-hot water and mix well, then cover and put to one side in a warm place for 10–15 minutes until the yeast is frothy. Pour the yeast into a mixing bowl and add the oil, salt and 200g/7oz of the flour. Now beat, either with a hand-held electric mixer fitted with a dough hook or with a wooden spoon (but either way beat it well!), adding the remaining flour little by little. When all the flour has been mixed in, and the dough is stiff and comes away from the side of the bowl, turn it out on to a floured work surface and knead. Return the dough to the mixing bowl, cover with a tea towel and leave somewhere warm until doubled in size. Turn the dough out on to the floured surface, summon all the anger and frustration you can think of, and punch the dough once, right in the middle, to knock the air out, then knead it a couple of times to remove any additional air bubbles. Finally, leave it to rest for 2 minutes to allow the gluten to relax a little. Shape the dough as required, put in a tin or on a baking sheet and leave until doubled in size. Meanwhile, preheat the oven to 200°C/400°F/gas 6. Bake for 20–30 minutes (or 12–15 minutes for rolls), then remove from the oven, turn the loaf upside down and tap it on the bottom. If it sounds hollow, it's ready. If it doesn't sound hollow, return it to the oven for 5 minutes and test again.

Tear-and-share flat breads

These flat breads are very versatile. The basic version here has basil leaves scattered over the top, but you could add some red onions and olives, maybe some peppers, or garlic, pesto or slithers of deseeded chilli … whatever you want, really. Let the dough prove once before placing it in the tin; it will prove for the second time as it cooks. Note that if you use bread-machine dough, there is no need to let it prove first.

> 1 recipe quantity Basic Handmade Bread dough after its first
> proving (see page 51) or Basic Bread-machine Bread
> dough (see page 49)
> extra virgin olive oil, for drizzling and greasing
> handful of torn basil leaves
> sea salt

Preheat the oven to 190°C/375°F/gas 5 and lightly oil a baking tray. Put the dough in the tray and squash it down, tugging it all the way into the corners until it fills the tray. Drizzle some oil across the top, and sprinkle with the basil leaves, then bake in the preheated oven for 15–20 minutes. Remove from the oven and eat warm straight from the tin or transfer to a wire rack to cool.

Unleavened breads

The difference with unleavened breads is the absence of any lightening, so although they can still include yeast, they're not left to prove and rise, which means they are flat rather than rounded. The most basic recipe for unleavened bread does not include yeast at all and is simply flour, water and salt mixed into balls, rolled out flat and dry-fried quickly in a frying pan over a high heat, like a savoury crêpe. Pitta bread is the same recipe but with yeast added, so it does have a certain puffiness. Naan breads are made by using live yoghurt as the rising agent instead of yeast, and chapattis and tortillas use baking powder. All are quickly made and quickly cooked.

Banana bread

Although this book is all about self-sufficiency and bananas are not exactly indigenous to the UK, this recipe is included because banana bread is made from over-ripe bananas, the ones that have gone black and the supermarkets or greengrocers cannot sell, and you can pick them up for next to nothing. Sometimes that's what self-sufficiency is about: spotting bargains and then finding nice ways to use them up. This bread is beautiful hot with butter or toasted the following day.

60g/2¼oz chilled butter, diced, plus extra for greasing
250g/9oz self-raising flour
1 tbsp baking powder
pinch of salt
60g/2¼oz caster sugar
1 egg, beaten
grated rind of 1 lemon
2 good-sized over-ripe bananas, mashed
splash of milk

Preheat the oven to 180°C/350°F/gas 4 and grease a 900g/2lb loaf tin. Sift the flour, baking powder and salt into a mixing bowl. Add the butter and rub in with your fingertips until the mixture resembles fine breadcrumbs. Add the sugar, egg, lemon rind, bananas and milk and stir well to combine, then pour the mixture into the greased tin. Bake in the preheated oven for 45–65 minutes until a skewer inserted into the middle of the loaf comes out clean. Remove from the oven and serve warm or cold.

Malt loaf

Although you might think that malt loaf is more cake than bread, the fact that we spread it with butter qualifies it as bread. The beauty of this recipe is that it doesn't give the horrible glued-to-your-teeth sensation that is the major downside to the bought varieties.

40g/1½oz butter, plus extra for greasing
110g/3½oz sultanas
110g/3½oz raisins
170g/6oz self-raising flour
tip of a teaspoon of bicarbonate of soda
pinch of salt
110g/3½oz soft brown sugar
1 large egg, beaten
1 tbsp malt extract

Preheat the oven to 190°C/375°F/gas 5 and grease a 900g/2lb loaf tin. Put the butter, sultanas, raisins and 150ml/5fl oz water in a saucepan and bring to the boil, stirring to combine. Reduce the heat and simmer for a few minutes, then remove from the heat and set aside to cool. Sift the flour, bicarbonate of soda and salt into a mixing bowl, add the sugar and stir well. Tip in the cooled fruit mixture, egg and malt extract and stir again. Pour the mixture into the greased tin. Bake in the preheated oven for 30 minutes on the top shelf of the oven and then another 30 minutes on the bottom shelf (reducing the temperature by 20°C for the second half of the cooking if you have a fan oven). Remove from the oven and turn out on to a wire rack to cool.

Gluten-free breads

More and more people are discovering that they are intolerant to gluten, which means that they cannot eat wheat (with all the many implications this has). Records show that up to 1 per cent of the population has coeliac disease, though because the current test for gluten intolerance means you have to eat wheat for 6 weeks prior to the test, many people never get tested and so don't become part of the statistics, which means the percentage could be much higher.

Bought gluten-free bread is expensive and can be unpleasant – most needs to be toasted to get even a reasonable result. It is therefore an excellent idea for coeliacs to make their own breads. Soda bread made with buttermilk works fantastically well with gluten-free flour and gives it a really good flavour, but it is not a bread to keep and does need to be eaten hot (any leftovers make fantastic breadcrumbs). Other suggestions are the rice, potato and tapioca flour recipe below (which uses xanthan gum to provide the stretchiness that is provided in normal bread by the gluten in bread flour) and the American corn bread recipe on page 57.

Gluten-free bread

Warming the dry ingredients at the start of the recipe helps to kick-start the ingredients into action, whilst placing a bowl over the dough while it is proving increases the humidity, so stopping the dough drying out and forming a skin over the top. This recipe also works well for pizza.

250g/9oz rice flour
150g/5½oz potato flour
100g/3½oz tapioca flour
1 heaped tsp xanthan gum
1 heaped tsp sea salt
1 heaped tsp bicarbonate of soda
2 tbsp olive oil, plus extra for greasing
7g/¼oz sachet dried yeast
1 heaped tsp soft brown sugar

Preheat the oven to 110°C/220°F/gas ¼, then switch it off. Put the flours, xanthan gum, sea salt and bicarbonate of soda in an ovenproof mixing bowl and stir together, then place in the preheated oven to warm through, stirring after 5 minutes. Also place an oiled baking sheet in the oven to warm. Meanwhile, put the yeast, sugar and oil in a bowl, pour in 400ml/14fl oz hand-hot water and mix well, then cover and put to one side in a warm place for 10–15 minutes until the yeast is frothy.

Remove the mixing bowl from the oven and pour the yeast mixture into it, then stir the ingredients just enough to bring the mixture together to form a soft dough. Shape into a ball, dust with flour and put on the warmed baking tray with the ovenproof bowl over the top. Put in the oven to rise for 30–90 minutes until doubled in size.

Remove the dough from the oven and increase the temperature to 220°C/425°F/gas 7. Keep the dough warm by laying a thick doubled towel over the bowl (if necessary). Remove the bowl and bake the dough in the preheated oven for about 1 hour until golden brown. Remove from the oven and eat while still warm.

American corn bread

Typical American corn bread is made from cornmeal (not to be confused with cornflour), which means it is gluten free. However, most baking powder contains wheat, so if you are coeliac, you'll need to buy the gluten-free version. If you don't have buttermilk, you can add 2 tsp lemon juice to 300ml/10fl oz milk to sour it.

1 egg
300ml/10fl oz buttermilk
1 tsp baking powder (gluten-free for coeliacs)
4–5 heaped tbsp cornmeal
oil, for frying

Preheat the oven to 180°C/350°F/gas 4. Beat the egg with the buttermilk and baking powder in a bowl, then stir in sufficient cornmeal so that the mixture has the consistency of double cream. Pour a little oil into a 25cm/10in heavy, ovenproof frying pan and heat until it is spitting hot, then pour the mixture in until it comes nearly to the top of the pan. Cook for 2 minutes, then transfer the pan to the preheated oven for 20 minutes until the cornbread is firm but still springy in the middle when pressed. Remove from the oven and eat still warm from the tin or transfer to a wire rack and leave to cool.

CAKES AND BISCUITS

The whole lifestyle of self-sufficiency is about producing the luxuries as well as satisfying everyday needs and wants. Cakes and biscuits are a luxury, but when you make them yourself they are a luxury you can afford. Apart from the obvious saving that making at home allows, the beauty of this is that it connects with so many other aspects of self-sufficiency, so cheese you have made yourself can be turned into a cheesecake, jam into fillings and garden vegetables into cakes, all made by using up the eggs from your own chickens. But if you have not made cheese or jam or grown your own vegetables, then it's no problem to pick up the ingredients from a supermarket.

Families always used to bake their own cakes until someone put out a rumour that it was difficult and time-consuming to do, and people drifted over to packet buying. There is some truth that the recipes did go through a stage of getting rather complicated. A typical example is the sponge cake. Sure you can do each individual section bit by laborious bit, but you can also do the all-in-one method using a food mixer and have it done and in the oven in less than 10 minutes, bake for 20, make the butter icing while it cools and have it assembled and ready for eating in under an hour.

This is cake and biscuit baking the self-sufficient way: big on time-saving shortcuts, big on truly delicious flavours and big on using up whatever is to hand, wasting nothing and keeping down the cost.

Basic sponge cake

You can use the traditional Victoria sponge method if you want, but the all-in-one food-mixer way gives a result that's just as good in a fraction of the time. You can also make a cake in a food processor, but less air will get incorporated, even if you remove the food pusher from the lid, and so the results are never as light.

225g/8oz butter, softened, plus extra for greasing
225g/8oz self-raising flour, sifted
225g/8oz caster sugar
4 eggs

Preheat the oven to 180°C/350°F/gas 4 and grease two 20cm/8in sandwich cake tins. Put all the ingredients in the food mixer bowl, turn it on (starting slowly if the flour is likely to coat your kitchen) and leave it mixing for a good few minutes. You will know when it's done because the mixture will turn light and fluffy. Scrape the mixture into the cake tins and cook in the preheated oven for about 20 minutes or until a skewer inserted into the middle of the cakes comes out clean. Do not open the door for the first 15 minutes or the cakes will sink. Remove from the oven and leave the cakes to cool for few minutes, then transfer to a wire rack to cool completely. Alternatively, you can cook the mixture in one deep tin, in which case it will take about 30 minutes, and then split it, or you can use the mixture for fairy cakes, which will take about 15 minutes.

Variations

Adapt this basic recipe by adding 1 tbsp cocoa powder for a chocolate cake, the juice and zest of 1 lemon for a lemon cake or ½ tsp instant coffee granules dissolved in 1 tbsp boiling water for a coffee cake – with chopped walnuts if wanted. Fill with jam or butter icing, plain or flavoured to suit, and top with sifted icing sugar, butter icing or a drizzled syrup. This recipe also works well for a steamed sponge cooked with fruit.

5-minute chocolate sponge

If speed and hot chocolate sponge are your thing (and, let's face it, for whom would they not be?), then this 5-minute microwave mug cake takes a lot of beating! The timing is for a 750W microwave oven.

> 4 tbsp self-raising flour
> 4 tbsp granulated sugar
> 2 tsp cocoa powder
> 1 egg
> 3 tbsp vegetable oil
> 3 tbsp milk
> sprinkling of chocolate chips (optional)
> 1 tsp vanilla extract

Put the flour, sugar and cocoa powder into a large coffee mug (roughly 400ml/14fl oz) and stir. Add the egg and beat the mixture together with a fork, then tip in the oil, milk, chocolate chips (if using) and vanilla extract and mix the whole thing together. If you don't have a large enough mug, divide the mixture between two mugs at this stage. Cook in a microwave for 3 minutes on high, then leave to stand for 2 minutes. Run a knife around the edge of the mug and turn the cake out on to a plate and have it with cream or ice-cream. Or, if you'd rather not make more washing-up, just take out a spoon (or two if you can bear to share it) and find a quiet spot to enjoy. Do not let the cake go cold, as it turns hard when it does so.

Cheesecake

This is a perfect summer's afternoon self-sufficient cheesecake, where every part of it can be made (including both cheeses), reared and foraged for – except for the sugar. Use a medley of any berries or other fruits you have grown or been able to forage. Alternatively, of course, it's no problem to buy what you need.

125g/4½oz digestive biscuits
60g/2½oz butter, melted

FOR THE TOPPING
250g/9oz ricotta cheese
250g/9oz mascarpone cheese
115g/4oz light soft brown sugar
a few drops of vanilla extract
2 eggs, beaten
115–175g/4–6oz mixed berries

Preheat the oven to 180°C/350°F/gas 4 and grease a 25cm/10in spring-form cake tin. Put the biscuits in a plastic bag and crush with a rolling pin. Melt the butter in a small saucepan, then remove from the heat. Pour in the biscuit crumbs and mix well. Tip the mixture into the tin and press firmly over the base. Put the ricotta, mascarpone, sugar and vanilla extract in a mixing bowl and beat together with a hand-held electric mixer or a wooden spoon until smooth. Add the eggs and beat well again, then tip in the fruits and fold gently into the mixture with a metal spoon until they are evenly dispersed. Pour the mixture over the base and spread out evenly. Bake in the preheated oven for 20–25 minutes. Remove from the oven and leave to cool, then put in the fridge for 1–2 hours to chill before removing the cheesecake carefully from the tin.

Garden vegetable cakes

The three garden vegetables that jump out as lending sweetness and a moist, succulent texture to a cake are carrots, beetroot and potatoes. This again is where so much of self-sufficiency interlinks, because not only are you baking a fantastic cake using vegetables from the garden, but if you have chickens you can use their eggs, you can use homemade butter for the potato cake and homemade cream cheese for the carrot-cake topping and even grind your own flour.

Carrot cake

This classic cake, which is sweet and moist and has a luscious creamy icing, is always a favourite.

butter, for greasing
4 eggs
400g/14oz caster sugar
300ml/10fl oz vegetable oil
250g/9oz plain flour
¾ tsp baking powder
¾ tsp bicarbonate of soda
¼ tsp salt
¼ tsp cinnamon
325g/11oz carrots, grated

FOR THE ICING
115g/4oz butter
225g/8oz cream cheese
500g/1lb 2oz icing sugar, sifted

Preheat the oven to 180°C/350°F/gas 4 and grease a 900g/2lb loaf tin or a deep 20cm/8in cake tin. Put the eggs, sugar and oil in a mixing bowl and beat together with a hand-held electric mixer or a wooden spoon. Sift in the flour, baking powder, bicarbonate of soda, salt and cinnamon, and add the grated carrots, then stir the mixture together. Pour into the tin and bake in the preheated oven for 40–50 minutes until a skewer inserted into the middle of the cake comes out clean. Remove from the oven and leave to cool in the tin for 15 minutes, then transfer to a wire rack to cool completely. Meanwhile, put the icing ingredients in a mixing bowl and beat with a hand-held electric mixer or a wooden spoon until smooth. When the cake is cool, smooth the icing over the top with a palette knife.

Variation

For a beetroot cake, substitute the carrot with grated beetroot and use 2 tsp cocoa powder instead of the cinnamon. This cake is too sweet to need any icing, so serve plain.

Mashed potato cake

This delicious and incredibly moist cake is guaranteed to wow everyone who tastes it. The sugar sprinkled on top forms a delicious crunchy topping, so it's best to mark out the slices first for ease. Ideally you should make this cake only when you've got some mashed potato going spare – so you're economically using up leftovers – but just in case you need to start from scratch, the recipe starts from the very beginning.

450g/1lb floury potatoes
knob of butter, plus extra for greasing
splash of milk, plus extra for brushing
450g/1lb plain flour
1½ tsp baking powder
200g/7oz caster sugar, plus extra for sprinkling
115g/4oz chilled butter, diced
115g/4oz chilled lard, diced
30g/1oz suet
200g/7oz mixed dried fruit

Cook the potatoes in a saucepan of boiling salted water until tender. Drain, mash with just enough milk and butter to moisten, and set aside. Preheat the oven to 180°C/350°F/gas 4 and grease a 25 × 25cm/ 10 × 10in baking dish, at least 3.5cm/1½in high. Sift the flour and baking powder into a mixing bowl and stir in the sugar. Add the butter and lard and rub in with the fingertips until the mixture resembles fine breadcrumbs. Stir in the suet and dried fruit. Now add the warm mashed potato (in stages, as you may not need it all) and mix to bind the dry ingredients into a soft dough. Transfer the mixture into the dish and smooth it level. Brush with a little milk and sprinkle with a little sugar. Using a knife, mark out 16 squares. Bake in the preheated oven for 1½–2 hours until golden brown and firm to the touch. Remove from the oven and leave to cool in the tin. Serve cold.

Hazelnut and honey cookies

If you do not want to cook all these cookies at once, wrap the dough and keep in the fridge for a few days, or freeze for longer.

  75g/3oz hazelnuts, plus 30–36 to decorate (optional)
  75g/3oz butter, softened, plus extra for greasing
  75g/3oz honey
  140g/5oz plain flour, plus extra for dusting

Preheat the oven to 180°C/350°F/gas 4. Spread all the hazelnuts out on a baking tray and cook in the preheated oven for 10 minutes, checking every couple of minutes after the first 5 minutes, as they burn easily. Remove from the oven and turn the oven off. Tip 75g/3oz into a blender or food processor and blend to a rough powder. Alternatively, use a pestle and mortar. Reserve the remaining nuts for decoration.

Put the butter and honey in a mixing bowl and beat with a wooden spoon until light and creamy. Add the flour and ground roasted hazelnuts and mix well together. Tip the mixture on to a floured surface and knead it gently, then roll it into a 15cm/6in-long cylinder. Wrap the cylinder in greaseproof paper and put in the fridge for 2 hours to firm.

Preheat the oven to 180°C/350°F/gas 4 and lightly grease three baking sheets. Remove the cookie dough roll from the fridge and slice into 30–36 rounds about 5mm/¼in thick. Place on the baking sheets and decorate with the whole roasted hazelnuts, if using. Bake in the preheated oven for 6–8 minutes until golden brown. Remove from the oven and transfer to a wire rack to cool.

Shortbread

So fast and cheap to make, this should be in everyone's emergency repertoire. If you want a more rustic look, form the dough by hand on a lightly greased baking tray.

140g/5oz plain flour
25g/1oz rice flour
50g/2oz caster sugar, plus extra for sprinkling
115g/4oz butter, softened

Preheat the oven to 160°C/325°F/gas 3 and grease two 18cm/7in sandwich tins. Put all the ingredients into a mixing bowl and mix by hand until they come together into a ball. Place the dough in the tins and press down all around, then prick biscuit-sized shapes with a fork on the top. Bake in the preheated oven for about 45 minutes until golden brown on top. Remove from the oven and leave to cool in the tins, then sprinkle with caster sugar.

Variations

For a jazzed-up version, dip half of each shortbread into some melted chocolate and leave to dry on the wire rack.

For a gluten-free version, replace the plain flour with 50g/2oz cornflour and increase the rice flour to 115g/4oz.

PASTRY

The pastry of a pie was once known as the 'coffin', because meat was cooked in a pastry case to keep it moist, and then the pastry was discarded before the food inside was eaten. The reason could have been that the craft took a long time to hone, and it wasn't until the Middle Ages that the basic pastry of fat and flour was perfected. Before that people used oil, which left the pastry soggy, soft and distinctly unappetizing.

Pastry today is made with half fat to flour. The fat can be all butter with a touch of icing sugar for sweet pastry, half and half lard and butter for a good shortcrust pastry or all lard for a hot-water crust pastry used for pork pies. The trick with all pastry making is to keep everything cold and to use your hands as little as possible.

Lard

Any day is a good day for a pie. But to make pastry, you need lard, which is pig fat. The best lard is always made by trimming the fat from your own free-range pigs and rendering it down, but you can also get it from your local butcher. Specify that it does have to come from a free-range pig, because barn-reared commercial pigs can produce a pappy, soft fat, while outdoor pigs have a much firmer, tighter fat. Ethically – and for flavour and texture – free range is always preferable.

PIES AND PASTIES, TARTS AND FLANS

Pies can be sweet or savoury, and, looking back at the original pasties, they were often both in one. In a book on self-sufficiency, it would be a travesty not to include pasties, as they were the original labourer's packed lunch, made by placing meat and vegetables (or anything else to hand, most often the leftovers from the previous night's meal) on one side of a circle of pastry, and a sweet filling of apples or plums on the other, and folding the pastry over the top of the lot and crimping it down on the other side in a half-circle case. It was ideal because it was a complete, filling, all-in-one meal, and the thick ridge that sealed it acted as a handle, so that the worker's dirty hands didn't touch the food. This sweet and savoury all-in-one version has dropped from fashion and really only comes into its own for the longest days out working, such as lambing or haymaking.

Nothing says self-sufficiency in quite the same way as a pie, because the filling for a pie is all about using up any leftover meat. Take a chicken you have reared yourself or bought (hopefully a free-range chicken), or a haunch of venison you have traded some other produce for, roast it one day, then strip it of every speck of meat for a pie the next (a pie is very easy to pad out, so a little meat can go a long, long way). The pies included here can be made with any white or red meat you want, though you'll note that the flavourings for the red-meat version are more robust. To help make either of the pies go further, use the really old-fashioned method of false meat balls by using herbs, breadcrumbs and finely chopped (cooked) offal bound with an egg to make little balls about the size of a golf ball, and pop them on top of the meat mixture before the lid goes on. This gives the extra advantage of lifting the pastry top away from the meat, so keeping it crisp and dry.

White-meat pie

Use cooked chicken, pheasant, rabbit or turkey meat (or a combination of some or all of these) for the filling for this pie. If you are pushed for time, forget the pastry, spoon the filling into a dish and top with mashed potato for a quick and easy pie.

50g/2oz butter
175g/6oz button mushrooms, quartered
1 carrot, diced
115g/4oz fresh or frozen peas
350–400g/12–14oz cooked chicken, pheasant, rabbit or turkey meat
    (or a mixture), stripped from the bones and diced or shredded

FOR THE PASTRY
350g/12oz plain flour, plus extra for dusting
175g/6oz chilled butter, diced

FOR THE SAUCE
50g/2oz butter
50g/2oz plain flour
150ml/5fl oz milk
150ml/5fl oz chicken stock
sea salt and black pepper

To make the pastry, sift the flour and a pinch of salt into a mixing bowl and add the butter. Using your fingertips, rub the butter into the flour until the mixture resembles fine breadcrumbs. Add about 4 tbsp water, stirring the mixture to form a firm dough. Turn it out on to a floured surface and knead lightly, then wrap in cling film and rest in the fridge for 15 minutes.

Preheat the oven to 180°C/350°F/gas 4. To make the sauce, melt the butter in a large heavy-based saucepan over a low heat, then stir in the flour and mix to a paste. Cook for 1–2 minutes. Remove the pan from the heat and gradually pour in the milk and stock, stirring continuously to prevent lumps forming. Once all the milk has been incorporated, return the pan to the heat and bring slowly to the boil, still stirring, until the sauce is smooth and has thickened, then reduce the heat and simmer for 5 minutes, stirring occasionally. Season to taste. Meanwhile, melt the butter in a frying pan over a low heat and fry the mushrooms and carrots until softened. Tip the mixture into the thickened sauce, along with the peas and diced or shredded meat and mix to combine.

Remove the pastry from the fridge and roll out on a floured work surface. Place a 25cm/10in flan tin or pie plate on top of the pastry and cut around it twice. Reroll the trimmings and cut out leaf shapes from them. Put one of the pastry circles in the tin. Pour the mixture into the pastry case, lay the lid over the top and crimp the edges. Decorate the top with the pastry leaves (sorry, all savoury pies have to have these), then stand the tin on a baking sheet. Bake in the preheated oven for about 1 hour or until the pastry is golden.

Variation

For a red meat (or game) pie, replace the white meat with the same weight of off-cuts of raw meat, browned in some oil in a frying pan until cooked. Add 150ml/5fl oz water or stock and 150ml/5fl oz red wine or beer, plus a squeeze of tomato purée, to the meat, along with a chopped onion and a bay leaf. Simmer the mixture to remove the harshness of the alcohol and until the meat is tender, then thicken the sauce using a paste made from the flour and butter (as for Peas à la français, see page 16). Add the mushrooms, carrots and peas and pour into the pastry case.

Open pastry flans are an ideal way to use up produce. If you have fruit trees or you can get permission to pick apples, plums, pears or apricots, then they can all be used for tarte tatin. Onion or leek tarts are beautiful served warm with soft homemade cheese, and nothing can beat a quiche made from free-range eggs and home-cured ham, or, even better, home-smoked ham.

QUICK PASTRY SNACKS

These make a perfect breakfast on the go. A tip when making any recipe using rough puff pastry, such as turnovers or sausage rolls, is to dampen the baking tray instead of greasing it, which creates steam and gives a much lighter finish. This pastry is a sort of cheat's rough puff pastry. It's quick and easy to make, and while it won't be as flaky as real rough puff, it will be much lighter than shortcrust.

> 225g/8oz plain flour, plus extra for dusting
> 175g/6oz chilled butter
> a little ice-cold water
> 4 bacon rashers
> 4 slithers of cheese
> 2 tomatoes (optional)

Sift the flour into a mixing bowl. Grate the butter into the flour and stir with a knife so as not to break up the butter gratings. Gently stir enough ice-cold water into the mixture to form a firm dough. Cover with cling film and leave to rest in the fridge for 30 minutes. Preheat the oven to 200°C/400°F/gas 6. Remove the pastry from the fridge and roll out on a floured surface. Cut into four 15cm/6in squares. Lay a rasher of bacon corner to corner on each one, with a slither of cheese in the centre and maybe a slice of tomato at each end, then bring the outer corners to meet over the top of the cheese at the centre. Place on a baking tray and bake in the preheated oven for 15 minutes.

Gluten-free pastry

The common complaint about most gluten-free pastry is that it tends to be crumbly and pretty tasteless. This recipe overcomes that problem to the point that couples where one partner has a wheat allergy and the other does not, as is so often the case, can both enjoy the same meal, which, if you are coeliac, you will understand is something of a rarity!

    115g/4oz cornmeal
    115g/4oz rice flour
    115g/4oz potato flour
    1½ tsp xanthan gum
    pinch of salt
    185g/6½oz chilled butter, diced
    1 egg

Sift the cornmeal, rice flour, potato flour, xanthan gum and salt into a mixing bowl. Add the butter and rub it in with your fingertips until the mixture resemble fine breadcrumbs. Beat the egg with about 200ml/7fl oz water and add gradually to the mixture, stirring to make a firm dough. You may not need all the liquid. Bring the dough together with your hands, then wrap in cling film and rest in the fridge for 15 minutes before using.

PASTA

A quick word about pasta, because the ability to make your own pasta in the self-sufficient kitchen is a must. Once you've got the basic recipe perfected, try making ravioli using homemade ricotta-style soft cheese (see page 83 for cheese-making ideas) and blanched chopped spinach with a grating of fresh nutmeg, and serve it with crusty bread and a homemade rustic tomato pasta sauce. Children adore rolling their own pasta, and even pasta haters among them will enjoy the fact that they have made it themselves.

Handmade pasta

Homemade fresh pasta cooks in seconds: just drop it into boiling water and, as soon as the water comes back to the boil with the pasta float-ing to the surface, it is cooked. It also dries fantastically well and keeps for ages if sealed. Use garden produce to flavour and colour the pasta – spinach for the brightest green, beetroot for red and fresh herbs for speckled – reducing the number of eggs used to take into account the increased moisture the vegetables bring.

100g/3½oz pasta (type oo) flour
1 egg plus 1 egg yolk, beaten

Tip the flour on to a clean work surface and make a well in the centre. Add the beaten egg and yolk and mix with your fingertips. As the dough begins to come together, knead it as for bread until an elastic dough is formed. Cover with cling film and rest in the fridge for 10 minutes, then take the dough ball and roll it out using a pasta machine or a rolling pin. The pasta should be dusted with flour after rolling or shaping and left to dry for half an hour before being cooked in plenty of boiling salted water.

Variation

For bread-machine pasta, put the ingredients in the machine on 'dough' mode and let the machine do the work, but remove the dough before proving starts. Rest in the fridge before rolling, as for handmade pasta.

CHAPTER THREE

·

The Home Dairy

Tactile, fun and immensely satisfying, turning your kitchen into a temporary dairy is not anywhere near as dramatic as it sounds, and can mean as little as using a bowl and a wooden spoon, right up to using all the kit and every inch of space you can muster to create your very own Cheddar-type cheese. If your interest lies in making a cooling milkshake, a healthy yoghurt or a stunning cheese board with hard and soft cheeses to share with family and friends, this is a zero-nonsense, stripped-down guide to home dairying and cheese-making that is a doddle to follow. Dairying is an essential skill in the self-sufficient kitchen.

An important aspect of the self-sufficient lifestyle is to create a balanced diet, and milk, cream, cheese and all their derivatives offer a tasty way of providing the calcium, proteins, fats and nutrients essential for a healthy body. Since humankind domesticated the second animal (the first was a dog, and nobody wanted to make cheese out of dog milk), we have been collecting milk and dabbling with dairy skills.

From the Romans, who bathed in milk, to the French, who took the strength of cheese (not to mention the smell) to new heights, just about every region in the world has milk and cheese feature in their history, and very much in their present.

Dairying, in particular cheese-making, is first a science, and second – albeit a close second – an art that can be picked up and perfected by anyone in any walk of life. Once the basic methods have been grasped, it is possible to go on and make a copy of just about any variety of cheese, such as Cheddar, Edam, ricotta, feta, Brie, cottage cheese and, of course, Stilton. But the basics have to be mastered first. This chapter teaches those basics, with one or two examples of easy, stripped-down dairy recipes at each step of the way, from the simplest method of making cream to the more taxing challenge of perfecting a hard cheese, all of which can be achieved in any kitchen. And it all begins with milk.

EQUIPMENT

Much of the equipment needed for small-scale dairy production will already be available in the kitchen of anyone who enjoys cooking, such as pots, pans and bowls, a food mixer or whisk, measuring jugs and sieves. The only consideration should be that all of the equipment used with milk must be scrupulously clean and sterile, including surfaces and surroundings, as milk will react with bacteria and turn bad very quickly. Making hard cheese involves some more specialist equipment (see page 84).

MILK

Every mammal produces milk to suckle its young, from elephants to moles, but the dairy industry has really sprung up around those animals that can be reasonably domesticated, such as goats, sheep, buffaloes and cows. Of these, the cow takes centre stage. Cow's milk is made up from millions of tiny particles of butterfat, on average about 12.5 per cent of the total, all kept in suspension away from one another in a solution of water. When we process milk in the dairy and make cream and butter and yoghurt and cheese, all we're doing in effect is finding different ways to separate those butterfat globules from the water and bring them together.

But it's the quality of that butterfat that will determine how good your dairy making will be. The creamier the milk, the more butterfat it will contain – on average cow's milk contains 66kcal per 100g/3½oz whole milk, whereas human milk is higher, containing 72kcal in the same amount. The richness of the butterfat, and indeed the colour, is directly influenced by what the cow has been eating. For example, the milk from a cow fed on spring grass will have a greater number of fat globules, which tend to be larger (making the milk thicker), and will have that gorgeous creamy yellow colour taken from the green pigment carotene in the grass. This makes it ideal for butter making, though not quite as good for producing hard cheese.

Goat's milk is not so easily influenced. The butterfat particles tend to be smaller in size and of a much lower percentage, only about 11 per cent, so the milk is skinnier – just 61kcal per 100 grams – and the colour whiter because goats don't use carotene. Many people who find themselves allergic to cow's milk are fine with goat's milk.

Sheep's milk, or ewes' milk, is actually higher in butterfat, as much as 17 per cent, making it perfect for cheese-making (think feta, manchego and ricotta), but because of its size, the animal produces far less in a single sitting (or standing), and therefore it can be quite an expensive alternative and slightly more difficult to find.

But, and this is a big but, if you're looking to be self-sufficient, there is nothing quite like having a house cow/goat/sheep and milking it yourself. Of course you need the land and all the other serious considerations such as time and effort, but the rewards are unbeatable!

For the rest of us, there's the supermarket, a health food shop or a really good deli, and don't be put off by frozen milk for dairying as it does freeze really well and works fine.

CREAM

For those people who do have their own house cow, making cream is as simple as taking a wide saucepan of at least 2- or 3-day-old whole milk and leaving it out overnight at room temperature. In the morning a soft crust of cream will have formed across the top, which needs careful skimming with a ladle. Alternatively, if you have a steady hand, make a tiny hole about the size of a small coin down one edge with the tip of a spoon, and very gently pour the liquid away, leaving the cream behind. Either way, what you have in the liquid is semi-skimmed milk, and in the solid, cream. This process only works with milk before it has gone through homogenization (emulsifying the milk to prevent cream separation), and therefore will sadly not work with pints bought from the shelf.

If you want cream for dairying rather than eating, however, many supermarkets and stores now stock a really interesting variety of creams that are perfect for the job, such as the Channel Islands' Jersey and Guernsey creams, which have a yellow tint to them and tend to be slightly richer due to the larger butterfat particles, making them perfect for things like butter making. Don't buy flavoured cream or cream containing anything synthetic: whilst these may be good in your coffee, they don't work for dairying.

BUTTER

Butter is just over-whipped cream. In fact, if you have ever over-whipped cream and ended up with a grainy liquid, the grains were butter and the liquid buttermilk – you were nearly there! All you had to do was continue to whip in order to bring more of the particles out and join them together to form butter.

In the old pre-gadget days before food mixers, it would be the dairymaid's responsibility to hand-churn cream into butter and she would often start at dawn by pouring the clabbered cream (the top of the milk that has naturally clotted together overnight) into a plunge-churn or barrel-churn, where she would work it by hand, keeping it in a perpetual state of movement for hour, after hour, after hour. Today we pour a carton of double cream into a food mixer and whisk it for long enough to shuffle over to a new track on an iPod or send a quick text message.

(If you want to have a test run, just to see how the process works, try this method, which fascinates my niece and nephew. Sink a jam jar and lid in a bowl of boiling water for about 15 minutes to sterilize them, then remove and leave to cool. Half-fill the jar with double cream. Secure the lid, wrap the jar in a tea towel and shake it vigorously. It takes a while, but eventually you get a distinctive *d-doink* sound of a small pat of butter forming inside.)

Before you start making butter, make sure the cream you're about to use is a good few days old. If it's shop bought, choose a double cream and only use it on or around its use-by date, as this makes it easier to work, gives a better yield and improves the flavour. (Many shops reduce the price of their fresh cream as it approaches the sell-by date. Buy it then: it's cheaper and works just as well.) If you use 300ml/½ pint double cream (30 per cent butterfat plus), this will produce about 225g/8oz butter and 300ml/½ pint buttermilk. It is important to leave the cream out overnight at room temperature so it can ripen – a natural process whereby the bacteria will act upon the lactose sugar in the cream. (If the butter were being made commercially, a 'starter' would be added. You thought butter pats in the shops had to be pure without anything added? Sadly not – reason number 472 to make your own.)

Pour the cream into a food mixer and fit the balloon whisk. Before you turn the food mixer on, drape some kitchen roll or a scrupulously clean tea towel around the top of the bowl because it does splash! Start at a medium speed, but be prepared to reduce it low as soon as you start to feel and hear the butter forming. This is the agitation process that will start breaking down the cream into solid (butter) and liquid (buttermilk), and should take only a couple of minutes. When the separation starts, you will hear the splashing inside the bowl get thinner and faster because obviously the butterfat globules that make the cream thick are being removed (buttermilk has roughly the same consistency as water).

At this point turn the food mixer down low and continue for a couple more minutes to make certain all the butter has been removed, then stop. Scrape the formed butter that has collected around the whisk into one piece and literally run it under the cold tap, turning it and turning it in your hand. This will clean the butter, although some of the buttermilk will remain. You need to remove as much of the buttermilk as possible because this will go off much faster than the butter and will spoil it. Therefore, place the butter on a board and take two wooden spoons, or Scotch hands (wooden butter beaters) if you have them, and pat the butter (which is where the phrase butter 'pat' came from) to remove as much milk as you can. As you pat it, you will see tiny pockets of milky liquid exploding free from the butter. Wash, gently knead and repeat this process until all the liquid has gone.

Use the butter as it is, or mix approximately ½ tsp flaked sea salt with every 225g/8oz butter, or to taste. To make spreadable butter, put it back into the food mixer and add up to 100ml/3½fl oz light olive oil and beat again lightly until creamed together. This increases the volume and, by introducing unsaturated fat, dilutes the less-healthy saturated fats.

If you want flavoured butters, try some of these options: add tarragon for melting over steak; mash with Stilton to stuff fillet steak; add lemon thyme for chicken or lemon thyme and garlic for chicken Kiev; or add minced and mashed anchovy fillets for lamb.

Buttermilk

Because most of the fat has been removed to make the butter, the liquid that remains is virtually fat-free natural buttermilk, with only about two-thirds of the calories of milk yet still high in potassium, vitamin B12 and calcium. It has a slightly sour, though pleasant, taste. Try using it in the following ways: chill and drink or pour over cereal; add to mashed potato; use it to make scones or soda bread; use it to make some soft ricotta-style cheese.

Clarified butter (ghee)

The reason why clarified butter is used in cooking, and especially Indian-style cooking, is because all the impurities, which burn and turn bitter during cooking, have been removed during the clarification process and so it can be heated to a much higher temperature than ordinary butter. As well as being the starting point for a perfect home-made curry, it can also be used as a 'lid' for homemade pâté, to seal out the air and help preserve it.

To clarify butter, put some unsalted butter in a heavy-based saucepan and heat gently until it melts. Do not let it boil. The butter will start to separate into two layers: a clear layer on top and a milky one below. Carefully pour the clear layer off into a separate container, and there you have clarified butter.

YOGHURT

Making yoghurt in the home is often the first venture into controlled fermentation and the use of live, healthy cultures that anyone new to dairying makes. Surprisingly, many of the health benefits surrounding yoghurt come not just from the fact that it is full of goodness, but also because it is so easy for the body to digest and therefore all the goodness is easily absorbed.

To make live natural yoghurt, you need, ironically, 2 tsp live natural yoghurt to use as a starter, as well as 1.2 litres/2 pints milk (skimmed, semi-skimmed or whole, goat's, sheep's or cow's – all work well, although the higher the cream content, the thicker and creamier your yoghurt will be).

Put the milk in a heavy-based saucepan over a low heat and heat to 38–43°C/100–110°F to kill off any existing bacteria. Pour the milk into a wide-mouthed vacuum flask, stir in the live yoghurt, seal and leave overnight (or for 10–12 hours). In the morning, tip the yoghurt into a dish, loosely cover with a plate and chill in the fridge for a couple of hours to thicken, then it's ready to eat as it is, or to add some flavouring. You can also stir it into curries and use it as an ingredient in naan breads.

As you become adept at making yoghurt and settle into a routine, you can simply keep a couple of spoonfuls from the last batch to create the next, so saving the need ever to buy yoghurt again. Alternatively, you can buy a commercial starter from a health-food shop. A starter, or culture, is essentially good bacteria, so this enables you to eliminate the bad and harmful bacteria acting on the milk and let in only the good. These healthy bacteria act on the lactose sugar in the milk, turning it into protein, which in turn curdles the milk into yoghurt, which is a mix of the curds and the whey. (Yoghurt was probably what little Miss Muffet was eating, comfy on her tuffet, when the spider came and sat down beside her.)

All yoghurts made with a live culture are probiotic, helping to establish and re-establish healthy gut flora (especially after a course of antibiotics), assisting in the prevention of gastrointestinal infections, improving our immune system and helping guard against infection.

Flavouring yoghurts

All fruit, fresh or canned, works well to flavour yoghurt, but soft fruit such as strawberries, raspberries and blackcurrants, hand-mushed with the back of a spoon and folded into the yoghurt, take a lot of beating. Stirring the yoghurt risks breaking the mixture back down into curds and whey, so try to minimize stirring and aim more for folding when you incorporate flavouring ingredients. If separation does occur, pour off the liquid whey and place the yoghurt back in the fridge to chill and set once again. Other flavourings include honey, nuts, muesli, raisins and sultanas, and avocado for use as a dip.

Frozen yoghurt

There are two main methods for creating this healthy alternative to ice cream: one involves churning, for which you will need to invest in an ice-cream maker, and the other involves still-freezing. This recipe is made in the still-frozen way, but both methods work equally well for yoghurt and ice cream.

Still-frozen yoghurt

You will need a spotlessly clean shallow roasting tin for this recipe. The reason for using a roasting tin is the fact that it's wide and flat and will therefore have a big surface area that will chill the mixture down quickly, thus avoiding most of the ice crystals that form during slower freezing. The metal in the tin is also a wonderful conductor of temperature, again helping with the cooling process. A handy tip is to freeze the empty tin before use.

Pour 570ml/1 pint chilled natural yoghurt into the roasting tin, then place in the freezer for 20 minutes. Remove the tin, tip the mixture into a food mixer and blend until smooth, then return to the tin and the freezer. Repeat this procedure every 20 minutes for just under 1½ hours. After the final blending, sweeten the mixture with a little honey and add some fruit, nuts or the seeds from a vanilla pod, then blend again until smooth. Return to the tin once more, cover with cling film to prevent ice crystals forming, and pop in the freezer until frozen. Hey presto: frozen yoghurt!

CHEESE

Patience is a virtue,
Possess it if you can.
Seldom found in woman,
Never found in man.

(ANON.)

Unfortunately if you want to make truly great cheese you're going to have to develop more than a little patience, because for some of the more distinctive cheese flavours, especially the hard cheeses, it can take several months, even years, before they're mature enough to eat. But, oh boy, if you can, the rewards will make the wait well worth it!

Luckily, not all cheeses take a long time. In fact, curd and cream cheese can be made in no time at all, and in this stripped-down introduction to cheese-making, the emphasis is very much on maximum flavour and stylish results with as little effort as possible. The golden rules of cheese-making are to work through the stages in sequence, take it slowly, and build up to the more complicated, more taxing cheeses only after you have mastered the basics.

This section is like having your first driving lesson, where you learn clutch control, braking and acceleration. It will enable you to move the vehicle around, but you won't be a driver until the subtleties sink in. The true art of cheese-making is all about those subtleties, and that will take years to learn. But, right now, just enjoy the freedom of stamping on the accelerator and producing tasty, classy cheese right out of your own kitchen.

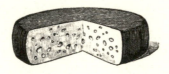

CHEESE-MAKING EQUIPMENT

There are a few specialist items of equipment that will be needed, mostly for making hard cheese, such as a thermometer, a palette knife for cutting the curds and a double boiler. If you don't already have a double boiler, you will need two saucepans (the smaller one with a lid) that can be stacked one inside the other so the inner rests on the outer's handles without the bodies touching. The outer one can then be topped up with boiling water to produce a bath that will help keep the inner pan warm, and allow the milk to heat up evenly without scorching. Alternatively, but less ideal, use just one heavy-based saucepan over a low heat, but keep a watchful eye on the milk so it doesn't catch. You will also need a cheese press to force out as much liquid from the cheese as possible and cheese moulds for shaping. (A homemade cheese press is simple to construct and works equally as well as anything you can buy; there are plans for one on page 89. Cheese moulds can be made or improvised, or found at speciality shops on the Internet.)

Basic ingredients

Milk: All pasteurized milk can be used, from cow's to goat's and sheep's milk, whole or semi-skimmed, but, as a general rule, the richer the milk, the richer and creamier the cheese.

Starter: This is a live culture of harmless bacteria, usually a lacto-bacilli starter, which can easily be purchased in liquid or dry form at speciality shops, good health-food shops and online.

Rennet: Also known as a coagulant, rennet acts to curdle the milk into curds and whey and can, once again, be found at speciality shops, good health-food shops and online. (The standard rennet comes from the stomach lining of young animals, so if you want to make vegetarian cheese, you will need to look for vegetable-based alternatives.)

Salt: Fine sea salt and a good flaked salt.

Curd cheese

Curd or cottage cheese is a soft cheese that is neither pressed nor matured and retains a high level of moisture in the curd. It can be made with any type of milk, including goat's and sheep's milk, and the higher the fat content, the creamier the curd. If made with skimmed or semi-skimmed milk, it is therefore low in fat, making it popular with weight watchers.

This is probably the simplest cheese in the universe to make, and the most versatile, as it can be cooled and scattered on a salad, used warm with added chopped herbs such as chives or basil, and be the filling for cannelloni and ravioli (how about a really funky self-sufficient homemade ravioli filled with cottage cheese, stinging nettles or spinach, and a little nutmeg?) Also, because it is based on the Indian recipe for paneer, it will accept toasted spices really well and is ideal for stuffing naan bread. In addition, if pressed under a light weight for 6 hours, it can be sliced, then popped in a tub and marinated in olive oil, rosemary and garlic, which will also help to preserve the cheese.

Basic curd cheese

> 2.25 litres/4 pints whole milk
> juice of 1 lemon

Pour the milk into a heavy-based saucepan and bring up to boiling point, then remove from the heat. Squeeze in the lemon juice and stir: the mixture will separate into curds and whey. Line a fine sieve with a muslin cloth, pour in the mixture and allow the whey to drain off. What's left in the muslin is curd cheese. To shape, twist the muslin down on to the cheese or pop it into a press and allow it to set for a couple of hours (the longer you leave it, up to a day, the firmer it will get); it should then be possible to slice with a sharp knife.

Variation

If you want a more mascarpone-type cheese, replace the milk with double cream and maintain the heat for 2 minutes before draining though the muslin cloth.

Crispy spiced curd cheese

This is a real favourite. It works as nibbles or as a crunchy protein-providing topping on a vegetarian curry.

> 225g/8oz fine semolina or polenta
> ½ tsp ground coriander
> ½ tsp ground cumin
> ½ tsp chilli powder
> 3 tbsp plain flour
> 1 egg, beaten with 2 tbsp water
> curd cheese made from 1 litre/1¾ pints milk, pressed for about 24
>   hours (see page 91), and cut into small cubes
> 3 tbsp sunflower or groundnut oil

Put the semolina or polenta and the spices in a shallow bowl and mix together. Put the flour and beaten egg on two separate plates, then coat the cubes of cheese in each in turn, and then drop into the spice mixture and stir, making certain all the sides are completely covered. Heat the oil in a frying pan and fry the coated cheese cubes until they are brown and crunchy on each side, turning as each side is done. Remove with a fish slice and leave to drain on kitchen towels. Serve hot or cold.

Soft cheese

Soft cheese, such as cream cheese, is made in much the same way as hard, but it is drained and briefly pressed or not pressed at all, and ready immediately without any need to mature. It is much simpler and quicker to make than hard cheese because it is eaten fresh, and it is perfect as a dip, a spread, to cook with or even in a fabulous cheesecake. Cream cheese is traditionally made with cream, but you can vary the recipe to use whole milk, goat's milk or even tofu for a vegan fat-free cream cheese.

Cream cheese

This cream cheese is made with whole milk. (Note that if you are using unpasteurized milk, you will need to heat it to 30°C/86°F and then cool to room temperature.)

> 1.2 litres/2 pints whole pasteurized milk
> ¼ tsp liquid starter culture or a pinch of dry culture
> 3 drops rennet
> sprinkle of fine sea salt

Put the milk in a heavy-based saucepan and heat to room temperature, then mix in the starter culture and the rennet, stirring vigorously for 5 minutes.

Cover and leave at room temperature for 18–20 hours, after which it should look like yoghurt. Line a colander with a muslin cloth and spoon the mixture into it. Tie the corners of the muslin together with the end of a string and hang it up to drain overnight, or for at least 12 hours. (Tying it to a tap over the sink works really well.) Open up the bag and stir the curds with a spoon, then hang for another 12 hours. Once the curds have drained, scrape the cheese out into a bowl and blend by hand until smooth, adding salt or herbs (such as chives) to taste. Chill, then eat immediately.

Hard cheese

There is nothing like a good Cheddar cheese, and the recipe that follows is based on a variant of that, but tweaked here and there to make it in a double boiler in an everyday home kitchen. It can be ready to eat in as little as 2–3 days, or waxed, stored and aged to intensify the flavour for several months. (See page 84 for the equipment you will need.)

There can be many steps in the cheese-making process, but

basically what you're doing is controlling the milk through three stages: fermenting, dehydration and solidifying. Fermentation happens when the bacteria is added to the milk and immediately seeks out the lactose sugars and turns them into lactic acid. Next the cheese is dehydrated by adding a rennet that separates the milk into solids (curds) and liquid (whey), before it is drained, shaped, pressed and left to solidify and mature.

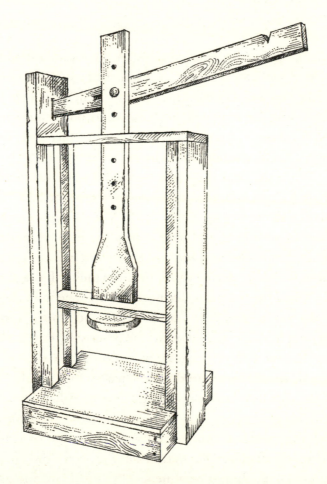

Design for a simple homemade cheese press

My Cheddar-ish cheese

This recipe makes approximately 450g/1lb cheese.

> 5 litres/9 pints whole pasteurized milk
> 300ml/10fl oz double cream
> 1 tsp liquid starter culture or ⅛ tsp dry culture
> ½ tsp rennet
> 2 tsp flaked salt

Mix the milk and cream together in the top of a double boiler and warm to 30°C/86°F, stirring to ensure the mixture does not burn. Take off the heat and add the starter, mixing well, then cover and leave in a warm place for about 1 hour. Meanwhile, boil some water in a kettle and swish out a mug with the boiling water, then pour in just enough water to cover the bottom of the mug and set aside to go cold.

When the hour is up, remove the lid from the double boiler and return it to the hob. Heat over a medium heat and take the milk/cream mixture all the way up to 32°C/90°F. Mix the rennet with the distilled water in your mug and pour it into the mixture, stirring carefully. Remove from the heat and cover once again, leaving it this time for about 1½ hours, during which time the milk will coagulate.

When the time is up, remove the lid. The milk should feel firm to the touch. Now take a palette knife and plunge it in at one side, drawing it all the way across to the other side. Repeat this process at 1cm/½in intervals until it resembles a neatly lined sheet of paper (albeit a round sheet!), then turn the pan a quarter turn and do the same again so the cuts now cross the original lines at right angles, making neat columns of 1cm/½in squares. Now's the tricky bit: cutting diagonally into the cheese so you end up with a pan full of 1cm/½in pieces. Return the double boiler to the heat, and, very slowly over the next 45 minutes, raise the temperature to 38°C/100°F, stirring occasionally to prevent the cheese clumping together.

Now line a colander with a muslin cloth, place it in the sink and carefully tip the whole mixture into the muslin, cover it and twist the cloth at the top so it forms a ball and leave it for at least 15 minutes. Using your hands, carefully mix in the flaked salt. Line a cheese mould with a separate piece of muslin and pack in the curds using your hands. Then put it in the cheese press under a 1.8kg/4lb weight for about half an hour.

Take the cheese out of the press and the muslin, and rewrap it upside down, then return it to the cheese press and put it under 3.6kg/8lb of pressure for a further 12 hours. Remove the cheese from the press and the muslin and gently wipe it all over with light salt solution and a small pad of muslin before resting it on a bamboo mat for 3 days, turning twice daily, until the skin feels hard and turns a pale yellow. Your cheese is now ready to eat, or you can dip it in wax for ageing and maturing.

If you found these cheese recipes fun, please go on and do more. There are some wonderful books and great sites online with recipes for all the famous, and not so famous cheeses, just begging to be made.

ICE CREAM

There are essentially two types of ice cream: one cream-based and the other made from custard or a crème anglaise (see recipes on page 93). Of course you *can* make these ice creams without an ice-cream maker, in the same way you *can* perform your own dentistry, but it's not for the faint-hearted because of the amount of work involved, and it's difficult to get a result that will wow the kids; not impossible, but difficult. Electric ice-cream makers can be picked up relatively cheaply and you're likely to earn your money back over the course of just one summer by cutting out the weekly tub from your shopping bill. However, in the true spirit of self-sufficiency, there is an alternative…

The hand-cranked ice-cream maker

Remember the poor old dairymaid and her butter churns? Well the hand-cranked ice-cream maker is exactly the same, only colder. Churning ice cream gives a lighter, fluffier, creamier texture because it is constantly being mixed as it cools, and there is no danger of ice crystals forming because everything is completely emulsified. Hand-cranked ice-cream makers are available to buy online and at some of the larger stores, but once you realize the principles of what's happening, which are really rather clever, it's simple to make your own.

The temptation is to fill the sink with ice and plonk a metal pan of your ice-cream mixture into it and stir like crazy until it goes hard. But that wouldn't work, and it wouldn't work because the ice in the sink is only 0°C/32°F, the temperature at which water freezes, which isn't cold enough to freeze the ice cream. What we need to do is make the ice in the sink colder, and to do that, we add salt. Adding salt will melt the ice, but crucially bring the temperature down to that at which salt water melts, about −2°C/28.4°F, which is cold enough to freeze ice cream. The other problem with using this method is the fact that once you reach that magic −2°C/28.4°F in the sink, it won't last long enough to work because the sink itself is being warmed up by the atmosphere. What you need to find is a container made of a material that doesn't conduct temperature, the best of which is wood.

So, to construct a homemade ice-cream maker, get a wooden box, line it with a black bin-liner (double bagged for safety), half-fill it with ice, measure out about a third of the quantity of ice in rock salt and stir it together. Then pour your ice-cream mixture into a metal pan and lower the pan into the ice, taking care not to let any of the salty ice spill into your ice cream. Take a wooden spoon and spend a pleasant 20–30 minutes folding the mixture continuously from the edge to the middle until it goes firm.

Of course, you could buy an electric ice-cream maker and sip a cool glass of homemade wine while you watch it work. But where's the fun in that?

Cream-based ice cream

This recipe makes quite a hard ice cream, a kind of old-fashioned break-the-spoon-to-get-it-out ice cream (and therefore benefits from softening by being placed in the fridge for half an hour before serving), though because of the high level of cream it does lend itself very well to hand churning and suits the old favourite flavourings such as strawberry and vanilla, chocolate and banana, even orange.

300ml/10½fl oz single cream
300ml/10½fl oz double cream
280g/10oz honey or caster sugar
½ tsp vanilla extract

Pour the creams into a heavy-based saucepan and warm over a low heat until tiny bubbles appear around the sides. Add the sugar and vanilla extract and stir until dissolved, then remove from the heat and allow to cool. Either churn in a hand-cranked or electric ice-cream maker, flavour and freeze or still-freeze (as for the frozen yoghurt on page 83).

Custard-based ice cream

For a smoother, more contemporary ice cream to which you can add crushed honeycomb or cake dough or even a smashed-up chocolate cream egg, try making a custard first. To make custard, you need an egg yolk. Years ago the whole ice cream with egg method would have been made raw, but that was before we discovered the link between raw eggs and salmonella. These days, especially if you're making ice cream for children, it's just not worth the risk, so the trick is to make custard and cook it, which kills any salmonella that may be lurking.

570ml/1 pint whole milk
2 egg yolks
2 tbsp granulated sugar
125ml/4fl oz double cream

Heat the milk in a heavy-based saucepan until just coming to a simmer, then remove from the heat. Put the eggs and sugar in a bowl and beat until smooth, then gradually pour in the hot milk, stirring constantly. When the milk has all been amalgamated, tip the mixture back into the saucepan and return to the heat, stirring all the while until it goes thick enough to coat the back of a metal spoon. Remove from the heat and leave to cool. Whip the double cream in a separate bowl until thick and fold into the cooled custard. Churn in a hand-cranked or electric ice-cream maker, then flavour and freeze.

Milkshakes

Opinion differs on a truly great milkshake, from a half and half mix of ice cream and milk, to yoghurt and fruit blended together (known as a smoothie). It basically boils down to the question: do you feel decadent or virtuous?

Everyone should have a little late-night decadence once in a while, and for this all you need is a scoop of ice cream and a slug of milk, and maybe a couple of strawberries or a sprinkling of cocoa powder, whizzed in a blender. Delicious.

CHAPTER FOUR

The Home Brewer

Almost all fruits, edible berries, flowers and root vegetables can be made into either wine or beer – which is handy. From hedgerow wines to 'turbo' cider, honey mead to real ale, home brewing is the perfect way to share self-sufficiency with friends. Even using a homebrew kit, a glass of beer or a bottle of wine is still cheaper than the average chocolate bar. Once the basic methods outlined in this chapter have been mastered, it is entirely possible to venture off the beaten track and start experimenting with things you can grow at home or easily forage, bringing the price down even lower. But even if you prefer to use a shop-bought kit, it will still cost you a fraction of the price charged at the shops. In fact, once all the equipment has been acquired – check out www.uk.freecycle.org on the net for second-hand gear – a tipple can cost next to nothing. But the cost is only one small reason why people brew beer and wine at home. The major reason is taste, and taste is the single factor that has bounced the concept of homemade wines and beer from the slightly seedy practice of men with beards in garden sheds to a fashionable, bright and trendy hobby that is simple, fun, cheap and immensely rewarding.

Just about any beer on the shelf, any red wine, any white wine can be copied, with exciting results. A cool crisp Chablis, a dark red Merlot or a lively lager can all be recreated in your kitchen. Today it is easier to make really great wine and beer than it has ever been before. The kits for home brewing have improved beyond recognition. The equipment is now less clunky and the recipes perfected. Self-sufficient wine and beer have also improved, largely, it has to be recognized, due to the Internet and the ease with which people can now share information. Things like dandelion wine and stinging-nettle beer have been stripped down, tweaked and made gorgeous. Mead, cider and perry are both exciting and moreishly drinkable.

The law

With very few exceptions (some dry states in America, for instance) it is perfectly legal to brew your own wine and beer, but it is *illegal* to sell it, as no duty will have been paid. As long as you use it only for your own consumption and never charge anybody who might share it with you, then you should be fine. However, you *cannot distil any alcoholic drink*. On this, there are no exceptions, and the reasoning behind it is far more to do with safety than finance, because it is quite possible for an amateur to unwittingly create alcohols that are unsafe and even life-threateningly dangerous.

Getting started

The beauty of home brewing is that it can be done in any kitchen any time of the year. The first thing to decide is what's your tipple – beer or wine? For someone just starting out, it's probably best to generalize and go for standards rather than specifics, so if you fancy a red wine, plump for a perfectly acceptable 'house' style, which is going to be fairly quick to produce and you know you'll be happy with the results, and wait until you are a little more confident before tackling something more challenging and hunting down a Chateauneuf-du-Pape. In this respect home brewing is very much like making cheese: starting off with ricotta and working your way up to a Cheddar- or Brie-type cheese. Of course if you are already specializing, then perhaps this will help to broaden your knowledge of some of the other aspects of brewing, such as mead, cider and perry, or tempt the wine connoisseur into dabbling with beer (or vice versa, of course).

This chapter examines the basic methods and processes involved in home brewing red and white wine, beer, lager, mead, cider and perry, with the emphasis firmly on self-sufficiency. Where possible, all the ingredients are home-produced, such as apples for cider, pears for perry and honey for mead. If you do not have access to these ingredients, then it may mean a trip to the shops, or what's even better is if you can trade whatever produce you do have with someone who has an orchard or a beehive. With a few exceptions, most of the equipment you need will probably be lurking in your kitchen. For anything that's missing, check out freecycle or speciality shops on the Internet.

MAKING BEER

In medieval Britain the water was so dangerous to drink that everyone stuck to drinking wine and ale, and it is estimated that an average man living in this period would have consumed about 4.5 litres/1 gallon of ale every day, starting with just over ½ litre/1 pint at breakfast and continuing to drink throughout the working day. Luckily a clean water supply was eventually given priority, as today's employers prefer a more sober approach from their workforce, being of the opinion that people tend to work harder when they're not sloshed.

Beer is simple to make at home and has the advantage over wine in that it is a faster process and can be ready in a matter of days, or, for a really exquisite drink, can be left to mature for a year or more. The two main forms of beer are ale and lager. Ale is the easiest and fastest to create of the two as it is brewed from top-fermenting yeast with a relatively short, room-temperature fermentation, whereas lager is the opposite: it is brewed from bottom-fermenting yeast over a longer period in cooler conditions. Ale uses hops, which often grow wild or in a garden using a tree as a support – so you can do some foraging for them.

EQUIPMENT FOR MAKING A SIMPLE ALE OR LAGER

Fermenting bucket

Plastic paddle

Sterilizer

40 × 570ml/1 pint bottles, along with caps and capping tool, or recycled flip-top bottles

Plastic siphoning tubs

Kit of your choice

Making lager from a kit

Kits are simple and make on average 23 litres/40 pints of pretty much foolproof lager. All you have to do is bring 3.4 litres/6 pints water to the boil, siphon it into a fermenting bin, mix in the contents of the kit along with any additional sugars, fill to the 23-litre/40-pint mark and that's it. Leave it to one side until it's ready to drink and then invite 40 friends around for a drink. As long as you follow the instructions in the kit, it really is difficult to go wrong.

Different kits will make slightly different beers, and once you get the knack it is entirely possible to customize your own version. As soon as you start tweaking it to produce something that's your own, then you can pull away from the kits and start mixing and matching by buying the individual components separately.

Making ale

The variations in making ale are as numerous as those in wine, so the trick is to start with a basic recipe and then adjust it to suit your own taste. Before you bottle your beer, make certain that your siphon and the bottles have all been sterilized in a solution specifically for the job. Use thick glass bottles with lids that can withstand a lively beer, and don't be tempted to use recycled screw tops, as the seal often fails, although recycled flip-top bottles are ideal.

Basic ale

This method is one step on from using a kit and encourages buying just a few bits of equipment. Note that if your tap water has a tang of chlorine or metal, you need to add a dash of salt and boil it first so it doesn't affect the flavour of the beer. For a fuller beer, increase the malt extract by as much as half again. Leave this ale to ferment for 3 weeks, when it will be ready to drink, or leave it to mature and mellow for months (if you can resist it).

25g/1oz hops (increase or decrease for a milder or stronger flavour)
450g/1lb malt extract
225g/8oz granulated sugar
juice of ½ lemon
pinch of salt
1 heaped tsp dry ale yeast
8–9 tsp granulated sugar

Leaving to one side a small portion of the hops, put the rest in a large saucepan with 3.5 litres/6 pints water and bring the whole thing to a rolling boil for 1 hour. Pour 1.2 litres/2 pints water into a separate pan, add the malt extract and sugar and stir over a low heat until the sugar has completely dissolved. This mixture is known as the wort. When the hops have finished boiling, strain the mixture into the wort and leave to cool. Pour 570ml/1 pint water through the drained hops into the wort to extract the last vestiges of flavour. Add the lemon juice, salt, yeast and remaining hops and stir continuously until everything has amalgamated. Cover and stand somewhere warm for 3 days.

Take a ladle and skim off the foam, then leave to stand for another 5 days before giving the beer a thorough stirring. Allow the sediment to settle over the next 24 hours, then fill nine 570ml/1 pint bottles to the neck, at least 2.5cm/1in from the top. (You may not have enough beer to fill all the bottles to the top.) Add 1 tsp sugar to each full bottle (and proportionally less to a non-full one) before securing the top.

Mixed-leaf beer

The really self-sufficient homebrew beer is made from scratch. Before hops were taken as the preferred flavouring, people would make light beer from any plants and leaves they could find. This is a modified version of one of the oldest known beer recipes in existence. It makes a light, refreshing drink that is ideal for a warm summer's afternoon. If you have trouble collecting all the suggested leaves at once, you can use just the stinging nettle or dandelion leaves.

> ¼ bucket mixed leaves, including some of the following: stinging nettles, dandelion, hop, a young twig or two of spruce and finally a little sorrel
> 25g/1oz cream of tartar
> 680g/1½lb granulated sugar
> ¼ tsp dried yeast

Rinse the leaves and leave to drip dry. Put in a large saucepan, cover with about 5.75 litres/1¼ gallons water and bring up to boiling point. Boil for about 15 minutes before straining the liquid and discarding the leaves and any twigs. Return the liquid to the pan and to the boil, then reduce the heat to a simmer and add the cream of tartar and the sugar, mixing until thoroughly dissolved. Take off the heat and leave cool. When it's just warm, add the yeast and stir in. Cover with a tea towel and leave for 4 days, then uncover and carefully scoop off any scum without upsetting the beer below. Siphon into bottles, leaving the sediment behind. Chill and drink.

WINE-MAKING

Making wine at home is simple, and it has been practised for the last 6,000 years. With all this practice we should be pretty good at it, and the truth is, we are. The kits available online and at speciality shops produce drinks that nobody would be ashamed of, with simple instructions that are easy to follow. They produce exciting and stylish red and white wines, and if you want to produce a safe drink from a kit then you should be encouraged to do so.

However, there are also many wines that you can produce self-sufficiently, and it's when you start dabbling in these that things get interesting. If you are the type of person who orders the taster menu in a restaurant, takes a shot from the bottle of liqueur with a pickled scorpion in the bottom in a Spanish bar or makes stinging nettle soup *and* tries it, then maybe you should consider making wine from scratch.

What is wine?

Wine is a combination of four things: water, sugar, yeast and flavourings. Sugar is added to the water and warmed up to make a lovely environment in which the live yeast can breed – a process known as fermentation. Much of the balance in creating a great wine is to do with the right proportion of sugar to yeast: too much sugar and the yeast can't use it all up and the wine tastes syrupy; too little sugar and you get the opposite effect, with a yeasty flavour. When the correct amount of sugar is used, the yeast will turn half of it into alcohol and the rest into carbon dioxide, which bubbles away.

The vast majority of wine is produced by using grapes as the key flavouring, but there are many alternatives you can explore. Country wines flavoured with fruits, berries, root vegetables and flowers are surprisingly good, and with a little practice on your part they can easily be the equal of many commercial wines available and quite often a lot better.

Principles of wine-making

- Flavour is taken from a plant/vegetable/flower/berry.

- Sugar and yeast are added to the flavour and fermentation begins.

- After about 10 days, the liquid is strained into a fermentation demijohn fitted with an airlock, where it will sit happily fermenting for a few weeks.

- The top, clearer, wine is siphoned off (racked) into a new demijohn and left to sit again.

- When it's ready, the wine is bottled.

EQUIPMENT

Large saucepan

Funnel

Demijohn

Airlock

Muslin cloth

Preparation

Before you start doing anything, the important thing is to create a good environment in which to work. Everything you use must be cleaned in a sterilizing solution, usually 1 Campden tablet per 4.5 litres/ 1 gallon water (maybe a teaspoon of citric acid, too, if you have any), which will be enough to inhibit bacteria from spoiling your wine. Use it before and after use on all your equipment, and to rinse out bottles and corks (avoid baking bottles in the oven or dipping them in boiling water to sterilize them, as this is not anywhere near as effective as a sterilizing solution).

Getting started

Country wines draw their flavour from the countryside. It does not mean you have to live in the country to make them, any more than you have to live on a farm to produce a farmhouse loaf of bread, but you do need to have access to the ingredients. Ideally, you will be able to source them from your own vegetable plot, or perhaps forage for them. If neither of these options is viable, then you can, of course, buy the ingredients, perhaps from a farmers' market to still give you that feeling that you are sourcing your wine ingredients straight from the countryside, though shop-bought produce will, of course, be fine if not.

When making jams and chutneys, it is perfectly acceptable to use second-quality fruit and vegetables, but to make wine, you need to select the best produce you have, discarding anything that looks bruised or iffy. Vegetables such as carrots, marrows, potatoes, parsnips and pea-pods should be scrubbed clean and chopped into chunks before being boiled in the relevant recipe. Leaves such as stinging nettles, parsley, cabbage and lettuce should be treated in the same way.

Flowers such as elderflower and dandelion produce very delicate, gentle wines, sometimes so delicate that many recipes call for the addition of dried fruit such as raisins, and the squeeze of a lemon for acid, to give the wine a little more body and character. To extract the gorgeous bouquet from any flowers that you want to impart into your wine, macerate them in warm water overnight before starting to make the wine.

Around March, when the sap is rising, it is possible to tap birch and silver birch trees, which can weep a good 1.2 litres/2 pints of sap in under a day (though if you do this, make certain that you plug the wound when you have finished or the tree will continue to weep and will eventually die). The sap can then be made into birch sap wine.

Speedy wine

This is a perfect recipe for anyone starting out on making wine because it's one of the fastest wines possible to make, and the result is a good table wine with about 8 per cent ABV. Of course, the wine made here is very young and so the flavour hasn't had much time to develop and mature, but it does pleasantly raise your eyebrows when you sip it. However, the longer you leave it, the better it gets. Store this wine in a cool place for 1 week before drinking, or leave to mature for 6–8 months.

450g/1lb granulated sugar
225g/8oz dried malt extract
570ml/1 pint grape, pineapple or cranberry juice
1 tsp general-purpose wine yeast

Pour 2 litres/3½ pints water into a large saucepan and heat gently while stirring in the sugar. In a separate container dissolve the malt extract in 250ml/9fl oz tepid water. Add the juice, mix and siphon into a demijohn. Dissolve the yeast in 3 tbsp warm water and add to the wine. Top up with 2.25 litres/4 pints water (to the neck of the demijohn). Shake the whole thing, fit an airlock and leave in a warm place to ferment.

Every day for 2 weeks make a point of picking up the demijohn and swirling it around to swish the sediment up into the body of the wine. Filter the wine through a muslin cloth placed in a funnel and return it to the demijohn with an airlock to sit in the warm for a couple more days. When fermentation is complete, with no more bubbles rising, siphon into bottles and seal.

Rose-petal wine

This wine has a slightly more complex flavour, and yet it is just so beautifully delicate at the same time, with a really summery floral scent. It takes about 6 months to be ready for drinking once bottled, but it's well worth the wait. If you are patient enough, wait for 2 years before drinking it for the best results.

1kg/2¼lb granulated sugar
2.75 litres/5 pints rose petals
juice of 1 lemon
1 tsp general-purpose wine yeast

Mix the sugar with 4.5 litres/1 gallon water in a large saucepan and bring to the boil. Tip in the rose petals and add the lemon juice, then remove from the heat and leave to cool. When the mixture is tepid, add the wine yeast and stir, then cover with a clean cloth and set aside. Stir once a day for a week, always covering in between times. Strain through a muslin cloth into a demijohn fitted with an airlock and leave somewhere warm for about 6 weeks to finish fermenting. Siphon into another demijohn with an airlock and keep for 6 months before bottling.

Jam wine

What better way to use up any old jams than to turn them into wine? Trawl through the pantry and store cupboard gathering all the old jars of jam and marmalade that you don't want or that have gone sugary. This wine should be left for a year before you drink it, and will keep for several years.

> 6–7 jars of jam
> 1 tbsp dried yeast
> 1 tbsp granulated sugar

Shake the jars' contents out into a fermenting bucket, add 4.5 litres/1 gallon boiling water and stir until it has all been amalgamated. Leave the mixture to cool to blood heat. Activate the yeast by mixing with the sugar and a little warm water, then add to the wine and stir well. Cover and leave in a warm place for 3–4 days, then siphon into a demijohn (beware of all the bits of fruit and pieces of peel within the mixture) with an airlock and leave for 6 weeks. Siphon into a clean demijohn with an airlock and leave until no more sediment is produced and the wine is clear. Siphon into bottles.

Pea-pod wine

This wine can be adapted for other vegetables, such as parsnips and beetroot. Just use the same weight of vegetables, and follow the method below. Store this wine for at least 6 months before tasting, though 1 year would be better. Drink within 3 years.

> 1.8kg/4lb pea pods
> thinly pared rind and juice of 2 lemons
> thinly pared rind and juice of 2 oranges
> 900g/2lb granulated white sugar
> ¼ tsp tannin
> 1 tsp yeast nutrient
> 1 tsp general-purpose wine yeast

Bring 4.5 litres/1 gallon water to the boil, add the pea pods and citrus rinds and reduce the heat and simmer for 30 minutes. Remove from the heat and leave to cool to blood heat. Place the remaining ingredients in a separate pan or brewing bucket. Strain the pea-pod mixture into the sugar mixture and stir until the sugar has dissolved, then pour into a demijohn with an airlock. Leave for about 6 weeks, depending on the temperature, until it has stopped fermenting, before bottling.

Elderflower wine

It would not be correct for a section on country wines to end without a tribute to the queen of them all, elderflower wine. Leave this wine for at least 3 months before drinking, or, if you are patient, wait for 6 months, when it will be at its best.

425ml/¾ pint elderflower heads
225g/8oz raisins
1.6kg/3½lb granulated sugar
juice of 3 lemons
1 tsp general-purpose wine yeast
1 tsp nutrient
1 tsp grape tannin

Bring 2.25 litres/½ gallon water to the boil in a large saucepan and add the elderflower heads, raisins, sugar and lemon juice. Add a further 2.25 litres/½ gallon water, mix well and leave to cool until tepid. Add the wine yeast, nutrient and grape tannin. Move the pan to a warm spot, cover with a clean cloth and leave to ferment for 4–5 days. Strain through a muslin cloth into a demijohn with an airlock and leave to ferment until the bubbling stops. When it's clear, siphon again into a clean demijohn with an airlock. Two months later, siphon into bottles and store in a cool place.

CIDER

For purity and simplicity in a glass, there is nothing to match cider. After dealing with wine, beer and lager recipes, where there are processes to follow, and we need to add this, then add that, suddenly to be confronted with a drink that's just pressed apple juice, and nothing else, feels … well it feels like it shouldn't work. Where's the yeast? Where's the sugar? How can it possibly ferment?

The answer is that Mother Nature very kindly made us a completely natural brewing kit, and named it 'apple'. Everything you need to brew cider is contained in that little round package. Within the cells of the skin are the wild yeasts. They react with the sweetness of the apple, the natural sugars, and during the course of fermentation turn the sugar to alcohol. Nothing added, nothing taken away – it's just so beautifully simple.

But where would the fun be if there were not a few challenges for the cider maker along the way? The principal obstacle is how to extract the apple juice. Apples are a hard fruit, and so the amount of pressure needed to press the juice out is high. This is why fruit presses, or cider presses, are constructed for the job. You can buy presses, but they don't come up for sale very often, and when they do the cost is normally too great to justify the purchase. The solution is, as usual in the self-sufficient world, to make your own. See my design overleaf, and also the apple press on www.cider.org.uk/millprss.htm.

The next dilemma centres on the apples themselves. Different apple strains will alter the taste: sharp apples will produce a sharp cider, and sweet apples a sweet cider. The best ciders are a blend of both, and a medium to dry cider can be obtained by mixing two parts sharp apples to one part sweet.

How to make homemade cider

If you have access to an orchard or can get out to one, then this is by far your best option, but if not head for a market or greengrocer where they sell loose apples as opposed to pre-sorted bags. Pick apples that are nice and ripe, but avoid any that are excessively bruised or battered (though windblown specimens are fine to use). Keeping them in a cool place, such as a garage or a barn, for a couple of weeks will soften the

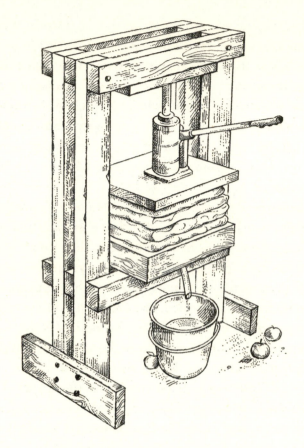

A homemade cider press using a car jack

skin, but do not be tempted to wash them as this will inhibit the natural yeasts. Once the 2 weeks are up, chop them into segments and press out the juice.

At this stage you can check the pH to make certain there is the right level of malic acid – the principal acid in cider – present. Most chemists sell litmus paper, and you're looking for a pH of around 4. If you feel it's too high, you can lower the pH by adding more malic acid, or if it's too low, you can bring it up with precipitated chalk.

Traditionally the juice would have been stored in wooden barrels and left to ferment, but nowadays it's easier to store it in a fermenting bin or demijohns. Fit an airlock, and leave it to ferment. Note that if you have enough liquid, you can use a dustbin, but make sure the construction of the plastic is not such that the dye will leach out and taint your cider.

After a day or so the wild yeast that has been pressed out of the skin will begin to be activated, and fermentation will start. Leave it for a couple of weeks. If at the end of this period the bubbles have stopped, then fermentation has stopped and you can bottle it. If they haven't stopped, then you might like to add a crushed Campden tablet to halt the fermentation manually.

Unlike with wine and beer, you need not worry about the ambient temperature and keeping it warm, as the wild yeasts are happy to cultivate as long as the temperature is above freezing. Most cider makers store their cider in an outbuilding, where the time of year will have an impact on the acid. Ciders made in warmer months tend to have a milder taste, whilst those made in cooler months retain a little more sharpness.

Allow it to mature for a couple of months before chilling and drinking. This cider will keep for up to 1 year.

Turbo cider

It is possible to make cider from cartons of apple juice and avoid all the rigmarole of collecting apples and pressing them, but bear in mind the fact that the juices you buy have been processed, and that means the chemical composition will be different from the freshly pressed apples used for proper cider. The result is not going to be quite the same as true cider– but it isn't called turbo cider for nothing and it is a lot quicker!

> 5 litres/8¾ pints additive- and preservative-free apple juice
> juice of 1 lemon
> 1 sachet fast-action bread yeast

Pour 4 litres/7 pints of the apple juice into a demijohn and add the lemon juice. Activate the yeast by dissolving it in a little warm water, and add it to the mixture. Put an airlock in place and place the demijohn in a warm place. After about 2 days, the foam collected on top should die down. Top up the demijohn with as much of the remaining apple juice as is needed to fill up to the neck. Leave for about 2 weeks, then siphon into two 2-litre/3½-pint plastic bottles. Chill and enjoy!

Perry

Similar to cider, perry is made by fermenting pears. Specially grown perry pears are best, as the flavour of eating pears is quite mellow, and when that's passed through the fermentation process the flavour can sometimes get lost completely. The trick (if you have only eating pears available) is to slice some of the pear skin and add it to the perry at the fermenting stage, something like half a pear skin to every 4.5 litres/1 gallon pear juice.

The other problem with perry is that although there is plenty of natural yeast contained within the skin, the pear offers very little nutrient and nourishment for the yeast to feed on, so it's best to add 1 tsp yeast nutrient to every 4.5 litres/1 gallon pear juice. Other than that, make it as though you were making cider.

MEAD

Thought to be the oldest form of brewing, mead is wine made from honey. There are lots of lovely stories about mead, about how it was made by monks who wanted beeswax for their candles, and making mead was a good way of using up the mountains of honey that accumulated. But the cutest tradition surrounding mead is how it used to be saved up and drunk at weddings, and the happy couple would then be presented with enough mead to drink for the first month of their marriage, coining the phrase 'honeymoon'.

Similar to all drinks, mead has a simple base-line entry, where a drink is produced just flavoured by the honey, but from there it can be lifted and personalized by adding spices such as cinnamon, cloves, nutmeg or ginger, and fruit such as orange zest, lemon, even apple.

Mead

Although honey is a natural sugar, the sugar content does vary from type to type. When making mead, it is recommended that you use a light-coloured set honey, as this tends to have a higher level of sugar, and the colour is more pleasing in the finished drink than a dark-coloured honey. Mead should be stored for 2 months before you drink it, and will keep indefinitely.

> 1.3–1.8kg/3–4lb honey (depending on how sweet you like your
>   mead)
> juice of ½ lemon
> 1 tsp general-purpose wine yeast

Warm the honey and gradually dilute it in 4.5 litres/1 gallon water until it has all been incorporated, then add the lemon juice and wine yeast and siphon into a demijohn fitted with an airlock. Store for 6 weeks, then siphon off into another demijohn. Repeat this process three more times before bottling the mead and leaving it to mature.

Variation

If you have only clear honey, not set, increase the amount by a quarter, decreasing the water accordingly to compensate.

NATURAL SOFT DRINKS AND CHILDREN'S FAVOURITES

Of course it would be wonderful if our children drank nothing but water, smoothies and fruit juice, but with temptation all around in cans of bright, sparkling, fizzy drinks, unless you're really, *really* lucky, that's unlikely to happen. So the next best thing is to make some healthier, delicious, additive-free alternatives, which can be kept in the fridge in plastic bottles or glass jugs (or in sterilized bottles out of the fridge) for up to 2 months, so at least you know what's going into your children's bodies. And then there's the bonus that they taste just as good to adults!

Traditional lemonade

> juice of 5–6 lemons
> 3 tbsp granulated sugar

Put 1½ litres/2½ pints water in a 2-litre/3½-pint bottle and add the lemon juice. Carefully tip in the sugar, then secure the lid and shake vigorously. Top up with water to the neck and shake again. Adjust the sugar and lemon to taste, if necessary. Chill and drink, or pour over ice.

Elderflower cordial

Like stepping into a cool shower on a hot summer's day, elderflower cordial refreshes and reinvigorates the senses. For the adult version, or to make it special, add it to sparkling wine or champagne.

680g/1½lb granulated sugar
2.25 litres/4 pints elderflower heads in full bloom, not pressed down
    (see note on page 262 regarding picking)
juice of 1½ lemons, along with the remaining ½ lemon, sliced
1 lime, sliced
1 mint sprig

Put 2 litres/3½ pints water and the sugar into a large saucepan and heat, stirring, until the sugar dissolves to make a syrup. Remove from the heat and add the elderflower heads, lemon juice, sliced lemon, lime and mint. Cover and leave for 24 hours. Strain through a muslin cloth into a 2 litre/3½ pint plastic bottle and chill. Mix with water to drink, or dilute it into a punch and add lots of diced fruit for a taste of summer.

Blackcurrant cordial

This cordial is best served diluted with ice-cold still or sparkling water. It can be frozen for up to 3 months, undiluted, in ice-cube trays/bags and used from frozen. The blackcurrants can be replaced with red or white currants, blackberries, blueberries or raspberries.

450g/1lb blackcurrants
250g/9oz white granulated sugar
250ml/9fl oz water
juice and thinly pared rind of 1 lemon

Place everything except the lemon in a saucepan with 250ml/9fl oz water and heat gently, stirring constantly, until the sugar has dissolved. Increase the heat and bring the cordial to a gentle simmer. After simmering for 5 minutes add the juice and rind of the lemon and simmer for a further 5 minutes. Remove from the heat and leave to cool for 10 minutes. Sterilize a glass bottle and strain the slightly cooled cordial through a fine (non-metallic) sieve into a jug, then fill the bottle. Leave to cool thoroughly before capping.

CHAPTER FIVE

Natural Solutions: Health, Beauty and the Home

FOR ANYONE LEADING A self-sufficient life, understanding which plants heal and which plants soothe and cleanse is almost as important as knowing whether or not they are edible. The practice of using plants to feed, cure, pamper and generally assist human beings in almost every sphere of their daily lives is probably as old as the human race itself. And with increasing global concern about environmental degradation and leading healthier lives, people today are keen to learn more about the tremendous benefits of natural products. This chapter explores some of the self-sufficient and natural alternatives to products that are used routinely in most modern homes: household cleaners, health, hygiene and beauty products and soothers for minor complaints. Using a little herb lore and some elementary botany and chemistry, you can create a range of natural products, from shampoos and hand creams to deodorants, face packs and bath bombs. You don't need any experience or specialist equipment to make the products described, just a little resourcefulness and an open mind. Most of the ingredients discussed in the pages that follow are natural and many can be grown or purchased from a health shop, or they may already be in your kitchen cupboard.

NATURAL CLEANING PRODUCTS

The majority of modern households contain an astounding array of cleaning products, from disinfectant, washing-up liquid, furniture polish, floor, oven, glass and drain cleaners to air freshener, lime-scale remover, carpet cleaner and fabric softener. The list goes on. Many of these items are expensive and sometimes harmful to humans and the environment. But you can trash the lot and replace them with just five natural products that you may already have at home: white vinegar, bicarbonate of soda (baking soda), cream of tartar, some lemons and a bottle of cheap olive oil. That's it. They will clean the entire house from top to bottom, leaving it sparkling and smelling great.

Although all five are natural substances, always test an inconspicuous area first to make certain they won't discolour, scratch or damage any of your surfaces. Don't worry about the smell of vinegar – as long as you only use white vinegar, not malt (which leaves a bad odour), the smell will disappear when the vinegar dries.

Most of the cleaning products mentioned in this section contain bicarbonate of soda, which is also a natural skin exfoliator. So rather

than stuffing your hands into sweaty old rubber gloves, use bare hands but moisturize them afterwards (see page 123). Bicarbonate of soda is an amazing product: it's so safe that you can clean your teeth with it; but pour it down the sink and it will clean the drains!

Kitchen cleaners

White vinegar is a natural general-purpose cleaner that disinfects and deodorizes. Clean your work surfaces using equal quantities of white vinegar and water and a squeeze of lemon, which has natural anti-bacterial qualities and a fresh, pleasant smell – simply wipe on and then wipe off. For tougher surfaces, such as the hob, the oven and the microwave, add baking soda to your cleaning mixture – apply and agitate with a cleaning cloth until all the stains have been removed, rinse the cloth and wipe clean.

For really stubborn stains and meat pans, cut a lemon in half, sprinkle baking soda over one half and use it as a scouring pad until all the stains have been removed, then rinse clean. Baking soda is the self-sufficient, greener alternative to commercial abrasive cleaner and can be used wherever you would normally use a commercial abrasive powder or cream. Combine it with lemon to cut through almost any grease and grime. This combination also makes a wonderfully effective washing-up liquid: add a teaspoon of baking soda and the juice of half a lemon to hot water and wash the dishes as normal. If you must use a commercial washing-up liquid, make sure it is eco-friendly and use half the usual amount in the sink with just a splash of white vinegar, which will make the washing-up liquid go further and the dishes easier to clean. To shine the sink, put a little cream of tartar, a natural bleaching agent, on a cloth and wipe it around the bowl and drainer. For an alternative to the standard washing powder for clothes, mix equal quantities of eco-friendly laundry powder and bicarbonate of soda, adding a splash of white vinegar in the final rinse as a softener.

Bathroom cleaners

For the general daily wipe around, use a trigger-spray bottle filled with a solution of white vinegar, lemon and water (three-quarters water to one-quarter vinegar, plus a squeeze of lemon). To clean the bath, shower and tiles (where body oils, fats, shampoos and gels accumulate) create a paste with two parts bicarbonate of soda to one part vinegar or lemon. Put a little of the paste on a sponge or cleaning cloth and wipe the area clean, making certain to rinse completely afterwards to avoid any smears. For the toilet, use equal quantities of bicarbonate of soda and cream of tartar, which will have a powerful cleaning, disinfecting and deodorizing effect, together with a bleaching action, leaving the bowl squeaky clean. Use the mixture on a damp cloth or sponge, wipe around the toilet, then rinse the cloth thoroughly and wipe the bowl clean. For cleaning mirrors and any glass, use half water to half white vinegar in a recycled spray bottle. Spray on and wipe clean. For a smear-free finish, dry with a piece of crumpled newspaper.

If your water is hard and you have a build-up of lime-scale on your taps or shower-head, soak some toilet paper in vinegar and place it on the affected area overnight – in the morning it will come off far more easily. To remove mould, mix half a cup of bicarbonate of soda with half a cup of vinegar or lemon and wipe over the affected area. If it doesn't disappear immediately, allow it to soak for a while or coat it two or three more times before rinsing off and wiping clean.

For a natural air freshener for the bathroom, or indeed anywhere in the home, use a spray bottle filled with water and a couple of drops each of the essential oils of lavender, rosemary and lemon. Finally, a small, shallow dish of bicarbonate of soda placed behind the loo will absorb, rather than simply mask, any unpleasant smells.

Metal cleaners

For a good brass cleaner, mix the juice of one lemon with cream of tartar or bicarbonate of soda: mix in enough of either of the dry ingredients to make a paste, then dab on and wipe away with a clean cloth. The length of time you leave the product in contact with the brass will depend on how tarnished the brass is.

A really good copper cleaner comes right out of the kitchen cupboard: simply mix a teaspoon of flour and one and a half teaspoons of salt with a mug of vinegar. Spray or wipe on liberally, leave for half an hour and wipe clean.

To clean silver, fill a washing-up bowl with hand-hot water then add a teaspoon each of bicarbonate of soda and cream of tartar, half a teaspoon of salt and a piece of aluminium foil. Immerse the silver and wash it with a soft sponge (always test a small section first). To clean aluminium, use cream of tartar mixed with water into a soft paste – wipe on and then wipe off.

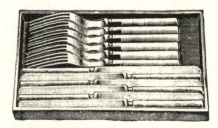

General-purpose cleaners

For an everyday, general-purpose cleaner – on windowsills, doors around handles, table tops, anywhere you'd normally run a cloth – mix a small mug of white vinegar with a slug of olive oil and a squeeze of lemon. To make a furniture polish, mix equal portions of olive oil and lemon juice. This also works well for any wood, including a hardwood floor. The mixture is best sprayed on using a recycled squeezy bottle – spray on, then wipe off.

Bicarbonate of soda will absorb most nasty smells from the carpet (including vomit, cigarettes, pet pongs and curry); for a spillage, remove as much as possible and then use half a teaspoon of bicarbonate of soda in a mug of warm water to dab away at the affected area. For a general carpet deodorizer, sprinkle dry bicarbonate of soda across the floor and vacuum up. To clean windows and mirrors, see page 120.

HOMEMADE BEAUTY PRODUCTS

Self-sufficiency doesn't mean that you can never take pride in your personal appearance or wear make-up again or that you have to wash your hair in dirty washing-up water and rinse it off in ice-cold water. What it does mean is that you have more options available to you because you're not restricted to what is on offer in the shops. You can experiment with all the natural products growing wild in the garden or tame on the windowsill. If you don't have access to a garden or lack the confidence to take the plunge, then all the ingredients mentioned here can be bought in a supermarket or health shop. But try to have a go at mixing your own: whatever their function, the most satisfying and effective way of obtaining natural products is to grow and prepare them in your own home. Shop-bought products are nowhere near as fresh, clean and natural as those you make yourself. So start small. Pick one thing you think might work for you, give it a try, then build from there.

Note: the products described here are pure and natural but always test a little on your skin first to make sure you will not have an allergic reaction. Rub a tiny amount on your wrist and monitor it for 24 hours. If there is no reaction it is safe to proceed.

Skin care

Skin is the largest organ in the human body and plays a critical role in, among many other things, protecting against infection and disease, helping to control temperature and eliminating waste. It is therefore a vital organ and, like any other part of the body, requires care and attention. Apart from drinking plenty of water and eating a healthy diet, one of the most important things you can do to help protect and nourish your skin is to cleanse and moisturize it regularly. Whether you work in the open air or spend all day in an air-conditioned office, developing your own skin care routine will help to keep your skin healthy, toned and soft to the touch.

Hand creams

For a basic but very pleasant elderflower hand cream, melt lard (rendered-down pig fat) in a saucepan and add some flower heads from a blooming elder (don't use the stalks) – the lard should look full of flowers but not be crammed with them. Use only the freshest white flowers as those with a yellow tinge that are slightly past their best can have an unpleasant 'tom-cat' odour that, although untraceable in the finished product, will be evident during the cooking stage! Keep the lard on a very low heat, melted and warm, not bubbling, for about an hour, then strain it through a fine mesh sieve or a piece of muslin. Add a few drops of your favourite essential oil before bottling.

For something more sophisticated, though arguably a little less self-sufficient, put some beeswax or cocoa butter into a water bath. To make a water bath, half-fill a baking or roasting tray with water, put another heat-resistant bowl into that and place the tray on the hob to heat. When the wax or butter starts to melt, put another bowl along-side it into the bath. Add to it two teaspoons of honey, two teaspoons of almond oil and the oil from two aloe vera leaves (the leaves are very fleshy: simply cut them and squeeze to release the oil or sap). Mix.

Then whisk the contents of the second bowl little by little into the butter or wax. Bottle the mixture while still warm and liquid.

Face and body creams

Face and body creams tend to be lighter and less robust than hand creams and are designed for different types of skin. They moisturize and enrich, replacing essential vitamins and minerals that are lost in the rough and tumble of everyday life. But no two skin types are alike, so it is important to understand your own skin and to develop a working knowledge of what each ingredient has to offer before you decide what to add to your homemade creams. Below is a list of natural ingredients (mainly oils) that can be added to the homemade creams – you can mix and match until you find a combination that works well on your skin. For example, for a dry skin, you might try a combination of ginger, a little honey and some lanolin in your cream and see how your skin feels after use.

- Almond oil for sensitive skin.

- Aloe vera for dry skin.

- Apricot kernel oil for older skin.

- Avocado oil for hydration and nourishment.

- Banana, mashed, for a wrinkle inhibitor.

- Benzoin oil for sanitization.

- Bicarbonate of soda for deep cleansing.

- Camomile oil for all skin types but particularly good for dry and hyper-sensitive skin.

- Cocoa butter for a protective, water-resistant barrier.

- Coconut oil for moisturizing and softening.

- Geranium flowers for dry, flaky skin.

- Ginger oil for dry skin.

- Grape-seed oil for greasy skin.

- Honey for antiseptic and antibacterial properties.

- Lanolin ointment for hydrating and soothing.

- Lavender oil for sensitive and normal skin.

- Light sesame oil for moisturizing.

- Mint leaves for zinging skin back to life.

- Myrrh oil for moisturizing.

- Peanut oil for softening all skin types.

- Rose petals or water for dry skin.

- Sandalwood oil for moisturizing normal skin.

- Sesame oil for a natural sunscreen.

- Strawberry juice for slowing down the skin's production of oil.

- Sweet almond oil for omega-3, which helps with the relief of allergies.

- Vitamin E oil for a good antioxidant.

- Wheatgerm oil, full of vitamins and minerals, excellent for a range of conditions, including skin that has been damaged by the sun.

- Witch hazel for acne and eczema.

- Yoghurt for bringing moisture to the surface of the skin, hydrating from the inside out.

All creams begin with a base, either beeswax, cocoa butter or shea butter. Melt your base in a water bath (see page 123). In a separate bowl, also in the water bath (so that they reach roughly the same temperatures), start adding your ingredient. For example, for a day cream, perhaps start with a couple of tablespoons of avocado oil to hydrate and nourish, a couple more of grape-seed oil to moisturize without leaving a greasy finish. If it's sunny, add a teaspoon of sesame oil as a sunscreen and perhaps a couple of fresh mint leaves to invigorate. Allow the oils and mint to infuse in the same bowl for half an hour. Then remove the mint leaves and add the remaining oil to the base little by little, whisking all the time. Bottle while warm.

Scent your creams using essential oils or flowers, leaves or petals: camomile oil is good for everything from dry skin to sensitive skin; geranium flowers and rose water or petals are great for dry skin; lavender and sandalwood are ideal for normal skin types. The idea is to mix and match, bringing in different ingredients to your cream base that you feel will work for you. As a rule of thumb, add essential oils at 5 drops per 100ml/3.5fl oz jar, general oils at 1.5 to 2 per cent of the finished product and 1.5 to 2 teaspoons of juices and honey. As you work through different formulations, keep a record of what you've mixed and how each product works on your skin. Bear in mind that ingredients will have different effects depending on the time of year, the climate, and various other conditions: skin generally becomes oilier in summer and dry and flaky in winter; hormones also affect the skin.

Dry skin

For dry skin, try a combination of two tablespoons light sesame oil, one tablespoon apricot kernel oil and a couple of drops of vitamin E oil or ginger oil (for the latter, grate some fresh ginger and squeeze out the oil) – you only need a small amount, about an eighth of a teaspoon, added to your cream base.

Greasy skin

For oily skin, add to your cream base two tablespoons of sweet almond oil, a quarter of a teaspoon of apricot kernel oil, a whole teaspoon of fresh strawberry juice, and maybe a few drops of Benzoin oil.

Cleansers, toners, face scrubs and face packs

Gentle, herby cleanser: Add a couple of fennel leaves, some thyme leaves and a squeeze of lemon to a mug of boiling water. Use warm but not hot. Apply with a cotton pad. No need to rinse off.

Face mask for dry skin: Mix honey and a couple of drops of camomile oil and apply to face. Leave for 5 minutes. Tone and moisturize after washing off.

Face mask for greasy skin: Combine natural yoghurt and honey with mashed strawberries. Apply to the face and leave for 15 minutes. Rinse off.

Face mask for tired skin: Purée one cucumber, sieve and mix with about a teaspoon of honey so that you have a thick paste. Apply to the face and leave on for 15 minutes. Wash and moisturize.

Face mask to help rebuild the skin's natural collagen: Blend together an avocado and a carrot. Transfer the mixture to a bowl. Add an egg white and three tablespoons each of honey and double cream. Beat together until smooth. The natural oils, vitamins and minerals in the carrot and avocado will tone the skin, the cream will add protein and the beaten egg white will act as a natural instant facelift. For an instant facelift on its own, beat two egg whites together, apply and leave for 10 minutes. Wash thoroughly after use.

Face mask to inhibit wrinkles: Mash together a banana and a spoon of honey and work the mixture directly into the skin. Leave for 15 minutes, then wash and tone with your favourite toner.

Stimulating face mask for all skin types: Blitz a marigold flower, a camomile flower, a carrot and some porridge oats in a blender. Add a teaspoon of almond oil. Apply to the face and neck and gently work into the pores. Leave for 10 minutes. Rinse.

Face scrub for dry skin: Oats are fantastic for dry skin. Wet your face, take a handful of oats and rub them gently into the skin. Tone and moisturize after washing off.

Face and body scrub: Mix milk and sugar together to form a sloppy paste, rub into the skin so it tingles. Wash thoroughly after use.

Toner to ping your face awake: Scrunch some fresh mint leaves in a bowl of ice water and splash on to your face.

Fantastic general toner: Mash an avocado and fork it over with the oil from three aloe vera leaves (simply cut the leaves and squeeze out the oil). Apply using a cotton wool pad then wash off.

Hair care

The treatments that follow have been used to wash and condition hair for generations but were replaced by commercial products in the second half of the twentieth century. But now they're very much back in favour, as the grandchildren, nieces and nephews of those who renounced the natural products are keen to return to the original treatments.

Homemade hair products are surprisingly easy to make and will enrich and enliven your hair with natural oils, herbs, minerals and vitamins. All shampoos, homemade or otherwise, clean the scalp first and then target the hair. If you have been using commercial hair products with chemical additives for a long time, you may find there is an adjustment period when you switch to natural ingredients, during which time your scalp rids itself of impurities. (The hair has a tendency to go limp after the first couple of washes using the natural product as the impurities are expelled from the scalp – but this soon changes and with continued use your hair should be in better condition than before!) One of those impurities is likely to be a chemical called sodium lauryl sulphate (SLS), the foaming agent used in commercial shampoos. SLS is generally regarded as a substance to be avoided as a result of its alleged toxicity. The absence of SLS in homemade shampoos means that they won't foam. But this does *not* mean that they won't work – the SLS in commercial products adds virtually nothing but visual effect.

A word about water: if you can avoid using chlorinated tap water, so much the better, but don't squander money on de-mineralized or de-ionized water. If you can't avoid chlorinated water, then simply boil it before use.

Shampoos

The best place to look for a really lovely, simple shampoo is in the herb garden. Rosemary should be at the top of every hair-care wish list. It is all things to all hair: it encourages growth, helps to restore colour, even to greying hair, and can be used on normal, dry or oily hair. To make a shampoo, steep around five to seven rosemary leaves in a cup of boiling water (if you don't have fresh rosemary, use a rosemary tea bag from a health shop). Add a teaspoon of bicarbonate of soda along with two or three drops of glycerine, wash as normal, rinse well and condition. Two or three drops of essential oil can be added to the treatment – lavender, rosemary, mint or vanilla are particularly pleasant.

Normal hair

Aloe vera is a good alternative to rosemary for normal hair. Simply replace the rosemary leaves with one aloe vera leaf and follow the instructions for rosemary shampoo given above.

Dry hair

Wash with a very gentle shampoo made from camomile tea, using the fresh flowers if you have them (if not use two camomile tea bags). Steep in a mug and allow to cool thoroughly. Add a teaspoon of aloe vera oil (simply cut the leaves and squeeze out the oil or sap) or aloe vera gel, and a teaspoon of baby shampoo. Mix thoroughly and apply, washing only once before rinsing. You could follow this treatment with the olive oil conditioner on page 131.

Greasy hair

Stinging nettles are excellent for all scalp problems but are particularly good for oily scalps as they help to cleanse and clear them. Make an infusion with boiling water and the tops of four or five fresh stinging nettles. Steep for a few minutes and sieve. Add to the nettle water a quarter of a teaspoon of bicarbonate of soda and a couple of drops of tea-tree oil, which is a fabulous antibacterial, antiseptic and antifungal agent that will help put some healthy oils back into your skin and hair. Mint and rosemary (either the leaves or the oil) are also good for oily hair, as are two or three drops of lemon or geranium essential oil, either added to the nettle water or as an alternative to it.

Conditioners

The best conditioner for dark to medium hair is a splash of cider vinegar in a cup, topped up with warm water (if your hair is bleached, add one or two drops of rosemary oil, or a couple of rosemary leaves). This will add vigour and shine like nothing else. For light to blond hair, use a squeeze of lemon juice in the same way.

For a light, general conditioner to nourish and enrich the hair, beat an egg either with an avocado or a banana. Apply directly on to the hair and leave for 15 minutes before rinsing. (This treatment is good for most hair types, apart from extremely greasy or extremely dry.)

Normal hair

Work some natural yoghurt directly into the hair, leave for a few minutes and rinse out.

Dry hair

In theory, an olive oil conditioner should be wonderful for dry hair but it can be slightly filmy and leave a residue. The best solution is to mix a splash of olive oil into your base conditioner, along with herbs that help to enrich dry hair, such as elderflower or rosemary for dry dark hair and marigolds for dry blond hair. Immerse the flowers in the oil (enough flowers so that the conditioner will become infused) and work into the hair. Two or three drops of lavender (see page 133) or sandalwood essential oil can be added to the mixture for really dry hair.

Greasy hair

The best conditioner for oily hair is half a lemon squeezed into a cup of warm water. Work into the hair then rinse out.

Natural hair colourants and highlighters

There are a number of natural teas that work very well as colourants and highlighters for the hair – they act on the pigments in the hair slowly and gently over a period of time. The more often you use the tea, the richer and deeper the result will be. Make the tea by adding whatever ingredient listed below is suitable for your type of hair to a mug of boiling water. Allow it to cool down completely. Wash and rinse your hair, apply the tea, then rinse.

To lighten fair hair, make a tea using camomile (in any form) or a chunk of rhubarb stalk. To darken hair, use cinnamon, sage or lavender (see page 133). To add daring red highlights to light or dark hair, use a tea made from hibiscus leaves.

Treatments for problem hair

To add volume, bounce and shine to dull or lifeless hair

The following four, separate, treatments all work well:

- Beat a raw egg with a teaspoon of olive oil, apply evenly, leave for a minute or so then wash off.

- Mix equal proportions of beer (not lager) and shampoo. Wash hair as with a normal shampoo.

- Add a teaspoon of tea-tree oil to your shampoo.

- Squeeze half a lemon into a mug of hot water and use as a final rinse – care should be taken with colour-treated hair as lemon is acidic, and may have a slight lightening effect.

For hair that looks greasy but is clean

Rub cornflower into the hair and brush out – the cornflower will absorb the grease. Particularly good for hat-wearers!

For dandruff and itchy scalp

Make two infusions, one water-based, the other oil-based. For the oil infusion, mix two tablespoons of olive oil, one of palm oil, one of coconut oil and a few drops of tea-tree oil. Massage into the scalp and leave for 15 minutes. Wash out thoroughly with a water-based infusion made from stinging nettles, sage or thyme leaves.

To help restore natural colour to grey or greying hair

Infuse sage or rosemary leaves in hot water. Allow to cool. Apply as a final rinse after shampooing and conditioning.

To strip out build-up of hairspray, gel and other products

Apply bicarbonate of soda to the hair. Work in gently, then brush out.

To give hair a light feel (particularly good for coarse, wiry hair)

Dilute a tenth of a mug of cider vinegar in a mug of hot water and use as a rinse.

To remove strong odours

Apply tomato juice directly to the hair. Work in and then wash out.

General problem-solver

Lavender can be beneficial to all types of hair but not everybody likes the smell. If you don't like the smell and are using a couple of drops of lavender oil in any of your treatments, you can mask it by adding a couple of sprigs of mint leaves or a couple of drops of eucalyptus oil.

Bath-time and personal hygiene

Everyone should be permitted the indulgence of unwinding and luxuriating in an end-of-the-day bath: the steam on your face; the sensation of soft water enveloping your body; the smell of essential oils and herbs; the sound of a bath-bomb fizzing; and perhaps even a glass of ice-cold white wine to hand. Blissful! Making bath products at home is easy and fun, and there's a real sense of achievement in knowing that you have created the things that are making you feel so good. And homemade toiletries also make wonderful gifts.

Bath-time bouquet garni

For a simple but great bath-time treat that deep cleanses the skin and leaves it feeling soft and silky smooth, take a handful of whole oats (which are fantastic for dry or flaky skin) with a spoonful of dry milk powder, another of bicarbonate of soda and any dry herbs you can lay your hands on: sage, mint, rosemary, thyme, bay, a stick of cinnamon or a vanilla pod. Scrunch everything together and place in a piece of muslin or a stocking, then tie with a ribbon (or some bailer twine if you're a smallholder!) and drop it straight into the bath.

Bath salts

Epsom salts (magnesium sulphate) is the main ingredient in home-made bath salts. They have a neutral pH of 6–7, so their impact on your skin is slight but their effect on the water and your muscles is *sublime*. Half-fill a breakfast bowl with the salts, add a tablespoon of bicarbonate of soda and a teaspoon of sea-salt crystals. Find an attractive recycled jar and fill it to the three-quarter mark (not to the top) with the salts. Then pour in a teaspoon of vegetable glycerine and four drops of your favourite essential oil, put the lid on and shake until all the salts are coated. Add to the bath, sit back and relax.

Bath oil

Select a natural oil, such as hazelnut, sesame, avocado or almond. You can also use baby oil or olive oil. If using olive oil, which is quite heavy, it should be mixed with a little of another oil, such as palm oil, to balance it out (add about 5ml of palm oil or your chosen oil to a

50ml/1.75fl oz mix of olive oil – in other words, about a tenth of the total treatment). Pour the mixture into a recycled bottle or jar and add your favourite essential oil: four drops of eucalyptus to invigorate or eight of lavender to rejuvenate or four each of sage, camomile and rose for a herby oil to pamper and soothe.

Fizz bath bombs

Fun to make and even more fun to use, bath bombs fizz and slowly dissolve a delicious fragrance and wholesome goodness into your bath-water. Although they are easy to make, there is one golden rule: make sure all your bowls and utensils are completely dry before using. If they are damp the chemical reaction will take place while you are mixing the ingredients, leaving you with little more than a damp squib when it comes to bath-time – not much fun!

To make bath bombs you will need five ingredients: three table-spoons of bicarbonate of soda, two tablespoons of citric acid, one tablespoon of cornflour, two teaspoons of almond oil and six drops of your favourite essential oil. Mix the soda, citric acid and cornflour in a dry bowl. In a separate cup, mix the oils, then pour them into the dry mixture and mix continuously for a minute. Pack the mixture into the compartments of an ice-cube tray – this is simply to shape them, they don't need to be frozen. Leave for a couple of hours, or until firm, then turn them out into a bag. Store the bag in a large glass jar to keep dry.

Deodorants

First, to answer the question that may be on the tip of your tongue: yes, homemade deodorants do work. And one of the most compell-ing reasons to make your own is quite simply that they are far better for you than many shop-bought deodorants. Most commercial deodorants work in two ways: as antiperspirants by clogging the skin's pores and as deodorants by neutralizing the smell of perspiration. But the ingredients that clog and mask the pores contain aluminium, which can be absorbed into the body. Opinions vary as to what effect the build-up of aluminium has on the body: some claim that it accumulates in the brain; others that it settles in the lymph glands and in women the breasts (if you're a woman and you are pregnant or breast feeding, *really* think hard about using an alternative, natural deodorant).

Each of the ingredients in homemade deodorant performs a very specific task: bicarbonate of soda absorbs the smell, rather than simply masking it; tea-tree oil – a natural antibacterial, antifungal agent – kills the bacteria that causes the smell; coconut oil soothes and moisturizes the skin; cornflour binds everything together, making it easy to apply; essential oils add fragrance – cinnamon for women and cedar for a men are pleasant options, but you can experiment.

To make a deodorant, quarter-fill a cup with bicarbonate of soda and add the same quantity of cornflour. Mix in enough coconut oil to form a paste. Add four drops of tea-tree oil and a couple of essential oil – that's it. Mix well. Apply the deodorant with your fingers or a soft cloth. This product won't sting after shaving or stain your clothes and you can use it anywhere on your body.

An alternative to the above is a 'deodorant stone' – a crystal of natural salt minerals that inhibits the growth of the bacteria that cause odours. Deodorant stones are hypo-allergenic and therefore perfect for most sensitive skins. They can be bought online or from good health shops.

The menstrual cup

The menstrual cup, designed by women for women, is a safe, eco-friendly, self-sufficient and convenient alternative to tampons and towels and of course avoids all risk of toxic shock syndrome. On average a woman will use up to 20 items of sanitary protection for each period, which adds up to several thousand throughout the course of a lifetime! A menstrual cup is reusable and can last for several years.

Shaped like a rubber cup and made from medical grade material, it is worn internally and works by forming a light seal on the vaginal walls so that your menstrual flow collects in the cup rather than being absorbed. It lasts up to eight hours and can then be removed, rinsed and reinserted. There are also fewer health risks, no toxic shock syndrome to worry about and no problems with dryness, which tampons can produce. In studies the only downside some women mentioned was that the cup can be a little messier than regular tampons and towels, but other than that, it seems to be a viable alternative. For more information, check out www.mooncup.co.uk.

HOMEMADE SOOTHERS FOR EVERYDAY AILMENTS

By extending our knowledge of the natural world it is possible to gain a deeper understanding of how our bodies and minds are influenced, both positively and negatively, by what we eat, smell and touch. This information can then be used to alter our attitudes and emotions and to rejuvenate and heal our bodies. When sickness or that grotty feeling strikes us down, there are a surprising number of homemade, natural, self-care soothers that can be used to help the problem. Although they are not remedies and will therefore not necessarily cure the condition, they will alleviate it.

Note: 1. None of the soothers described in this section should be used in place of a doctor's advice. If symptoms persist, consult a doctor. 2. Homemade soothers should never be taken by anyone who is pregnant, who thinks they might be pregnant or who trying to become pregnant.

Oral soothers, teas and infusions

Bad breath: Chew a strong herb such as cardamom, fennel, parsley (the latter is especially good for combating the smell of garlic), dill or aniseed, or drink a tea made from mint leaves or fenugreek.

Bloating: Drink a tea made from dandelion root (a good diuretic) or either chew raw angelica or drink a tea made from it.

Cellulite: Dandelion-leaf tea helps break down waste and toxins in the body that are thought to be the cause of cellulite.

Common cold: Drink a tea made from elderberry extract and ginger and never underestimate the soothing effect of a thick chicken soup if you have a cold.

Constipation: Make an infusion of dandelion root, ginger, burdock and liquorice. Use this concentrate to make tea, which should be drunk warm twice a day.

Coughs: For an expectorant: sip carrot juice. To soothe: make a paste of raw garlic, onions and honey, leave to infuse overnight and take a teaspoon every three hours. Drink elderberry tea to boost immunity and fight the infection.

Fatigue: Ginseng tea or capsules.

Flatulence: Eat fresh pineapple or drink a glass of pineapple juice after each meal.

Hangover: Make a dandelion tea and allow to cool. Put a couple of teaspoons of the tea into a blender with a whole banana and some honey and top up with milk. Blitz and drink.

Headache: Drink beetroot tea, preferably made from raw rather than cooked beetroot (don't use pickled beetroot).

Indigestion: Apples, carrots and the juice of raw potatoes all have antacid properties.

Menstrual cramps with light bleeding: Drink a tea made from cramp bark, blue cohosh, ginger, camomile and prickly ash.

Mouth ulcer: Squeeze a little fresh lemon into a cup of warm water and add a couple of drops of tea-tree oil. Use as a mouthwash.

Nausea: Chew fresh ginger or drink it as a tea.

Premenstrual syndrome: Take 500–1,000mg/0.017–0.035oz of evening primrose oil a day or two before symptoms usually start and continue taking daily right up to the second day of your period. In extreme cases, consult your doctor, who may suggest higher doses for a limited time.

Run-down: This is when your body is most susceptible to illness, so eat two raw cloves of garlic a day to boost the immune system and to revitalize your body from the inside out.

Sore throat: Blackberry tea to sip.

Thrush: Despite widespread belief, live yoghurt doesn't help. But adding essential oils of tea tree and sweet thyme, together with a few dandelion leaves in a warm bath might.

Toothache: Drench a cotton bud in oil of cloves and place on the affected tooth until the pain subsides.

Water retention (including swollen ankles): Drink dandelion-leaf tea and increase your intake of vegetables that have diuretic properties (for example, carrots, onions, cucumbers and leeks).

Skin rubs and aromatherapy

Note: Always carry out a small skin test to check for allergies before using any of the soothers suggested below. Using a cotton pad, apply a little of the treatment on to the fleshy skin under the top of the arm. Leave for 24 hours, checking regularly for any sign of inflammation. If no adverse reaction occurs after this period then it is safe to proceed with the treatment.

Bruising: Arnica cream rubbed gently on to a bruise will help bring down inflammation and swelling.

Blocked sinus: To ease daytime symptoms, put a couple of drops of eucalyptus oil on to a tissue and inhale; at night time add a couple of drops of the oil to your pillow. For more extreme cases, add the oil to boiling water in a basin, place a towel over your head and inhale the vapours.

Burns: Cut open an aloe vera leaf and apply the sap directly to the burn. Alternatively, apply a compress that has been soaked in cold tea made from the green leaves of ragwort (St James' wort), lavender oil or camomile flowers (the shop-bought version is a lotion) or from witch hazel.

Cracked or infected skin: Marigold flowers steeped in boiling water and allowed to cool, then gently wiped on with a clean cloth twice a day.

Common cold: Add eucalyptus oil and clove oil to your bath.

Cold sores: Scrunch a marigold flower in your hand and apply directly to the cold sore.

Dermatitis: Make an infusion of marigold flowers and chickweed and dab on to affected areas.

Dry skin: Cut open an aloe vera leaf and apply the sap directly to the affected areas.

Eczema: Crush one or two vitamin B tablets into a fine powder in a pestle and mortar, add a little wheatgerm oil, olive oil, safflower oil and sunflower oil, mix and apply to the affected areas.

Haemorrhoids: Apply a cold wash of witch hazel and marigold flowers.

Head lice: Squeeze unscented body lotion to half-fill an eggcup, then add essential oils: one drop of lavender, one of geranium and two of eucalyptus. Mix together then massage into the head and leave for half an hour. Comb thoroughly with a nit comb before shampooing. Rinse off, then use a final rinse of clean, warm water in a mug with two drops each of lavender, geranium, eucalyptus and rosemary together with two teaspoons of white vinegar. Dry naturally.

Insomnia: Sprinkle lavender oil on your pillow.

Leg cramp: Rub with arnica cream.

Sadness: Before going to bed, add some pine needles, willow bark and larch bark (the inner part) to a mug of boiling water. Place it, still steaming, on your dressing table to scent the room while you sleep. Do not drink.

Sore tired eyes: Put a whole rosebud into a cup of boiling water and allow to cool back to room temperature. Dab the rose water directly on to the eyelids.

Stiff muscles: Add rosemary oil to a hot bath. When dry, apply arnica cream.

Thrush: Crush a clove of garlic in a light olive oil – mix until it forms a paste. Apply to the affected area. Leave for 10–15 minutes. Wash away then soothe with a cream made by half-filling an eggcup with unscented body lotion into which has been added two drops of myrrh oil, two of lavender oil and one of tea-tree oil. (This cream can also be applied to a panty liner.)

Wasp or bee stings: Scrunch a marigold flower in your hand and apply directly to the sting.

Weak or split nails: Mix tea-tree and marigold oils together and rub on to the nail.

·

CHAPTER SIX

Arty Crafty Bits

SELF-SUFFICIENCY IS ALL ABOUT doing things for yourself, but it's also about giving (because nothing is quite as personal and says that you care quite as much as something you have made yourself) and about not wasting anything. It's that crossover that this chapter explores. If you have sheep, you have to get them shorn; and if you have to get them shorn, you have to do something with the wool; and from that the logical progression is to knit. If you have bees, there is all that wax with which to make candles. If you have trees, or use split wood for the fire, then you could hand-carve spoons or eggcups. If you have reeds or willows, you could make a wicker basket. If you have leftover scraps of fabric, you could make a rag rug... The list goes on and on. The basic materials for all these projects are the by-products of self-sufficiency – the bits that are left over as you live the life. And if you don't live the life – if you have never sheared a sheep in your life and have no inclination ever to do so – but would still like to make crafty things, then simply buy the materials or source them direct from a smallholding.

Arty crafty bits are the nice things in your home. They are the bits that make you smile and the bits that make your home so very, very personal to you and your family. Whatever your comfort level on the scale of self-sufficiency, be it a chilli plant on the kitchen window-sill and a little homebrew happening in the back room, or a full-on 8-hectare/20-acre smallholding with enough meat and vegetables to keep your whole family fed for a year, there are always moments when you can indulge in a little creativity. It might be making a candle or knitting a rug, carving a spoon or weaving a basket, but it will be homemade and that is what makes it special.

BASKET-MAKING

This is a beautiful art, and totally absorbing. Forget everything for an afternoon in the comforting knowledge that at the end of it you will have produced something practical that will be handy for decades to come. People have been weaving baskets as a means of carrying things for some 12,000 years, and probably for millennia before that, because of course the evidence will remain intact for only so long (though you'd have to admit that a basket made 12,000 years ago and still recognizable today is pretty good going).

One of the reasons why baskets would have lasted so long is the material they were made from. Although you can weave baskets from anything that's flexible, the old basket-makers would have used hard materials such as oak, ash and hickory, and there is a long history in North America of using long-leaf pine needles. Today the favoured approach is to use reed and cane because they soak quickly and become pliable and easy to weave, whereas the old oaks and ashes would have taken days to absorb water and soften. If you do decide to use these traditional materials, you will need to work outside. Boil them in something like a Baby Belling or on a camp stove and then allow them to cool (this is the quickest way to soften them), and make sure you wet them frequently when you're working them at the first sign of cracking or brittleness.

Unless you are determined to be traditional, however, this is where the self-sufficient urge to recycle comes to the fore, because you can use anything that's flexible and can be cut into strips, from magazines and newspapers to leather, fabric (including denim) and plastic bags, on to string, wool, wire or rope, horsehair, willow and straw.

Techniques

There are four main techniques in basket-making, with lots of embellishments and subtleties that can be added to each.

1. A **woven** basket starts with a frame of ridged spokes around which a more pliable material is woven in and out in a weft pattern.

2. A **twined** basket is when two or more flexible materials are twisted between each spoke of the frame.

3. A **plaited** basket is when strips are woven together without a separate frame to create a chessboard pattern.

4. A **coiled** basket (the most intricate, the most difficult and probably the most beautiful style) is when a spiralling oval or circle of strands is stitched in place using one thinner strip.

See the diagrams overleaf for examples of these techniques.

Weaving a simple basket

You will need 10 strips of reed to form the base and the uprights, and then some weaving reeds, which hold the sides of the basket together. Lay five of the reeds on a flat surface rough side up (the smooth side is the neat side and that will make the outer edge), equally spaced, with

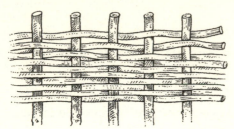

weaving

The four main techniques
used in basket-making

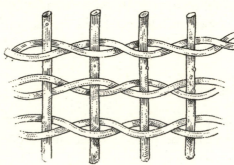

twining

plaiting

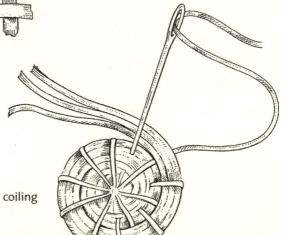

coiling

a gap the same width as the reed between each strip. Take the second five strips and weave them through, maintaining the gaps all the while, until you end up with a woven square in the middle of your reeds, all neat, straight and tidy. This is the base of your basket.

All around the edge of the base, tease the strands into bending upwards. Pick one strand, and, with a sharp knife, cut a vertical slit (just a little longer than the width of your weaving reed) at the point where the strand bends up. Poke one of the weaving reeds into the slit – this will keep the reed in place as you begin to weave it in and out of the uprights. When you have finished the second layer, all the vertical strands should be standing straight up. If they are pointing in, your corners are too tight and you should loosen them a little. If they are pointing out, gently pull the weave a little tighter until all the strands are standing correctly. Continue weaving in and out of the frame for another couple of rows until you are four rows high. When you get to the end of your first weaving reed, cut a slit in an upright reed, as before, and poke its end into it, so that it is invisible from the outside, then start a new reed in the same fashion, and carry on weaving.

Now gently support the top of the basket with one hand while tugging the strands. This helps to compact the weaves. Stand the basket on a flat surface and check to see if it sits flat. If it wobbles or is uneven, carefully tug the centre strands until they are just higher than the corners – this should enable the basket to stand on the four corners, thus eliminating the wobble. Now return to weaving.

When it's about six or seven layers high, stop weaving. Make certain the weaves are nice and tight and well compacted down on one another, and trim the vertical strands about 2.5cm/1in above the top line. If your reed has dried out by now, damp it down again, then fold the strands over the top and tuck them inside the basket (it often helps to use a small screwdriver to help poke the ends into a pocket on the inside weave).

To rim the top, wrap a new strand around the outside of the top edge (the 'rim strand'), and, taking a thinner strand, sew it over the top of the rim strand and through the weave, back over the top of the rim strand and back though the next gap in the weave, so it's like a big, looping, running stitch back and forth, going all round the basket, which will keep the rim strand firmly in place.

Try these basic techniques a few times until you feel reasonably comfortable with the process before venturing on to something larger and more complicated. The more you do, the faster you get and the more confident you feel. And don't think that your trial efforts will go to waste, because if you weave flat lids for the small baskets and secure them along one end with a couple of woven hinges to form lids, they make really lovely boxes and are especially good to use in place of wrapping paper for birthday and Christmas gifts.

CURING AND TANNING

Within this neat little package we call our bodies is the exact amount of oil to tan our own hides. The same goes for all animals, from a fox to a cow, and that oil is found in the brain. Lecithin is the body's natural tanning agent, and if you go back to 20,000 BC, people would have mixed the animal brain in a water solution and actually used it to tan the hides (in fact, the native Americans used mashed brains for tanning until the end of the 19th century). Today, despite all the computers and advances and everything else, that traditional method is still used, although we have tweaked some of the less hygienic aspects. To soften an animal skin, tanners throughout the Middle Ages and onwards would have worked the skins in a solution of faeces, urine and rotting animal flesh to tenderize it, and this was done by steeping the skins in a huge vat and then *treading it in for hours on end*, in the same way that wine-makers used to tread grapes. I'm assuming that these were probably men and (as a wild stab in the dark) also probably bachelors, certainly until baths and soap were invented – not to mention bleach. For this reason, and a very good reason it is too, tanneries were always sited a long way outside of the village.

Though the tanners themselves were often amongst the poorest in the community, they were in elite company, as it says in Genesis that God himself made clothes for Adam and Eve out of animal skin before he evicted them from the Garden of Eden. From the leather sandals of the ancient Egyptians to the leather coats, wallets, handbags, boots and sheepskin rugs of today, curing and tanning rawhide into leather is something we cannot imagine living without.

With the discovery of certain chemicals, and particularly acids, the methods changed to those we know today – virtually all hides are now commercially tanned using chemicals. Curing the hide follows exactly the same principle as curing meat, and involves salting to preserve (otherwise the skin will begin to rot when it is first removed from the animal). Tanning is altering the chemical structure of the hide to make it durable and waterproof. Cure a hide and it is still a skin. Tan a hide and it becomes leather.

Curing small-animal fur

Of course, curing animal fur can be done using the old traditional methods of faeces, urine and rotting animal flesh, but that's a slightly scary and very smelly method, as well as being an utterly foolproof way to lose every friend you've got. It's much better to seek a less alarming alternative, and there is one that is still natural, and works with smaller skins such as rabbit, squirrel and most small-animal furs.

For the best results, you need to work the skin within 1 hour of the animal being killed, and you should keep it in a cool, shady spot throughout the process. Remove the skin carefully, making sure there are no tears, and tack it to a wooden board, fur-side down and reasonably stretched out. Take a handful of table salt and sprinkle it liberally over the skin until the whole thing is covered, then massage it in with the tips of your fingers. Wipe the salt away with clean water and a sponge until most of the salt has gone. Then make an alum solution by dissolving 1 tablespoon alum in roughly 600ml/1 pint water and, using the same sponge, wipe the alum/water solution over the skin once every 6–8 hours for 3 days, then leave for a further 10 hours to dry. When the skin is dry, remove the tacks that held it to the board and roll the skin like a giant cigar quickly one way, then the other, back and forth until it feels soft and pliable. It's now ready to use.

CANDLE-MAKING

Nothing inspires intimate conversation and romance quite like a room lit with candles, and a room lit with homemade candles can boast an ambience of sexy self-sufficiency. There are many beautiful candles you can buy, but virtually all of them can also be made at home and are perfect as gifts, to sell as a little cottage industry, to pamper yourself (with a candlelit bath, glass of ice-cold white wine and some relaxing music) or to set the scene on a romantic evening.

Making candles is easy, and every candle is created using one of two methods: heating wax and pouring it into a mould or rolling a flat sheet of wax into a fat cigar. The materials are simple: wax and wicks, plus scented oils if you want to go the whole hog.

Wax

You can buy wax online or from any craft and hobby shop, but the thrifty way is to save up all the stubs from old candles and render them down. Most wax is based on paraffin (a by-product of oil refining), and candles made of paraffin wax burn in on themselves. By contrast, candles made of beeswax (a natural alternative, which can be quite expensive) run. Soy wax, invented in 1992, is a natural, long-lasting, low-soot option that is becoming increasingly popular. Other natural waxes include palm wax and vegetable wax.

Wicks

To make your own wicks, take a length of strong cotton, such as kite string, and soak it in a solution of 2 tbsp table salt and 4 tbsp borax (sodium borate) dissolved in a mug of warm water for 20 minutes. Take it out and hang it up to dry for 5–7 days. When it's completely dry, dip it into melted wax and hold it up so that most of the wax runs off. After a few minutes it will be cool enough to lay flat. You can then cut it into the lengths you require, keeping what you don't need for another time.

Scented oils

Adding a few drops of an essential oil to your candle will give it therapeutic qualities, but do ensure the oil you use is natural and undiluted. Coconut oil is lovely for a bright summer's evening; lavender will help you sleep (to be avoided at all costs if you are planning a romantic evening for two, and never allow a candle to burn while you sleep); bergamot is uplifting; and citronella is a natural fly deterrent.

Making a pillar candle

Small plastic milk cartons make perfect moulds for pillar candles. Clean and dry a carton and cut it to the height you want the candle to be. Fix the base of the wick at the bottom in the centre with a little dribble of wax (just enough to hold it in place). Wrap the top of the wick around a wooden chopstick (or something similar) and balance it across the top of the carton so that the wick is in the centre. Heat the wax you are using in a pan until it has melted and turned clear, then fill the carton not quite to the top, tapping all around the outside to release any air bubbles. Allow it to cool and set completely before carefully cutting the plastic away.

For a multi-coloured candle, pour in the first colour and when it's just set but not yet firm, pour in the next layer. Adding the second layer when the first is not quite set means that the two waxes will bond together, and you get that lovely shading in at the point where the two meet.

Making a no-heat beeswax candle

This is an ideal fun-time treat for children because it does not involve hot wax. Beeswax comes in sheets and is quite easy to buy if you don't have your own bees. Lay out the sheet with a wick placed along one end, sticking out at the top slightly, and roll it into a cylinder – tightly or loosely, it doesn't matter. When it's done, simply trim the ends.

Making a hand-rolled candle

On the same theme as the beeswax candle, take a tray and lay a piece of greaseproof paper on it, smoothed out so the paper is completely flat, without a wrinkle. Scrunch the edges of the paper up by about 2cm/¾in (to keep the wax in place) and form into a rough square, about 30cm/12in across. Heat the wax and, little by little, build up a puddle of wax on the paper; each layer will set very quickly. When it's cool, but still pliable, trim off the rough edges of the square to give a nice neat shape (saving the trimmings for re-melting), lay a wick at one edge of the square and roll as above.

Making a sand candle

Fill a bowl with damp sand and make a smooth dip in the middle by pressing down with a tablespoon. Make sure it's as smooth and symmetrical as you can get it. Put a wick in the bottom and secure it across the top with a wooden chopstick, then pour in the hot wax. Let it cool completely, then lift it out of the sand, trim the wick and gently tap the candle to remove any excess sand.

MAKING PAPER AND GREETINGS CARDS

Until the industrialization of the 19th century, all paper was handmade one sheet at a time. The word 'paper' is derived from the Latin *papyrus*, which described the ancient Egyptians' form of paper – a flat woven sheet made from strips of the papyrus plant. Despite this, however, paper was not actually invented by the Egyptians, but rather by the Chinese, and to this day some of the most beautiful paper still comes from China.

Making paper at home is all about recycling: taking old newspapers, old utility bills (nothing more satisfying than putting a bill into a blender and blitzing it) and turning them into crisp new sheets ready to be used. (Note, though, that the ink from newsprint does come through, so you may need to add a little bleach to your pulp solution.) In fact, in both Britain and America, around 70 per cent of the material used to make all the paper each year comes from recycling. Paper manufacturers collect old newspapers and magazines and subject them to a simple process that can be recreated in any kitchen, though the process is a little soggy – which makes it ideal for children! But it's not just wood and recycling that can be used to make paper, and more industrious makers use rags, cotton and even elephant dung, though quite how many self-sufficient households would have an elephant is questionable.

How to make paper

EQUIPMENT

Washing-up bowl

Blender

Deckle (see below)

2 tea towels

Rolling pin

Iron

The most important thing for making paper is a deckle. A deckle is the frame in which the paper is made. You can buy them from craft shops and online, and if you are going to turn this into a small business, then it's worth the investment. But if you are only going to make a few odd sheets, then it's cheaper to make your own deckle.

To make a deckle, take an old picture frame (car boot fairs and recycling centres are ideal places for finding old pictures), the inside measurement of which is just a little bigger than the piece of paper you want to create, but smaller than a washing-up bowl. You also need to source some fine mesh that is the same size as the frame (the ideal is the gauze used in a screen door or the fine mesh for windows on a chicken house to keep the flies out). Take the glass, picture and backing out of the frame and cut the gauze so it fits snugly into the frame and staple or pin it in place. That's the deckle.

For an even quicker version, get a wire coat hanger and bend it into a rough square with the hook at one corner. Pull a stocking (or one leg of a pair of tights) over it from the opposite corner to the hook, right down to the foot, and tie a piece of string at the corner where the hook is so the stocking is as tight as a drum. This works well as a one-off, but is unlikely to last any longer than that.

Prepare the paper you are going to use by shredding it, ripping it into strips or tearing it into coin-size pieces. Note that, as a rule of thumb, every two A4 sheets of paper will make one A4 sheet of home-made paper, though this obviously depends upon how thick you want your paper to be. Half-fill the bowl with warm water and soak the pre-pared paper for about 1 hour, then drain through a colander. Half-fill the blender with water, and add a little of the pulped paper, taking care not to add too much in one go as it will just clump. Blend it until it is completely smooth without any lumps, adding more pulp little by little.

Meanwhile, rinse out the washing-up bowl and half-fill it again with warm water. Slide in your deckle so it rests on the bottom and add a spray of laundry starch to help stiffen the paper. When the blending of your pulp is complete, pour it into the water and swish it around so it settles evenly. If you want to make a large or thick sheet, and so need more pulp, blend some more paper until you are happy that the amount in the bowl is thick enough to create the sheet. Swish the whole lot once more, if necessary, and let it settle (shake the deckle a little if you feel it is still not landing evenly), then carefully lift out the frame and rest it over the bowl to drain. When it has stopped dripping, gently press down with the tips of your fingers to help squeeze out any excess moisture.

Lay a clean tea towel over the deckle and place a plate on top of that. Holding all three layers (deckle, tea towel and plate) together, invert them on to a flat surface. Lift off the deckle and slide out the plate, so the tea towel is resting on a flat surface with the sheet of paper in the middle of it. Lay the other tea towel over the top and use the rolling pin to roll the paper 'sandwich' to squeeze out as much water as possible.

Remove the top tea towel and let the paper dry for a good couple of hours (it should not be left to dry out completely, just until it's mostly dry), then iron it with a medium-to-low iron, still with the tea towel as a backing. Leave it for 12 hours, then peel the paper away from the tea towel. Leave it for another 12 hours, and your homemade paper is ready.

If you are an incurable romantic and want to use your homemade paper to write a love letter, add a couple of petals or leaves for a girl, or straw or herbs for a man, into your pulp at the blending stage after the pulp has been blended until smooth.

Making a greetings card

In the UK alone it is estimated that in excess of £1.5 billion each year is spent on buying greetings cards. There are masses and masses of cards available, but none of them compares with a handmade card, as any parent will testify the first time their little one hands them a card they have made themselves. Sending a homemade card says so much more than one bought from a shop, so the next time someone you know has a birthday, don't buy a card (and certainly don't send an e-card!) – make one.

Of course, the best way would be to attach a sheet of your home-made paper to the front of a folded piece of thick card so it sits in the middle and write your message on that. Alternatively, you can use stencils or Clip Art from the computer, or for a birthday you could print off a montage of events that have happened on that day in history, or famous people who also have a birthday on that date, by going to www.brainyhistory.com.

For something different and a little special, try hand-stitching a card by drawing a pattern on a separate sheet of paper (or trace a picture) and lay it on top of your card. Take a pin and work your way around the outside of the picture, making holes at regular intervals, so that when you take the top sheep away the pin marks outline the image. Then sew around it using a backstitch or zigzag stitch.

WOOD CARVING

It may sound obvious, but the first thing to do when you want to carve something is choose the wood. The difference between softwood, such as pine, and hardwood, such as oak, beech and ash, is that while the softwood might be easier to carve, it will not last as long or carve as nicely as a hardwood. Make sure the log is well seasoned (one that has been cut for at least a year, so has weathered its way though each of the four seasons) and looks undamaged.

When using wood in its natural form, it is important to follow the line of strength, which, in a tree, runs from bottom to top, not side to side. When you look at a tree stump, you can see the rings that mark its growth. Never be tempted to create an item across these rings, as it will curve and twist. Instead, always follow the grain, whether it's the trunk of a tree you are using or a branch, and try to use wood from the middle of the tree/branch, where the rings are closest: you will get the prettiest patterning and the least curving and twisting.

One of the nicest and easiest things you can carve from wood is a spoon. The feel of a hand-carved spoon is unlike anything mass-produced. It feels chunky and solid and deliciously tactile, and when you use it to stir a cooking pot, it sits snugly in your hand. For anyone who cooks, a hand-carved spoon is as personal and important as their favourite knife.

Wooden spoons have, unfortunately, gained a negative connotation from being used as the description of a booby prize in a competition. In Wales, by contrast, beautifully ornate hand-carved wooden spoons were given as love tokens, and were known as love spoons. The origin of the Welsh love spoon is somewhat hazy, but it doesn't take much imagination to piece together the intimacy of the gift: literally, it is something that the woman would put in her mouth and use to feed herself, but it's also a figurative representation of her man's desire to provide for and look after her. It's lovely. As to the symbols that were carved on the spoon handles, such as diamonds, hearts, crosses and birds, they spoke (and still do speak) a language of their own.

Carving a wooden spoon

Making a spoon, whether it's a love spoon or a practical spoon for cooking, takes a little bit of time and effort, but it's well worth it, and once you get the basic shape you can whittle anywhere: on a park bench while the dog charges around, sitting on the back doorstep or even in front of the fire with the log basket between your knees.

EQUIPMENT
Pencil
Fretsaw
Stanley knife with a brand-new blade
Gouge knife (optional)
Sandpaper – different grades from coarse to extra-fine

Choose a log about 30cm/12in long and at least 10cm/4in in diameter, following the guidelines above, and split it top to bottom down the centre. This is the time to spot any flaws that may affect your spoon, such as rot-spots, cracks or infestations. If you see any of these, discard the log and start again. If the wood looks good, then measure about 4cm/1½in back from the centre (no need to be too accurate) on one of the halves, and split it again, top to bottom, at this point so you end up with effectively a thick plank (once again checking both sides for flaws).

Now take the pencil and draw an outline of your spoon. This is going to be the actual outline of your spoon, so try to get it as symmetrical and straight as possible, either by drawing around another spoon or by making a template out of cardboard first. Using a vice or a work bench, carefully cut out the shape of the spoon with the fretsaw. What you should end up with is a spoon shape if you look down on it from above, but very thick – sort of the spoon equivalent of a platform shoe.

Now it is just a case of carving away the excess wood with the Stanley knife, little by little. Before you start, put a thick plaster on your thumb or wrap some leather around it to protect it. Then, beginning at the back of the spoon, work down the handle of the spoon until it is roughly the right shape, but do not worry too much about getting it perfect, as the sanding at the end will smooth it out and round it off. When you get to the back of the bowl, work from the outside to the centre, making sure you leave enough wood so it's nice and proportionally deep. Turn the spoon over and start working down the handle once again. If you have a gouge knife for scraping out the bowl, then so much the better. If not, continue using the same knife and work it as though you were making a ham-fisted attempt at scooping out the innards of a hard-boiled egg.

Once the basic form of the spoon has been realized, and you are happy with the depth and shape of the bowl, take the coarsest grade of sandpaper and begin smoothing it. Wipe the spoon regularly with a clean cloth, and as soon as most of the obvious cut marks have disappeared, work down through the grades, spending more time on the finer grades than the coarse ones. When it's finally completed, a little oil will help to protect it and also bring out the grain. If your spoon is to be used, use a light olive oil; if it's just decorative, use linseed oil.

Once you get the hang of carving spoons, you'll find it's both addictive and therapeutic, and you can go on to embellish the handle or even the bowl with beautifully intricate patterns. You can also use the same method to make bowls, ladles and eggcups. If you have a child, you could also make them their very own wizard wand, like Harry Potter's, by working intricate designs, as for the spoon handle, on a suitable length of wood.

PYROGRAPHY

Also known as branding, firework or pokerwork, pyrography is writing with fire, and it is a skill that is recognized to have been in existence since the 1st century BC, though it probably dates back much further. At its most basic level, pyrography is used to personalize an item such as a wooden spoon (or a wizard's wand) by burning the name into the wood of the person to whom it belongs, or the craftsman who created it. At its most artistic level, it is used to create wonderful pictures, with a subtlety of shading and texture you simply could not craft on any medium other than wood.

Technology has advanced even this most ancient form of writing and there is specialist equipment available, which looks like a cross between a thick pen and a soldering iron, that can be bought and plugged into the mains. Alternatively, you can use a soldering iron, or be authentic and get a poker with a sharp pointed end and rest it in a hot fire to heat up.

Writing with fire

You can use pyrography to decorate eggcups or spoon handles, to draw a picture, to burn the name of a house on a house sign (or that of a horse to pin on a stable door – unless it's the type of horse who would eat it!) or even to sign a fine piece of work as its creator, just as many distinguished cabinet-makers used to do.

Use a pencil to trace exactly what you want to burn first, and then, when you're happy with your design or lettering, take your red-hot iron and lightly follow the pencil mark with the tip. The heavier you press, the darker the scorch will be, so use a heavy hand for the main image/writing and a lighter hand for shading.

SOFT FURNISHINGS

This term encompasses a wide variety of items that make our homes more attractive and more comfortable to live in. From cushions and quilts to curtains and blinds, via lampshades and chair covers, soft furnishings are what turn a house into a home. Better still, you can do most of them yourself (actually, all of them yourself if you are handy with a needle, a sewing machine, knitting needles and a crochet hook), which means you won't be paying large sums of money for custom-made curtains or buying 'ethnic' rag rugs from trendy stores: you'll be making them all yourself.

Knitted blankets

Some soft furnishings, such as knitted blankets, are very easy to make. If you can knit, then you can knit a square. And if you can knit a square and sew, then you can sew the squares together to form a knitted blanket, since most blankets are a collection of squares fitted together. (If you can't knit at all, flip to page 169, where knitting is explained and a website source is given.) From a baby's coverlet to a teenager's Bart Simpson, Harry Potter or Girls Aloud bedspread, and on to a touch of home for a young adult in university digs, a wedding present for a daughter or something just for you – it all starts with casting on the first stitch and knitting that first square. Once the top of the bed looks beautiful, turn your hand to a hot-water bottle cover or a new throw for the sofa. Once you can knit, anything (well, anything knitted) is possible.

Patchwork quilts

A step up from a knitted blanket is a patchwork quilt, which combines two skills: *patchwork* and *quilting*.

The origin of patchwork (shapes of fabric sewn together to make a pretty pattern or block) is thought to date back to the 12th century, when pieces of fabric were stitched together to make underwear for Mongolian soldiers to wear beneath their heavy armour, so protecting them from the bitter winters. One of the best books on patchwork quilting, which will show you many different pattern blocks, is *The Sampler Quilt Book* by Lynne Edwards.

The beauty of a homemade patchwork quilt is that so much of it can be made from recycled material. The only stipulation, certainly for the beginner, is that you use only 100 per cent cotton, as manmade fabrics tend to stretch out of shape. The exception to this rule is denim (which often has Spandex or Lycra in it these days), as the toughness of the close weave keeps the shape nicely; though if you have lots of old pairs of jeans you want to turn into patchwork, never use the knees – you can spot them a mile away! The ideal materials are old shirts or off-cuts from dressmaking.

As for quilting, this was popular for making blankets and was used by the ancient Egyptians as a means to keep warm against the cold desert nights. Quilting is taking a sandwich of top and bottom layers of fabric, with a layer of wadding in between, and sewing them together with a simple running stitch, in and out, about 8 stitches to 2.5cm/1in. The bottom layer, known as the backing, is normally a single piece of fabric, such as broadcloth or muslin, whilst the top will be patchwork if you are making a patchwork quilt, but could just be a piece of fabric if not.

Making a patchwork quilt

Start small with a lap quilt (a scaled-down version of a bed quilt) or a baby's cot quilt – or even a picnic quilt – and aim to move up bit by bit to something more ambitious, rather than starting out on a king-size quilt straight away and getting daunted and dispirited (then hiding the part-worked quilt in the cupboard under the stairs, never to be seen again).

EQUIPMENT

A2 cutting mat

45mm/1¾in rotary cutter (dressmaking scissors will do at a push, but it's difficult to get any real accuracy with shears, as you need to lift the material in order to get the blade of the scissors underneath it)

Ruler

Sewing machine

Before you start cutting and sewing your patchwork, put all the fabrics you intend to use through the washing machine, even if they are brand new, as this gets rid of any dust from the manufacturing process and will help to preshrink the fabric, hopefully eliminating that danger later on. Iron the fabrics, then lay the first fabric you are using on the cutting mat, and, using the rotary cutter, cut out the required shape. Continue cutting in this way, using all the fabrics you intend to use, until you have cut all the shapes required for the quilt. Sew the shapes together following the instructions in the book mentioned above, or any other good patchwork book, or following information from a website.

Whether you are going to freestyle the quilting stitching (i.e. just stitch as you want) or work from a template, it is a very good idea to draw an accurate scaled-down image of your finished quilt so you will have something visual to refer to as you progress with the quilting. If you are using a template, once you have drawn it, make photocopies of it and lay them across the patchwork to make up the sections of the design, and then machine sew (or hand sew if your patience and skills extend that far) each section in place through the paper and material. Later you can tear away the paper so that you are left with only the material – the paper will come away easily along the sewing line once it's done.

When you are ready to assemble the layers of the quilt and stitch them together, take your bottom broadcloth or muslin layer and lay it out. Then take your wadding and lay it neatly on top. Then take your patchwork top with the template sections sewn on to it (as a rule of thumb, the top should be smaller all around than the backing and the wadding) and pat it down flat, then pin it to the lower layers in a square grid, working from the centre out. When it's pinned, start sewing your quilting pattern, again from the centre out, using quilting thread rather than ordinary cotton thread, which is tougher and has a tendency to saw through the quilt over time, leaving gaping holes. When you have finished all the stitching, tear the pieces of paper away to reveal your lovely quilted pattern.

Finishing off the quilt by binding, or edging, is done either by taking a separate strip of fabric and sewing it all the way around the outside, or folding the overcut of the backing and the wadding to the top and sewing it all the way around. As a final little embellishment, embroider a label with your name into a discreet corner for future generations to see, as quilts often become family heirlooms and are handed down for decades, even centuries to come.

Making rag rugs

Rag rug-making started off as a way of producing floor and bed rugs in times of hardship, such as the beginning of the 1900s and during both world wars, because these rugs are made from cast-off clothing such as old T-shirts, dresses, leggings and maternity wear, basically anything that can be cut into strips – an early form of recycling. Originally the base would have been made from hessian, but most rag ruggers now prefer canvas.

There are lots of different methods of rag rug-making and they can pretty much all be used on the same rug, but the two most popular are *pushing* and *hooking*. Pushed rugs are made by taking short scraps of material and prodding each end through the backing from behind using a pointed, but not sharp, tool. By contrast, hooked rugs are worked from the front, and they involve holding strips of fabric behind the canvas and hooking loops of them through to the front in a criss-cross pattern with a large crochet hook or rag rug hook. As each strip is used up, another strip is added to give a continuous long strip.

Once the rug has been completed (whichever method you used to make it), paint the back with latex glue to seal all the ends. When the glue is dry, lay the rug on a backing – something like an old tablecloth or bedspread works well – and trim around the edges, then hand-stitch the backing to the rug. Don't worry if it looks a little homemade: that's the look you're working for. My rag rug has been in front of the fire for two years now with regular washes and still looks fabulous!

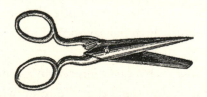

Making curtains

Some soft furnishings, such as curtains, need to be taken a bit more seriously. During the 17th and 18th centuries, the government of Britain was desperate to impose some sort of tax on the people, and although they would have loved to levy an income tax, at the time this was felt to be too intrusive into people's private affairs. In its place they decided to tax the property in which people lived, and set an unpopular charge based upon the number of windows in each house, a window tax, which gave birth to the phrase 'daylight robbery'. Many people bricked up their windows to avoid the tax, which must have made it very dark and dingy inside, especially as electricity hadn't been invented then, so the need for pretty curtains to cover the ugly bricked-up gaps must have been high.

Nowadays, the choice of what to hang in our windows is wide: from simple unlined tab-topped curtains to elegant lined goblet-pleated creations. There are also many different styles of blinds, from the classic roller blind to the more challenging Austrian version. You *can* buy curtains and blinds, of course, but making them is very rewarding and gives immense satisfaction. Walking into a room that has lovely curtains is one thing, but walking into a room that has lovely curtains *made by you* is quite another.

Curtains aren't just functional: they're also a statement. They're the accent in a room that will make it feel warm and inviting or cold and dull. They can make or break a room. Curtain-making is all about the fabric. There's the colour to consider, the weight (a heavy or light-weight curtain fabric) and the print: subtle like a moiré watermark or bold and bright. Let the material say something about you and your home.

Because they have such a great impact on a room, changing your curtains allows you to alter the feel of the room whenever you want. Make four sets of curtains and change them with the seasons – not for every room in the house, just the important ones like the bedroom and the sitting room. Swapping curtains might take you a couple of hours, but the impact on a room is as strong as if you'd redecorated, only without all the mess. And changing something so bold is a great way to beat the feeling of being stuck in a rut.

If you want to take your self-sufficiency into the realms of soft furnishings by making your own curtains, arm yourself with a good instruction book and start with something simple. A pair of unlined curtains made from plain fabric is the safest starting point, and from there you can move on to adding linings, then interlinings (to help the curtains drape beautifully and also to act as wonderful insulation) as well as dealing with pattern repeats and matching patterns across widths, and experimenting with the wide range of available headings. Once you start, you'll be hooked.

As for blinds, you can buy kits for making roller, Roman and Austrian blinds. Again, start with a simple roller blind before experimenting with the more complex Roman or Austrian ones.

MAKING YOUR OWN CLOTHES

From 1964 until 2006, *Top of the Pops* was one of the highlights of the week for pop-music fans. Hit groups and singers of the day would perform in front of a live audience, and the programmes were broadcast to large television audiences. For many years it was without doubt the trendiest programme on TV, and everyone watched it for the music and the fashion tips because it showed real people dancing to real music. And then this happened...

It was a normal week with a guest list that would justify rolling out the red carpet and popping champagne corks. The bands were giving it their all on the stage and the spectators were dancing and flirting and showing off for all they were worth. Then came a slow song, and to emphasize the change in tempo, the camera took a long, slow sweep across the audience, and there, right in the centre, looking gorgeous, was a lady knitting. *And nobody thought that was odd.* The coolest, most fashionable place to be in the country, with millions of people watching, and she had taken her knitting. 'Just doing an arm of this cardi I've been working on.' Presumably when the music sped up and she really got going, she could turn out a jumper, several scarves and a hat all in the space of a three-minute boogie-woogie. Knitting was *in*.

Now, some decades later, knitting is back in fashion. Women who can remember their mothers click, click, clicking away with the needles find themselves drawn into wool shops and flicking through pattern books. Babies born in the 21st century are once more spending their early months in hand-knitted booties and peeping out from under warm woollen hats, and the fashion pages of magazines are full of hand-knitted jumpers and cardigans. Forget Granny's scratchy cardigan, or the awful Christmas jumper brigade: this is sharp and sexy fashion for the 21st century.

Women have been making their own clothes for centuries: from knitted hats and shawls to hand-sewn dresses, tops and skirts. Dressmaking and knitting are essential skills in the self-sufficient home because not only are you making something unique and beautiful but it's also a perfect way to recycle your old clothes. You could unravel a no-longer-loved jumper and knit it up again into something you will love.

Chic, sexy or practical (or all three at once), creating your own fashion by knitting and sewing is a brilliant way to show the world who you really are, and that you're not simply an 'off-the-peg' type of person. Whether you spend your days bumbling around on a farm in jeans and a jumper or you need a smart skirt and cardigan for the office, it's perfectly possible to create your own wardrobe.

Knitting

The image of knitting being something done by grannies in rocking chairs does not belong in today's world, and neither is it a fair representation of women knitting their own high-end fashion right now. The craft of knitting deserves better, and in the hands of the current generation, it seems to be getting respect at last. The end of the 20th century saw a rise in sales of high-street fashion, but as that century gave way to a brand-new one, fashion started to become a little more down to earth again: fewer fantastic and, frankly, unwearable garments – more knitwear and crafty 'home-styled' creations. Television picked up on the trend and fanned the fashion flames, with style, designer and home TV shows becoming must-see events. This insight into the minds and methods of fashion designers and style gurus meant that looking good no longer meant having a purse stuffed full of money and a day's off-the-peg shopping, it meant creating something unique at home … and one way to do that was by knitting.

Knitting involves creating a loop in a continuous length of yarn around the tip of a knitting needle, and using another needle to thread the next loop on to the one before, thereby locking it in place, thus creating material that can be shaped into a garment. If you're a knitting novice, www.knittinghelp.com is a fabulous site for beginners that shows the knitting basics of long-tail casting on, and plain and purl stitches, which make up the three most important elements of knitting and with which virtually any pattern is then possible. You can knit at home in front of the television, on the train or while you're waiting your turn on the Xbox or Wii, anywhere in fact, and when your few spare knitting minutes have run out, you can just put it down ready to pick it up again later. No fuss, no hassle: the perfect pick-up, put-down hobby.

From chunky jackets and slimming skirts to beanie hats, funky gloves and beautiful lingerie, knitted clothes are the perfect dress-up or dress-down outfit for occasions from a garden party to mucking out a horse; and, if the wool has been spun with a fleece from your own sheep, they are the epitome of self-sufficiency.

To knit, you need knitting needles and some material to knit with. Traditionally this would have been wool, but there are many recycled alternatives, such as T-shirt or silk sari material, which you simply strip cut, starting at the bottom and working your way around and up in one running cut so you end up with a continuous strand, and then knit in the usual way. Although T-shirt material is mainly recycled into rag rugs (see page 165), it can also work for short jackets or long skirts. Other unusual materials are banana fibre; rabbit, goat, yak or cat hair; plastic bin liners (strip cut as you would a T-shirt) or even old video tape!

The most common misconception of knitting is that once you start you end up with dozens and dozens of scarves. Not true: once you start you end up with dozens and dozens of socks instead. Life could be worse. Yet once the complexities and subtleties begin to sink in, the transition from socks to everything else is swift. A competent knitter can easily turn their hand to most patterns – and there are patterns available for most things.

Whilst it's true that knitting is a way of having beautiful things to wear that may be financially out of your grasp otherwise, knitting is equally about individuality, about making a statement. Whether you're dressing up a knitwear top with a flirty skirt or dressing it down with a pair of old favourite jeans, the result is the same: you made it, you love it, and nobody else in the world has one the same.

Dressmaking

The difference between dressmaking (I use the term in its general sense to cover all forms of making clothes from fabric, including tailoring) and knitting is that with knitting you are starting from scratch and creating the material for the garment, whereas dressmaking begins with finding the right fabric for the clothes you want to make. Another interesting difference between knitting and dressmaking is that traditionally, tailoring was once seen as a male profession, whereas even today, fewer men knit than women.

Note that if you are going to take up dressmaking, a sewing machine is pretty much a must. Yes, you could stitch everything by hand, but the results will never be as good, and there are only so many hours in the day. So buy a good, lightweight machine (not one that is so heavy that you can't lift it on and off the table without risk of serious injury) and get sewing.

There are hundreds of different fabrics, many of which are suitable for dressmaking, including cotton, leather, Lycra, denim, silk and satin. Hunting for the right fabric (the right colour, the right texture), maybe combining fabrics that complement each other, and choosing a stylish pattern is what dressmaking is all about. Whether it's making a simple top or creating a complete outfit, the fabric is where it begins and ends. For ideas, inspiration and guidance on what to do, and how to do it, check out www.burdastyle.com/creations, which showcases everyday people creating high-end fashion in their own homes.

Dressmaking, or at least dress-mending, also plays an important part in self-sufficiency. As our mothers and grandmothers were well aware, the ability to patch up and repair clothes, to make do and mend, makes the household income go further and avoids (or at least delays) the buying of new clothes.

NATURAL DYES

The synthetic fabric dyes available commercially can be disappointing and a bit samey, not to mention toxic, and more and more people are developing allergies to these commercial colourings, which can make clothes feel itchy, and, at worst, can lead to blotchy irritated skin. Not nice. Yet the crazy thing is that we are surrounded by natural dyeing plants, spices and berries that will colour clothes with more vibrancy and depth than any shop-bought equivalent. If you live more than a minute away from the shops you will probably pass half a dozen different dyeing ingredients growing wild, and available for free, along your journey.

All you need to do is collect the plants or berries – adding different ingredients together will heighten or lower the shade and tone – and put them in a large pan (not one you might cook in afterwards). Add some alum (a stabilizer available from most chemists) to set the colour, water and the fabric you want to dye, and bring the whole lot up to boiling point, then turn off the heat and let it cool gently for anywhere between a couple of hours to a whole day. The longer you leave the fabric steeping, the richer and darker the colour will be.

NATURAL DYES

Colour	Plant
Red and pink	Cranberries, dandelion root, raspberries, red onion skin
Orange	Beetroot, dahlias, heather, marigolds
Yellow	Field mushrooms, nettles, St John's wort, saffron, turmeric
Brown	Cinnamon, onion skin, tea bags, walnut husks
Dark brown	Gypsywort, hawthorn berries
Green	Foxglove, grass clippings, lily-of-the-valley, nettles, sorrel
Blue	Cornflower, wild pansy

There are no formulae, as different plants picked from different spots at different times of the year will each produce a shade that is either darker or lighter, so it really is a case of playing around: adding and taking away until you get something you like. One trick, however, if you find the colour very dark is to add a capful of white wine vinegar to lighten the shade. This works especially well with the berries and takes away a lot of the darkness, bringing out more of their natural reds.

Once the right colour has been reached, take the material out and wash it in clean, warm water and hang it out to dry. This method of dyeing is perfect for shirts and blouses, tablecloths and curtains – indeed, for most fabrics, including off-cuts for patchwork and quilting and even wool for knitting.

CHAPTER SEVEN

·

Livestock

A FEW DECADES AGO FEW OF US would have thought to question where our food came from. But nowadays we're better informed, more inquisitive and not so trusting. We want to know exactly how and where our Sunday roast has been reared, the conditions under which it was produced and the processes the meat was put through before it reached the shelves. These things make a difference to us, and they certainly make a big difference to the animal. This chapter explores how we can feel in greater control of the food we eat. It will be of practical use to those who simply want to shop a little more ethically, to those who have room for a beehive or a handful of chickens and time on a Saturday afternoon to cast a rod into a river, as well as to smallholders with space for pigs, poultry, sheep, goats or cattle.

KEEPING BEES FOR HONEY

The production of honey is a miracle of the natural world. The end products – the beeswax and the honey – are almost secondary to the privilege of witnessing the complex community of bees manufacturing their product. So, in less time than it takes to watch a commercial break, this is how honey is made.

The bees gather nectar from flowering plants and store it in their 'honey stomachs'. They then return to the hive and pass the nectar on to other worker bees whose job it is to chew it, breaking down the complex plant sugars into more digestible forms, effectively creating the early stage of honey. The honey is then put into the honeycomb. But before it is sealed with a wax lid for long-term storage, another group of bees stands outside, fanning their wings to dry the honey and remove any excess moisture. Ingenious!

The blossoms that are visited by the bees will obviously influence both the taste and the colour of the honey: colours can range from strong browns and ambers through to very light, almost transparent yellow with a touch of gold; likewise, the tremendous variety of flavours depends on the flowers used and their region of origin, but they vary from delicate, soft and floral tones through to richer, almost nutty tastes. The majority of honey sold in shops is a blend of several different honeys from separate locations. But sampling a single honey made from one source is like tasting the countryside inhabited by the bees.

Honey is a natural sugar – a healthy alternative to refined sugar – and can replace refined sugar in most recipes. It goes well in coffee, tea and milk and can be mixed in cakes, drinks and yoghurts, and with flavoured vinegars for fantastic salad dressings. It also provides a stunning glaze for most meats. Beeswax can be used to makes candles, soap, lip balm and furniture polish.

For anyone thinking of keeping bees, the initial cost of the starter kit, including the hive, would be roughly equivalent to an average week's wages in the UK. But after the initial outlay, a standard-sized hive can produce between 27–45kg/60–100lb of honey a year for about an hour's work a week. A standard hive is around 0.9m/3ft high by 0.6m/2ft wide, so space should not present a problem for most people. What may be an issue, however, is that bees need a lot of flowers to make honey – around two million of them for just 0.5kg/1lb of honey (not to mention some 55,000 miles of flight)! But crops and plants can't pollinate without bees, so if you live reasonably close to an arable farm, the farmer may welcome your plans and donate a corner of a field to your apiary. Even if you live in a suburb, it is possible keep a hive at the end of the garden, although success will depend on the plants and flowers that surround you. The more built-up the area, the less practical it would be. If you are interested in keeping bees, browse the Internet for reliable, practical guidance on how to get started.

KEEPING HENS FOR EGGS

The humble egg is possibly *the* most exciting single ingredient to come out of the self-sufficient garden and goes with more things than Joseph's Technicolour Dreamcoat. If you've never had a proper, fresh egg, the first time you crack one open prepare to be wowed. The yoke is an intense yellow, almost orange, and sits pert on top of the white. It doesn't 'wash' across the frying pan when it's cooked, as older and shop-bought eggs sometimes have a tendency to do, but remains firm and compact. And it has a distinctive, rich, nutty, creamy taste. Once you've had a fresh egg straight from the chicken, you'll never want a shop-bought one again.

Laying chickens, or 'layers', need a safe shelter, known as a coop (which should be dry and draught-free and able to be locked at night), and a run where they can peck and scratch about. The main differences between meat birds and layers are the types of breeds and the method of feeding. Unless you intend to breed, avoid getting a cockerel – a hen can lay eggs even if a cockerel is not present, but they won't be fertilized. Cockerels are the ones that make a lot of noise and crow to announce the arrival of dawn … and they will crow from there on pretty much throughout the day. If you live in a built-up area or have any neighbours, they may not welcome the new alarm clock. Layers tend to be leaner than meat birds and produce one egg a day when they are in full lay.

There are many breeds to choose from, and some are very pretty. But always consider buying ex-battery hens. These are chickens that have worked hard to produce eggs day after day in confined and often terrible conditions. After a year of intensive egg production they are replaced by a new batch of layers. The future is bleak for those that are removed – they are either sold off very cheaply or culled. But for anyone wanting to keep a handful of chickens for eggs, they are ideal, and still more than capable of producing a plentiful supply of eggs. They seem pathetically grateful for the new lease of life and will often follow you around (if you stand still long enough, they will sometimes even hop on your foot and fall asleep). So give some thought to mixing ex-battery hens in with your flock (half and half is a good proportion). There are rescue centres for battery hens in most towns and these are easy to find on the Internet.

Many feed manufacturers produce compound pellets, which are high in the protein and minerals necessary for egg development. This is by far the best form of feed as it ensures a regular laying pattern (one thing guaranteed to put a chicken off laying is a fluctuation in its feed).

However, some feeds include chemical additives that influence such things as the colour of the yolk, so be sure to check the ingredients before feeding. The chicken obviously derives everything required for the daily production of an egg (yolk, white and shell) from the food it is fed. But in order to digest this food, it also needs grit, which it swallows and stores in its crop. This helps to break down the feed so that it can be absorbed more easily. Bags of chicken grit can be purchased at any feed vendor; but if your chickens are free-range, they will naturally pick up small stones from the ground and these have the same effect.

If a hen's feeding routine is altered too much, the hen gets upset, its body becomes confused and egg production shuts down. So if it's not practical for you to leave feed down permanently (a practice known as 'ad-libbing'), be sure to follow a reasonably strict feeding routine. Hens need to feel safe and comfortable in their surroundings and also benefit from a routine in their care in order to produce eggs regularly. Try to feed them around the same time each day and set up a pattern of tasks that they can recognize, such as cleaning out their coop once a week. This pattern needn't be set in stone, but the more constants there are in their life, the more comfortable they feel and the better the egg flow will be.

In addition to food and water, housing and bedding, chickens love a bath. Their idea of heaven is a dust-box filled with dry sand. It doesn't need to be large, but it should have shuttering around the outside and dry sand in the middle. This sandpit also gives you the opportunity to de-flea and de-louse the chickens by adding powder to the sand periodically (always read the label on any treatment you introduce as there may be a period during which you cannot eat the eggs).

Chickens are affectionate, extremely funny and make great pets, especially if you have children. Always check that there are no laws preventing you from keeping livestock before purchasing. And never keep a single chicken – they are social animals and should always be kept in groups of two or more.

KEEPING LIVESTOCK FOR MEAT

There is something truly wonderful about eating meat you have raised yourself. It's a special moment when you open the oven door and take out a golden, beautifully roasted chicken that you have hand-prepared yourself to share with friends and family. The sense of achievement, of satisfaction and *providing* is fantastic. Equally satisfying is the fact that you know where your meat has come from, what the animal has been fed, and that it has been well-treated and has lived a happy, contented life. But just how practical is it to keep animals for food, and what does it involve?

Space

Space is obviously a major consideration if you are thinking of keeping animals. Keeping a single animal alone is not an option – you should always have at least two. Agencies such as the Department for Environment, Food and Rural Affairs (DEFRA) and the Royal Society for the Prevention of Cruelty to Animals (RSPCA) have minimum welfare standards on space, but these represent the absolute minimum and should be exceeded, if at all possible. An enclosure should be big enough for the animal to function normally, as nature intended (I refer to this area as 'comfort space'), and should make them feel safe and content. Overleaf is a rough guide, taken from my experience, to the space needed for the five animals that are most often kept for meat in the UK. It should be stressed, however, that by far the best option is to keep all livestock as naturally as possible – and that means free range.

SUGGESTED ENCLOSURE SIZES FOR LIVESTOCK

	Number of animals		
Type of animal	2	3	4
Chickens	2.5 × 2.5m/8 × 8ft	2.5 × 3m/8 × 10ft	3 × 3m/10 × 10ft
Pigs	6 × 9m/20 × 30ft	7.6 × 9m/25 × 30ft	9 × 9m/30 × 30ft
Sheep	0.2 ha/0.5 acre	0.3ha/0.75 acre	0.4ha/1 acre
Goats	0.2 ha/0.5 acre	0.3ha/0.75 acre	0.4ha/1 acre
Cattle	0.8ha/2 acres	1.2ha/3 acres	1.6ha/4 acres

Before buying livestock, check with your local authority that you won't be infringing any rules or bye-laws. Also think about notifying your local vet in case any problems arise. In addition, it is important to make enquiries with the appropriate authorities about obtaining a 'holding number' for the land and a herd or flock number for the stock. These numbers are legal requirements for anyone keeping livestock in the UK.

Identification

It is the owner's responsibility to ensure that their animals have the correct identification tags and marks in accordance with current regulations. Even if you have just a couple of pet pigs in the back garden, the rules still apply. To keep up to date with the latest UK regulations, check the DEFRA website regularly.

Chickens

The main problem presented by chickens is their vulnerability to attack. Foxes, domestic dogs, cats and even rats can attack and kill a growing chicken in seconds, so it's essential that the enclosure is secured by a stout wire fence. Speciality shops and web suppliers offer electric fencing, which is a worthwhile (although somewhat pricey) option. But there are also things you can do yourself to safeguard your livestock. The most obvious is to ensure the birds can't fly away and get nabbed by a passing fox. Clipping the flight feathers of each bird is therefore vital. You should only clip the flight feathers of one wing. This will unbalance the bird and prevent it from flying high or with sufficient control. Cutting flight feathers on both sides would impede its flight but would still mean it could take off and fly in a straight line.

Allow the chickens the free run of their enclosure during the day but ensure that they are locked safe in their coop at night, which is when they are most vulnerable to attack (although daytime attacks are certainly not unheard of). Chickens like a snug house with a perch so that they can fall asleep on it, snuggled up and touching one another. This keeps them warm and seems also to give them comfort. If there are too few chickens in a large house, they will get cold, lose condition and can even die. Housing should be dry and airy, and there should be unlimited access to water.

Chickens only eat in the light, so ensure that they are fed properly during the day. The feed for a meat bird is different from that of a layer (see page 177). A good, balanced diet is essential. Corn works well for a bird over 6 weeks old and has the advantage of having a high fat content, which helps them gain weight; it also gives the skin a gorgeous yellow colour. But it should be fed to layers only as a very rare treat as the protein levels in corn are inappropriate for egg production – it's about as healthy as feeding a child burgers and chocolate. Milled pellets are another option, but always check the ingredients for any chemical additives (some have been banned in EU countries).

Many commercial chicken units attempt to 'finish' a bird quickly, in just 42 (broilers) to 56 (free range) days after hatching. ('Finished' is the term used to indicate when an animal is ready for slaughter.) The birds are fed an intensive, high-protein diet to increase their weight rapidly. They are usually hybrids and bred as eating machines, to the extent that their legs often don't develop quickly enough to keep up with their general growth rate and aren't able to support their bodies. The demand for cheap meat means that farmers produce the chickens in the most cost-effective way possible, to the extreme detriment of the bird. By contrast, a non-commercial, free-range bird that is allowed to develop naturally may take up to 6 months to reach an ideal weight. Not only will it have a far superior flavour, it will also have lived a longer, happier life.

Pigs

A single pig is about as destructive as a medium-sized nuclear bomb. But this natural power can easily be turned to the owner's advantage. Pigs will clear any old scrap of land, eating all the weeds and roots, bugs and slugs and snails in the process. They can therefore be used to dig over last year's vegetable patch, fertilizing as they go, so that it's ready to be planted again. But the big downside to this is that the pig won't differentiate between the area that needs clearing and your glorious flower borders!

The easiest way to keep a pig in one place is to run electric wire through plastic 'keepers' (an old watering hose is perfect) that have been attached to wooden stakes positioned every 1.8–2.4m/6–8ft around the area you want to enclose. Snip off several 2.5cm/1in lengths from the hose (the number will of course depend on how many posts you use for your enclosure) and secure two of the plastic keepers (hose sections) to each of the wooden stakes with U nails: one keeper should be about 15cm/6in above the ground, the second should be about 20cm/8in above the first keeper. Run a single line of wire around the enclosure, feeding it first through all the top keepers and then, going around a second time, through all the bottom keepers (so you are running one strand of wire twice around your enclosure). Then attach a pulsar to the wire. It will emit a pulse of electricity every 3 or 4 seconds that will give the pigs a mild electric shock if they touch the wire. The pigs may attempt to break out of the enclosure a couple of times until they become familiar with the fencing. But thereafter it should prove to be an effective deterrent, although pigs are intelligent animals and notorious escapologists, so nothing apart from a solid brick wall can really guarantee their confinement! The great advantage of electric wire is that you can move it to another location, depending on your needs. Pulsars can be purchased on the Internet or at speciality shops.

The best and most cost-effective time to buy a pig is just after it has been weaned from its mother, at around 8 weeks old. It is preferable to buy a traditional, rare breed rather than a commercial breed. Not only does this contribute to the continuity of the breed, but rare breeds grow more slowly than commercial breeds, which gives a greater depth of flavour to the meat. Commercial pigs are bred as meat machines and give a leaner carcass, but this can be at the expense of flavour (commercial breeds 'finish' in around 4 months, compared with 8 to 10 months or more for traditional breeds). Whatever your preference, the piglets should be podgy, lively and inquisitive. Keep them in groups of two or more. If your intention is to eat them, don't make the mistake of giving them a name, as this makes it even more difficult to part with them when the time comes to take them to slaughter.

Most breeders give their weaners an ivermectin injection at 8 weeks. This covers them for the next 6 months against internal and external parasites. Always check with the breeder that this has been given. If it has not, then consider having a worm count carried out at around 4 months old to see if they need worming.

A pig house, or ark, is a corrugated metal construction with a solid wall at one end and an opening at the other. Arks come in various shapes and can be bought or made at home, and usually have skids or handholds so that they can be moved easily from place to place. Despite popular belief, pigs are clean, fastidious animals and like to go outside to do their business, even at night. For this reason, a pig house seldom needs to be cleaned out, but the bed should always be topped up with fresh straw.

Pigs need fresh water and 'hard feed' throughout their lives – this usually comes in the form of milled pellets. The pellets contain different concentrations of protein. The amount of protein required depends on the stage of development, but a 17 per cent protein diet often works well. As a general rule of thumb, a traditional breed of pig should be given 0.5kg/1lb of feed per day for each month of its life up to a maximum of 2.3kg/5lb of feed at 5 months (so a 2-month-old piglet would need 0.9kg/2lb of hard feed, whereas a 7-month-old pig would still be on 2.3kg/5lb a day, and so on for the rest of its life). But nothing beats the 'stockman's eye', the ability of experienced owners to gauge the condition of their animals simply by looking at them. Supplementing the diet with vegetables is fine, but slop, meat and food, including raw peelings, that has spent any time in a kitchen is now prohibited in the UK for animals (even chickens) classed by DEFRA as farm animals, whether they are intended for consumption or are just pets. Failure to comply with this regulation attracts not only a hefty fine but a mandatory prison sentence. Many people 'finish' their pigs with a high concentration of barley in the last few weeks of life. Although this fattens the pigs, it can adversely affect the texture of the meat. It's always best to keep everything as nature intended and not to finish them unnaturally fast.

There is an optimum amount of feed a pig needs in order to grow and mature. After obtaining a certain body mass, they tend to put down fat alone. So increasing a pig's feed in the last months of its life and taking it to slaughter as late as possible does not necessarily result in a better carcass. All the breeds finish at different weights, and it is important to research the optimum killing weight of the breed you have chosen.

Weighing a pig at any point in its life involves some string, a tape measure and a simple calculation. Run the string around the pig's middle, just behind the front legs, and make a note of where it meets. Then measure the string. Next, take the measurement from between the ears to the root of the tail. Then calculate as follows:

$$\text{Girth}^2 \times \text{length} \div 400 = \text{live weight}$$

This calculation must be done in inches. It will give the 'live' weight of the pig in pounds (lb). To convert to kilograms, divide the final weight by 2.2. To obtain the carcass weight (accurate to within 3 per cent), reduce the answer by a third.

Pigs are adorable and can bring immense pleasure, which means that taking them to slaughter can be extremely difficult. But take heart from the fact that you can gradually learn to disassociate the meat you eat at the table from the pigs that you were so attached to.

Sheep

Don't be fooled into thinking that, because we may see sheep grazing happily in the field day after day, they're easy to manage. They're not. Keeping sheep properly involves considerable care and attention. The industry assesses a sheep's condition by means of 'condition points', which range from 1 to 6: 1 denotes a sheep in extremely poor condition, with bones that can be easily felt through the fleece; 6 denotes a sheep in show condition; a sheep reared for meat would require about 4 condition points. It takes around 6 weeks of hard work and good feed to increase a sheep's condition by just half a point, which means that a sheep in poor condition can take up to 36 weeks to bring into its prime.

Sheep need routine worming and should be sheared once a year. Dagging – trimming the wool from around the anus and tail – is also crucial as flies lay their eggs in the faeces that gather here and can cause major problems, especially when the maggots hatch and start burrowing into the skin, causing a condition called 'fly strike'. Drenching – administering oral medication and supplements, such as selenium and cobalt – is important for ensuring adequate nutrition if the ground is lacking in essential vitamins, minerals and enzymes. And then there is foot trimming, which involves cutting back the hoof to prevent the accumulation of muck, dirt and germs. If left unchecked this can turn into 'foot rot', a painful condition that can make it uncomfortable for the animal to stand upright or walk and will result in a rapid loss of condition.

If you intend to keep just a handful of lambs, think about asking someone nearby with a flock, and expertise, if you can buy some ewes with lambs at foot to run on your land. Even the most experienced shepherd will tell you that sheep are born to die. So, as a condition of the sale, ask if they could buddy your husbandry and help keep an eye on your flock. Sometimes you can do everything according to the book – be vigilant and meticulous in your husbandry and feeding regime, for example – and still they'll find a way of either committing suicide or dropping dead. That's sheep for you!

But on the plus side, sheep don't require housing as long as there is somewhere in the field they can find shelter (for example, a bank to lie against or a couple of trees to stand under). Although they need access to water, they drink very little and obtain most of the moisture they need from the grass. Spring grass is wonderful for sheep, full of nutrients and energy, but in the autumn its goodness wanes and they will require hard feed. In a small flock, getting sheep to come to a bucket to feed is important. Always feed them at the same time of day in roughly the same area. If possible, construct a small enclosure from hurdles so that they become accustomed to entering the area to eat. This will mean that when you need to catch them for anything they will enter the enclosed space willingly. Always touch them while they are feeding. Run your hand down the backbone to determine how prominent and knobbly it is – as above (page 185), this will give you a rough guide to the animal's condition (a woolly sheep is virtually impossible to judge by eye) and will familiarize the sheep with human contact. A flighty, nervous sheep that is not used to being touched can turn nasty when handled.

Lambs are classified as lambs for the first 12 months of their lives but thereafter are referred to as hogget. Most farmers aim to lamb their ewes in early springtime, when the grass is rich and sweet and will give the babies a good start. They are generally ready for slaughter at between 8 and 11 months (6 months in some commercial breeds). As with chickens and pigs, consumers have been brainwashed into believing that eating them early is best. But the argument for this is purely financial because the flavour of hogget, and even mutton (24 months plus), is far superior to that of lamb. With this in mind, it is entirely possible to plan so that a dozen or so sheep can keep a family in fresh meat for a considerable period of time, without the need to kill every one of them within 12 months.

Goats

Hang knickers on the line and a goat will eat them – the knickers and the line. Given the chance, they'll eat anything. But apart from this minor irritation, they are quite easy to care for and can be affectionate. They are also more intelligent than sheep, which isn't difficult. In addition to producing delicious meat, a goat can keep a family in milk, butter, cheese and yoghurt with very little effort – milking twice a day takes about 40 minutes in total (20 minutes per session). An added attraction is that Cashmere and Angora goats have stunning coats that can be spun and made into fabulous clothing (including the warmest, most luxurious socks imaginable).

Like all undomesticated animals, goats are happiest living outside. They don't do well in draughty or wet conditions and will need a lean-to or an overnight barn in which to shelter from extreme weather (snow, ice and heavy winds and rain). The roof of the shelter must be high enough for the goat to stand upright on its hind legs (which they have a tendency to do) and still have room to stretch out its head. The shelter must be dry and draught-free and should allow for approximately 6sq m/65sq ft of space for each animal housed under the shelter.

The ideal turnout area for a goat is a combination of woods and pastureland, preferably with a hill or steep bank, as their natural urge is to climb. They are browsers, so although they will eat grass, they are not predisposed to it as sheep are. Greens, raw vegetables and peelings, branches and cut grass are among their favourite foods and they require uninterrupted access to fresh, clean water. Goats thrive in small

groups, but will pine and lose weight if left on their own. Fencing should be strong and a minimum of 1.8m/6ft high as they are adept jumpers and may well spot greener grass on the other side of the fence. More goat meat is consumed throughout the world than any other red meat. It is a surprisingly healthy option as it contains minimal calories and less cholesterol and saturated fats than chicken, pork, lamb or beef.

Cattle

Beef cattle represent the biggest time commitment of any of the animals mentioned in this chapter (they are usually taken to slaughter between 24 and 30 months). Calves are generally weaned at between 6 and 12 months, and this is an ideal time to buy them. If you have the option of buying them younger, think about having a mother with calf at foot: not only will the animals have companionship but it will also mean that you can learn how to hand milk (any excess milk can be fed to the pigs, who fatten nicely on it). It's likely that you will encounter greater problems if you buy a calf that is younger than 6 months. On the whole, cows are easy to take care of. In the summer they live out all the time, and although it is possible to continue this through the winter months, especially if you can forage them on crops such as kale, you may find their condition will tail off as they start using up their bulk to keep warm. It is therefore best if you have somewhere to bring them in, such as a stone barn with a straw area for them to sleep on, and a rack for fodder.

Cattle don't usually suffer from problems with their feet and there is no routine medication to worry about, apart from worming of the calves – they are highly susceptible to worms and must be treated. But they seem to develop immunity with age, so adult cattle don't require treatment.

The chances are that unless your turn-out meadow is extremely rich in nutrients, you will have to finish the cow artificially on concentrates. These are mainly made up from by-products, such as bread waste, root crops and extracts from the brewing industry, all of which are designed for maximum weight increase. A concentrated mix suitable for your area and requirements will be available from food suppliers, so it's worth talking to them directly.

The United Kingdom, the European Union and the United States have rigorous programmes for the testing of bovine tuberculosis, which have resulted in the virtual eradication of the disease. All cattle in these regions (including water buffalo and bison) have ear tags and passports, and essential information is recorded at a central database. In the UK this centre is the British Cattle Movement Service (BCMS). As soon as a producer registers the purchase of cattle with one of these bodies, it automatically triggers a bovine tuberculosis testing programme that has to be adhered to. All tests are carried out by a vet.

Before taking cattle to slaughter, the abattoir will need a clear tuberculosis test certificate and the animal's passport as proof of age. Contact your abattoir at least two months before you intend to take your cattle, and discuss with them the necessary routine and requirements so that the day passes smoothly.

FISHING

The Food and Agriculture Organization of the United Nations (FAO) estimates that the number of people throughout the world involved in fishing is a staggering 38 million. For some people, fishing is a recreational sport, with the river bank or sea shore offering an ideal escape from the stresses and strains of modern life. For others it is a serious profession and, certainly in poorer regions of the world, can mean the difference between life and death. For the self-sufficient 'surf and turfer', fish represents an important part of a healthy, balanced diet. Omega-3 fish oils, found in oily fish, such as mackerel, salmon and trout, are beneficial in the prevention of heart disease. It is also believed that a regular intake of omega-3 can improve your general well-being and help combat depression.

At its most basic, fishing involves a rod, a line, and time. Lots and lots of time. The equipment ranges dramatically in price and quality, and it's not uncommon for a serious angler to spend as much money on tackle as many people would spend on a run-around car. But it doesn't need to be that expensive. The best place to search for a starter kit is on the Internet, perhaps sourcing a second-hand rod and line on one of the big auction sites. Once you have the equipment and are reasonably happy with how it all works, find an experienced fisherman, buy them a coffee, and find out where the best fishing sites can be found. Alternatively, if you're interested in sea fishing, contact the local coastguard, who is often an invaluable source of information on tides, currents and good fishing spots. Finding the right location is crucial and often provides the key to actually catching fish as opposed to subjecting others to lengthy stories of how they got away.

The world of fishing is a complex one, filled with different hooks, line strengths and baits and techniques, all designed to catch different fish. To become proficient takes years, but the joy of landing a couple of fresh mackerel that can be turned into a stunning fishcake, or a trout, simply baked with a knob of butter and a couple of wedges of lemon, makes every second of effort worthwhile. And it's not as if the apprenticeship is arduous – it simply involves standing on the shore looking out to sea, or sitting on the bank of a river enjoying the beautiful surroundings and keeping an eye on the fish piling up in your 'keep net'. However, an apprenticeship it is, and nothing can take the place of practice, which may not make you perfect, but it should at least get you something good to eat for dinner.

Mackerel fishcakes

A light and zingy summer night's dish makes a great end to a day's hard fishing.

> 3 mackerel, gutted, skinned and boned, then finely chopped
> 4 spring onions
> 4 field mushrooms, finely chopped
> 2.5cm/1in piece root ginger, finely chopped
> 2 tsp oil
> sea salt and freshly ground black pepper

Put all the ingredients in a bowl and mix together. Shape the mixture into patties and fry in a tiny amount of oil on both sides until the cakes are golden brown. Serve immediately.

CHAPTER EIGHT

Meat Preparation and Basic Butchery

A HIGH PERCENTAGE OF THE cost involved in the production of beef, pork, lamb and chicken lies in the processing of the meat – in other words, the butchery. What very few people will tell you, however, is that basic butchery can be quite easily undertaken at home. I teach beginners on a regular basis and I'm always encouraged by how quickly most people catch on. With a little knowledge and a basic understanding of the anatomy of an animal, cutting a beast down into the primal cuts is relatively straightforward. And once you can butcher one animal, you can pretty much negotiate your way through most of them (with the exception of venison, as deer have an extra leg joint). The primal cuts of meat on lamb, pork and beef are essentially the same, even though they have different names and there are different ways of butchering the animal to achieve the various cuts.

Hanging meat

It is important that meat is allowed to hang before it is butchered. This process improves the taste and tenderness and enables the meat to dry out. Meat should always be hung in a cool, dry environment, such as a refrigerated store. If you don't have access to one, the abattoir where the animal has been killed will be able to hang it for you. To follow are the ideal minimum and maximum hanging times for lamb, pork, beef and chicken:

Lamb: Minimum 3 days; maximum 7 days.

Pork: Minimum 3 days; maximum 10 days.

Beef: Minimum 10 days; maximum 28 days.

Chicken, dry plucked: Minimum 24 hours; maximum 10 days before 'drawing' (see page 205).

Chicken, wet plucked (see below): Wet-plucked chickens must be drawn immediately after plucking and should never be hung.

All poultry should be cooked or frozen within 7 days of drawing.

Beef can be hung for longer than lamb or pork as it decomposes from the outside in; pork and lamb decompose from the bone outwards, which means that deterioration cannot be detected easily. A plucked chicken should either be allowed to rest in the fridge for a minimum of 24 hours before drawing (see page 205) or hung by the feet according to the times specified above and depending on whether it has been dry plucked or wet plucked (wet plucking is where the bird is dunked in a hot bath of water to help loosen the feathers).

EQUIPMENT

Before butchering your meat it's advisable to buy a pack of cheap laminate flooring from your local DIY shop. Glue the tiles together so that they form a board that can be placed on top of your kitchen table to protect it from being damaged during the preparation of the meat.

Knives used for butchery need not be expensive, but it *is* essential that they are razor sharp. To prepare a carcass you need the following:

Butcher's knife (a stout, sharp knife with a blade about 30cm/ 12in long)

Boning knife, about half the size of a butcher's knife, with a thinner, narrower blade

Chopper for chopping the chops

Stanley knife for scoring skin

Hack saw

If you are planning on butchering regularly it is worth investing in a bone saw, which will enable you to slide through even the thickest bone very easily. However, the blade of a bone saw will rip flesh rather than cut it – cutting your finger on a hack saw is painful, but cutting it on a bone saw could do serious damage, so take particular care when using.

LAMB: THE PRIMAL CUTS

The primal cuts of a lamb are shoulder, breast, loin and leg. A lamb carcass comes complete from the abattoir. (Anything over a year, such as hogget or mutton, is split in two, so the spinal cord can be removed by the abattoir.) To butcher a lamb to obtain two shoulders, two breasts, two loins and two legs, follow the steps below.

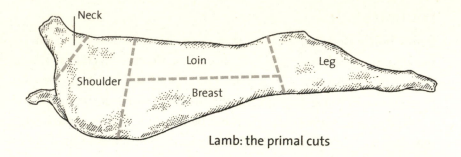

Lamb: the primal cuts

1. The first cut is to separate the shoulders entirely from the carcass. Place the carcass on its side. Count back three ribs from the head end and, using the butcher's knife, cut down (from the outside of the carcass) between the third and fourth ribs from the bottom of the carcass to the spine. Saw through the spine and continue the knife cut between the corresponding ribs on the other side. The carcass is now in two separate pieces. Starting at the neck and working down, cut lengthwise down the spine, splitting the shoulders so that the torso is divided in two, so now you have two shoulders with the neck attached (with the entire carcass in three pieces). Then cut the neck into half rings by chopping it diagonally through the vertebrae with the chopper or the saw – these cuts are called scrag end of neck and can be used for stewing.

2. Now move to the back legs. The outside of the carcass should be facing upwards. You will see where the waist of the lamb dips in. Mark this with the butcher's knife and cut through to the backbone. Turn the meat over and do the same on the other side. Saw through the backbone, detaching the two back legs from the loin and the breast. Now saw between the legs to give two legs with the chump end attached.

3. This leaves the loin and breasts. Lay the meat on its back and saw all the way along the spine, splitting the carcass lengthways into two sides. Detach the breasts from the loins by drawing a line

(inside the carcass with the butcher's knife) down the middle of each half and then cutting through with the saw.

The primal cuts are now complete: two shoulders, two breasts, two loins and two legs. You can then cut the meat down even further, as required: for example, by chopping the chops, boning and rolling part or all of the loin, dividing the shoulder, taking off the chump end for lamb steaks or mini roasting joints, and either leaving the legs whole or cutting through them to make more manageable half legs. The choices are up to you – see the illustration below.

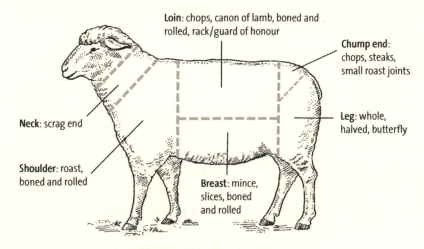

Loin: chops, canon of lamb, boned and rolled, rack/guard of honour

Chump end: chops, steaks, small roast joints

Neck: scrag end

Leg: whole, halved, butterfly

Shoulder: roast, boned and rolled

Breast: mince, slices, boned and rolled

Lamb: cuts and joints for cooking

Lamb and parmesan bake

This fragrant dish really brings out the flavour of the lamb. Use some diced shoulder of lamb, or, if you don't mind the bones, you can use stewing lamb cut into pieces or even cutlets or chops. If you have less meat than I suggest, don't worry because this recipe can make a little meat go a long way. If the oven is already on at a lower temperature than the one suggested, you can leave the dish in for up to 4 hours.

280g/10oz day-old bread, preferably from an uncut loaf
2 garlic cloves
handful of picked rosemary leaves
1 tsp dried oregano
115g/4oz fresh Parmesan cheese, in chunks
3 tbsp olive oil
1.3kg/3lb lamb
1.3kg/3lb new potatoes, unpeeled and halved (or quartered old ones)
225g/8oz cherry tomatoes, halved (or chopped larger ones)
1 glass white wine
sea salt and freshly ground black pepper

Preheat the oven to 175°C/350°F/gas 4. In a food processor, whizz the bread into breadcrumbs. Add the garlic, rosemary, oregano and Parmesan and blend the mixture again until it is all in fine breadcrumbs. Drizzle some olive oil in the bottom of a casserole or roasting tin, add a layer of potatoes and season. Then add a layer of lamb pieces, some tomatoes and a layer of the breadcrumb mixture. Repeat the layers, finishing with a layer of the breadcrumbs. Drizzle with a little more olive oil and pour the white wine (and an equal quantity of water) down the side of the casserole – basically you want to cover the first layer of potatoes with liquid. Cover and bake in the preheated oven for at least 2 hours. Uncover for the last 20 minutes to brown and crisp the top. Serve with a Forager's wild leaf salad (see page 267) or Peas à la français (see page 16).

PORK: THE PRIMAL CUTS

The primal cuts of a pig are shoulder, hand and sprig, loin, belly and leg. Pigs come split in two, lengthways, from the abattoir, so they are slightly easier to butcher than lamb as you are only negotiating half the carcass at a time.

1. Lay the half carcass down with the inside of the animal facing the board and the outside facing towards you. The first cut is to take off the head using a butcher's knife and a saw. (The abattoir splits the head in two with the rest of the carcass, so this cut will remove it from the animal's shoulders.) Run your index finger around the neck, just behind the ear – this will give you an imaginary line to follow. Starting at the far side of the neck, draw the knife cleanly towards you in a downward motion, cutting right through the meat down to the bone, so that the knife ends the cut parallel to the table and with the handle closest to you. Now take the saw and saw through the back bone. Then remove the cheeks, known as bath chaps, and the ears: the ears should be sliced off at the base with the butcher's knife; the bath chaps should be removed with the boning knife, by slicing right the way down to the jaw bone and lifting the cheek away.

2. Next take off the back leg using the butcher's knife. The leg is the most expensive and highly prized cut of pork, so care should be taken to get it right! Lay the half-pig on the board, skin side up and with the legs towards you. Using the butcher's knife, mark the narrowest part of the waist, just before the rump. Cut down with the knife until you reach the backbone, then either chop through with the chopper or, in the case of a larger pig, saw through, detaching the back leg and chump end from the body of the carcass.

3. Now turn the carcass over to expose the inside and the ribs. The next cut is to describe a line with your knife all the way down the centre from the shoulder to the bottom of the carcass. (This line will be going across the bony ribs, so the intention is not to cut the carcass entirely, but to create a guiding line.) Position the carcass so that the shoulder is furthest from you and the waist nearest to you. Allow the carcass to hang over the side of the table so that the body is curving slightly. Using the saw, start cutting along your guiding

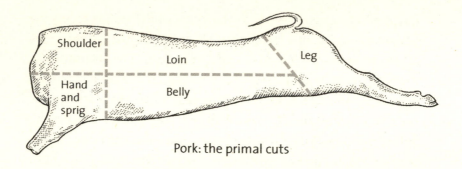

Pork: the primal cuts

line through the ribs all the way down until each of the rib bones has been split. Through the same line you have just sawn, finish the cut with the butcher's knife going all the way through the flesh until the complete carcass has been split in half lengthways.

4. Next, take the side with the trotter attached and, skin-side down, count along three ribs. Cut right through between the third and fourth ribs with your butcher's knife, transferring to a saw when you reach bone. This cut will separate the hand and the sprig from the belly. Set these to one side and pull the shoulder with the attached loin towards you. Again, count down three ribs and cut between the third and fourth ribs, in just the same way as the belly was separated from the hand and sprig. This now gives the shoulder and the loin and completes the primal cuts (shoulder, hand and sprig, belly, loin and leg) for the first half of your pig. Now that the carcass is in manageable pieces, it can be further subdivided.

5. Repeat cuts 1–4, above, on the other half, or second side, of your carcass.

The primal cuts are basically the same as those of a lamb, but a pig's carcass is much bigger, so there are more cuts and more options (see illustration below): for example, the hand and sprig can be divided into hand, hock and trotter; the leg can be cut into as many joints as possible and is perfect for turning into gammon (see page 220); the loin can be made into chops, back bacon, spare ribs and tenderloin; and the belly will give streaky bacon and rashers (from the thick end of the belly). Use the Stanley knife to score the skin of the joints for perfect crackling (see page 209).

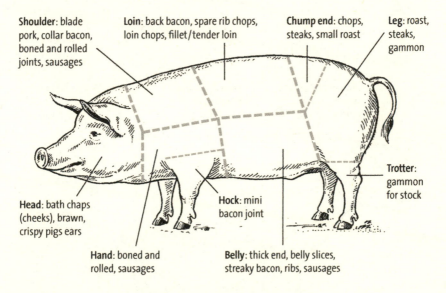

Shoulder: blade pork, collar bacon, boned and rolled joints, sausages

Loin: back bacon, spare rib chops, loin chops, fillet/tender loin

Chump end: chops, steaks, small roast

Leg: roast, steaks, gammon

Head: bath chaps (cheeks), brawn, crispy pigs ears

Hock: mini bacon joint

Trotter: gammon for stock

Hand: boned and rolled, sausages

Belly: thick end, belly slices, streaky bacon, ribs, sausages

Pork: cuts and joints for cooking

BEEF: THE PRIMAL CUTS

Cattle are quartered at the abattoir. The method of butchery and the primal cuts are the same as for pig and lamb, even though the names for them are different. In bullocks the primal cuts are ribs, sirloin, rump, brisket and flank. However, the size and weight of a cow or bullock of course present particular challenges in terms of manoeuvrability. After obtaining your primal cuts, it's simply a matter of preference how you divide them further into the particular joints, steaks and cuts (see the illustrations overleaf).

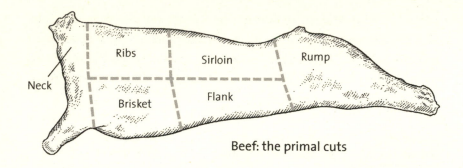

Beef: the primal cuts

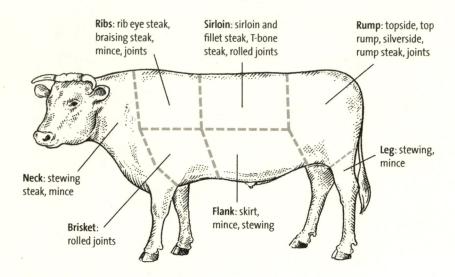

Ribs: rib eye steak, braising steak, mince, joints

Sirloin: sirloin and fillet steak, T-bone steak, rolled joints

Rump: topside, top rump, silverside, rump steak, joints

Leg: stewing, mince

Neck: stewing steak, mince

Brisket: rolled joints

Flank: skirt, mince, stewing

Beef: cuts, joints and steaks for cooking

POULTRY AND GAME BIRDS

Once you are able to pluck, draw and prepare a chicken for the table, the process is pretty much the same for all poultry and game birds, including duck, turkey, goose, pheasant, partridge and guinea fowl. (Game is seasonal, and can only be shot in certain winter months, when the young have fled the nest. It makes sense to be aware of the different seasons for each bird, as fresh birds will not be available out of season.)

Plucking

For anyone prepared to take on the challenge of plucking chicken and poultry, the financial savings can be immense, especially around Christmas time, when unplucked turkeys and geese sell for a fraction of the price of oven-ready birds. But it's not all about saving money. Plucking a bird can be incredibly therapeutic and satisfying: the time, trouble and attention to detail that goes into the preparation of a bird for the table allows you to develop a true understanding of the connection between meat and the animal.

Follow the instructions below for plucking and, if possible, pluck while the bird is still warm.

1. Lay the bird on its back and, starting at the breast, use the thumb and forefinger to pinch a few feathers together, ideally no more than six or so. Peel them down and away from the body, working in the opposite direction from the way in which they lie. Plucking the tougher parts of the bird's skin, such as the legs, back and wings, involves expansive arm movements and usually results in feathers filling the air in a manner reminiscent of a children's pillow-fight! But for the breast, under arms and top of the thighs – in other words the bits prone to fat – you need a more gentle peeling action, taking out just a few feathers at a time. The temptation to grasp a huge clump of feathers and yank it out is strong, but the chances are that if you do this the skin will rip. So take your time and peel the feathers out gently.

2. Pluck around the middle of the bird until you have a bald band. Then carry on plucking from there down to and including the legs. (There are two forms of plucking: rough plucking, which involves

removing the majority of feathers without worrying too much about those that remain, but with the idea of going back over the bird a second time; and smooth plucking; a longer process but with the benefit of only plucking once.) Once the legs and undercarriage (including the parson's nose) are clean, work down to just slightly below the head, leaving the wings until last.

3. The wings are fiddly and can take as long to complete as the rest of the bird. Some people therefore prefer to snip off the last section of the wing tips with a pair of shears. Even so, it's a good idea to have some pliers handy for the wing primaries – the long, tough flight feathers – as they can be difficult to pull by hand. When you have finished, the result should be a clean, smooth bird with just a ruff of feathers around the head.

No bird should be eaten fresh as the muscles need time to relax and pass through the period of rigor mortis. Once your bird is plucked, let it rest in the fridge or hang it by the feet (game birds should be hung by the neck), according to the times given on page 194. It can be kept for up to 10 days and still remain perfectly safe to use as long as the skin is unbroken and it has been dry plucked (as advised by the Food Standards Agency). If you are hanging more than one bird at a time, take care not to let the plucked birds touch each other until they are completely cool as this can turn their skin green.

Dressing

Now it's time to prepare, or 'dress', the bird for the table.

1. Start by taking off the head. Using a good, stout, sharp knife, such as a butcher's knife, cut through the neck, skin and bone, a little way up the neck from the body so that there is no risk of breaking the crop (this is a sack at the base of the neck where food eaten by the chicken is stored temporarily).

2. Take a small, sharp paring knife, such as a boning knife, and cut very carefully around the leg just below the knee joint. Be sure to sever the outside only just deep enough to separate the skin without slicing any deeper. Then snap the leg back at the joint and wiggle it. The foot should be separated but still attached by long, white sinewy tendons. Grasp the foot with one hand, brace the thigh with the other and pull the two apart, bringing the tendons out from inside the leg.

Drawing

'Drawing' (short for 'withdrawing') a chicken means gutting it, removing the entrails and all the parts that are not edible. It's worth taking a little extra time and care to do this because if you get it wrong, things can soon become stinky and unpleasant.

1. Start by swivelling the bird until the head end is facing you, breast down. Then with a small sharp knife cut the skin from the neck just enough to see the meat underneath begin to uncover, then stop. Peel the skin open like a pair of curtains and turn the bird over so it is facing breast up.

2. Now you are looking down on the exposed neck. Beside this, on the right, is a small sack, which is the crop. If the bird has been starved for 24 hours (highly recommended if you are processing a chicken or a bird over which you have control of the feed), the crop will be baggy and empty. If not, it's likely to be taut and full of undigested food. Using the tips of your fingers, gently tease it away from the sides of the inside of the bird at the neck end until it's loose but still attached at the other end. The reason for this is that you are going to draw the whole of the insides out through the bottom of the bird.

3. Now spin the bird around so that the legs are spread out in front of you. Using your fingers, pinch the bit of skin between the breast bone and the vent (the vent is essentially the anus). The vent is easy to spot and the skin above it often looks crinkled and slightly baggy, not unlike elbow skin. It feels empty when you pinch it. This is the entrance into the body cavity. Pick up your sharpest knife and make a couple of incisions like an upside down V just beneath the breast bone. Don't worry about being too precise as there are no tubes or innards lurking just inside, you have already pinched it to prove that. Now holding the knife like a pen, so that you are less likely to slash, continue each cut from the upside down V to either side of the vent and stop. Try to be as delicate as possible – you don't want to slice into the tubes connecting the vent or to go down too far, so just cut either side of the vent.

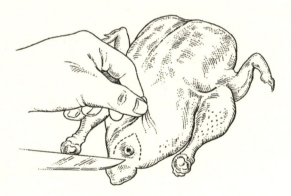

How to make the vent cut

4. Put the knife down and poke your fingers inside the bird – don't be tempted to use anything other than your fingers. There may be a membrane to break but it should give way easily. Still with your fingers inside, slide them along the top of the bird and gently take hold of the gizzard, the first major organ you come to (it's a large, hard, round organ, often surrounded by fat) and tease it out as far as

the tubes will allow. It should come fairly easily. Go back in, find the liver (the next large organ after the gizzard) and pull it out to join the gizzard. (This will make a fantastic chicken liver parfait, but always check it for any marks or discolouring, and if in doubt, chuck it out.) The next large organ will be the heart, which should also be withdrawn (but not yet removed).

5. By now you should have created some space inside the bird. Using a very soft scooping action with the tips of your fingers, start drawing out the main, squishy tubes, starting at the back, towards the bird's neck. Work the tubes towards you, taking care not to break them as they come. Keep going back in and scooping more out. The very dark tube is the bowel tract, so try really hard not to break that. Eventually the crop at the top will come free. Draw it back through the body cavity. The result should be an empty bird with all the innards spilled out the back end, though still attached to the underside of the vent.

6. Turn the bird over and, with the care of a surgeon, cut around the rest of the vent, without nicking the tubes, so that everything falls away. Make one last check that nothing is left inside and that it's clear and clean. Wash under a tap inside and out and you will have an oven-ready bird!

BUYING WHOLE BODIES OF MEAT

Although the thought of keeping our own animals for meat may be appealing, not everyone has the space or the time to commit to their care. If this is the case, let someone else rear the animal for you and then buy it from them either slaughtered or alive (if the latter, you would need to arrange for its transportation to slaughter). Buying a whole carcass, effectively buying meat in bulk, has a number of benefits: it is cheaper, you can make use of every part of the animal (nose to tail), sample every cut of meat, and you can determine how it was treated when it was alive, what it was fed, whether it was free range, healthy and happy (which makes a big difference to the taste), and the processes it went through after it was killed.

Many farms, homesteads and smallholdings have websites with pictures and descriptions of how and where their animals are kept. It obviously makes sense to look for one that keeps animals the way you would keep them yourself. Always keep an eye out for those that seem to have a passion for what they're doing and a sense of pride – looking after livestock is more than just a job, it's a lifestyle, and there's nothing better than someone who's passionate about their world. It is also extremely important to support animal welfare. Make sure that the animals are happy, extensively reared and free range – apart from the ethical considerations, contented animals that have lived complete, rounded lives, will always taste better than animals that have been stressed and confined. Don't be afraid to contact the farmer and chat about the issues that concern you. The distance that has developed between the producer and the consumer can be a source of frustration to farmers. They are often delighted when someone takes an interest in where their meat comes from. Ask if it's possible to see the animals for yourself or whether the farmer can select a beast for you that he would choose for his own family. Many farmers know and use their local abattoir regularly, and arrangements can be made for your beast to be taken directly to slaughter, so the next time you see the beast is when you collect it or have it sent to you from the abattoir. You have the option of either butchering yourself – the cheapest option – or asking the abattoir to butcher according to your specifications.

Depending on the size of your freezer and your family's appetite, you may decide to keep the entire carcass yourself. But splitting it with other people is a wonderful way to share the cost and to bring families and friends together.

NOSE-TO-TAIL EATING

Using every bit of the animal by cooking and eating it from nose to tail, being creative and enjoying every single cut, is the perfect way to show respect for the beast and get the most out of what you have. The Victorian country kitchen was a haven of thrift, but the concept of using every part of the animal has waned dramatically over the years. The modern fad for lean meat – boneless, skinless chicken breast, boned and rolled pork joint or reduced-fat beef mince, for example – means that some of the most delicate and delicious cuts are scraped from the butcher's floor at the end of each day and tossed into the bin. A terrible waste!

Pork is often regarded as the most versatile of all the meats because it can be made into ham, sausages, bacon and so on. But it still only has a carcass–meat percentage of 51–57 per cent. The rest of the animal – fat, offal, head, trotters, blood, and so on – is mostly classed as waste. On a shorn lamb, the ratio is roughly 54 per cent. On a goat, it's only 44 per cent.

Nose-to-tail eating is about using all the animal, or as close as possible to it. In a pig that's everything except the oink. The reason to eat this way is not simply because you're using the rough cuts that nobody else wants, it's mainly because these cuts are packed full of flavour and taste wonderful.

If you ask your local butcher for pig's skin they will probably give it to you for peanuts. Take it home, score the outside with a sharp knife, sprinkle generously with sea salt and pop it into the bottom of the oven on full power for 45 minutes. When it's done, move it on to a wire tray so that the air can cool it thoroughly all over, and there you have homemade pork scratchings – perfect to snap off and crunch with an ice-cold glass of beer or to jazz up a creamy garden soup!

Much of the older style of cooking was based around this idea of using cheaper, secondary cuts, such as the skin, cheeks and offal, because the primary cuts were so expensive. But increased affluence has meant that many of these recipes have been largely forgotten. Although they have moved further into the spotlight in recent years, dishes such as liver and bacon, kidney pilaf and faggots were sadly neglected for many years. But not only do they taste delicious, they're packed full of goodness. Liver is rich in iron, an essential part of the human diet. Kidneys are high in vitamin A (also known as retinal), which is important for good vision and bone growth. Take these out of the diet and the body needs to search for replacements elsewhere, which these days often come in the form of artificial tablets.

Buying nose to tail means getting the best deal on meat and then making the most of it. Instead of buying pieces of chicken, buy a whole bird, then either joint it into the cuts you need or roast it whole. Many people plump for the breast, but it only has half the flavour of dark meat, which is the muscle that has worked on the legs and wings to keep the bird running and flapping. In free-range birds especially, this meat is rich and dark because of the amount of blood required to keep all the parts of the bird active, and it therefore has much more flavour. Once the majority of the meat has been stripped from the bones of the chicken, simmer the carcass in water with an onion and a carrot. As soon as it has reduced and intensified, drain the liquid into a bowl and use as stock – perfect for a fish or vegetable risotto or delicious chicken gravy. If you don't need the stock straight away, take an ice cube bag and pour the cooled liquid in. The stock will freeze really well, then wherever you normally use a stock cube, simply pop out an ice cube and treat it in exactly the same way.

Secondary cuts, sometimes known as Cinderella cuts, such as brisket, blade or belly, are all versatile, full-on flavour alternatives to the more expensive cuts. Offal is incredibly cheap and can either be coated in flour and flash fried or minced and made into faggots (offal meatballs). Traditionally, many of these poorer cuts would have been used in stews that would have been prepared in the morning and put on the stove to simmer and tenderize all day long. The family would then return in the evening to fill their empty stomachs with a piping hot, nourishing meal.

Faggots

Serve this winter warmer with creamy mashed potato and thick onion gravy – just the thing for cosy nights in front of an open fire.

> 1 pig's caul (lacy fat) or 8–10 thinly sliced streaky bacon rashers
> 225g/8oz day-old bread, preferably from an uncut loaf
> 900g/2lb pigs' heart and liver
> 450g/1lb belly pork
> 2 large onions, chopped
> 2 tbsp chopped sage
> 1 tbsp chopped parsley
> sea salt and freshly ground black pepper
> sufficient pork or beef stock to form a 2.5cm/1in layer in the
>   roasting tin

Put the caul, if using, in a bowl of warm water and let it soften for 15 minutes. Preheat the oven to 180°C/350°F/gas 6. Put the bread in a food processor and whizz to form breadcrumbs. Tip them into a bowl. Next whizz the liver, then the heart, then the belly pork, adding them to the bowl in turns, and finally the onions. Add the herbs and seasoning and mix well. Cut the softened caul into roughly 10cm/4in squares. Take a handful of meat and form it into a ball the size of a tennis ball. Place it in the centre of a square of caul and wrap the caul around it. (If using streaky bacon, you will need to stretch each rasher with the back of a knife, then cut in half. The bacon can then be wrapped around the faggot to form a cross with the loose ends underneath.) Repeat until all the mixture has been used up. Place the faggots in a roasting tin with about 2.5cm/1in stock in the bottom and bake in the preheated oven for about 40 minutes to brown lightly and cook through.

For the family that rears its own happy, healthy animals and then eventually takes them to be slaughtered in order to eat their meat, it is crucial that every part of the beast is used and that nothing has been wasted. Waste from an animal that has been in your care since the day it was born can fill you with rage. Careful planning on how to get the best from every part of the animal is essential. Pigs are straightforward because any trimmings can go in the sausage pile. The head can be made into brawn, the skin into crackling or pork scratchings, the cheeks (bath chaps) into a delicious change from chops and steaks, even the blood can be caught and made into blood (black) pudding.

Lamb (up to 12 months old), hogget (12–24 months) and mutton (24 months and over) also have the potential for many more dishes than the standard roasting joints. Lamb belly, or breast of lamb is soft and succulent when slow roasted. Neck makes fantastic stewing meat, and the shank, the lower part of the back leg that was for many years one of the cheapest cuts but recently seems to have won favour with chefs and diners alike, needs to be cooked long and slow until it is beautifully succulent.

Bones are fantastic boiled up for stock (but always roast the bones first to reduce the fat and intensify the flavour). And what about the much-neglected marrowbone? We're all so used to giving marrowbone to the dog that we've forgotten what a great source of natural minerals and calcium it is. Marrowbone is perfect as a flavouring for soups and stews but absolutely delicious when cooked, spooned out from the centre of the bone and then spread on toast.

Marrowbone on toast

Hearty and good for you – the perfect combination! Serves 1 with a side salad.

> 4 pieces of marrowbone, roughly 7.5cm/3in long
> sea salt
> 1 slice lightly toasted fresh bread

Preheat the oven to 200°C/400°F/gas 6. Place the marrowbone on a baking tray and sprinkle with sea salt, then roast for about 35 minutes. Remove the tray from the oven and, while the marrowbones are still hot, scoop out the soft centre with a narrow spoon and spread on the toast.

If you're going to eat the marrowbone rather than let the dog have it, here are some canine treats to compensate.

Liver cake

Slice this tasty treat and watch your dog go berserk for it – ideal for training. It also freezes well.

> 450g/1lb liver
> 1 egg
> 1 garlic clove
> 225g/8oz self-raising flour

Preheat the oven to 180°C/350°F/gas 6 and grease a 900g/2lb loaf tin. Put the liver in a blender or food processor and blend. Add the rest of the ingredients and blend again. Scrape the mixture into the tin and bake in the preheated oven for 1 hour or until a skewer inserted into the middle of the cake comes out clean. Leave to cool.

Light snack for dogs

Using the lights (lungs from a sheep, pig or cow) as a dog treat is a great way to use up any lungs that are not needed for anything else, such as faggots (or ask your butcher for some lights). Slice the lights, place on a baking tray dusted with flour and leave in the bottom of a low oven (150°C/300°F/gas 2) for at least 1 hour. Turn the oven off and leave to dry out completely. (You can use the same method for drying a pig's ears and tail.)

CHAPTER NINE

Curing and Preserving

IT IS INCREDIBLE TO THINK that the common kitchen refrigerator has been around for less than a century. Prior to this there was a predecessor called an icebox, which was, literally, a lined cabinet that contained space for a solid block of ice (which had to be changed daily) and shelving around it to store things. But before that, throughout 1 million of years of evolution, where humans walked, talked and ate, we had to find other ways to stop our food from spoiling.

Preventing food from going bad would have been a major concern, as very few families had an appetite healthy enough to devour an entire animal such as a pig in one sitting, so ingenious ways were found to keep food edible. Yet what early preservers probably hadn't anticipated was that not only did the food remain edible but the processes also subtly changed the flavours and textures and created delicacies we still adore to this day – things like ham, bacon and sausages, pickles, chutneys and jams.

In a book on self-sufficiency, it could be argued that this chapter is the jewel. Certainly this is the one that has the potential to widen the most eyes and drop the most jaws, as the mysteries of making great bacon and sausages, pickles and chutneys are explained – the biggest of which is how ridiculously easy it all is. Anyone can turn out excellent home-cured bacon and gammon using nothing more complicated than the standard salad tray fitted at the bottom of most fridges, or snazzy homemade sausages that not only taste better than anything you can buy in the shops but are much better for you too.

The craft of preserving

Although the craft of preserving has changed from one of necessity to one of preference, there is still much that can be taken from it by anyone who grows their own vegetables, forages or rears their own animals for meat. Preserving can also be of just as much use to a busy family looking to batch-cook meals and store them safely for later, or indeed to the health conscious among us who have been frightened away from some of our favourite foods by the commercial processes and additives, and would dearly love to create them at home so we know exactly what everything contains.

Because the subject is so diverse, each of the following seven sections (Kitchen Charcuterie; Pickles, Chutneys and Sauces; Bottling; Smoking; Drying; Jam; and Freezing) begins with its own introduction, followed by (where possible) a breakdown of the equipment and ingredients needed. Where relevant, I offer a choice between shopbought equipment and home-produced versions made up from knickknacks around the home and garage, which are a fun alternative and ideal if you are just starting out and want to see how things work out before you invest (though to be honest, very little specialist equipment is needed anyway). Don't forget that most of these techniques were invented hundreds, if not thousands, of years ago, when 'state of the art' meant harnessing a donkey to a treadmill.

KITCHEN CHARCUTERIE

From the French for flesh (*chair*) and cooked (*cuit*), charcuterie is the art of preserving meat (primarily, though not exclusively, pork) by curing it to produce bacon, ham, sausages and gammon, the influence from which goes right the way back to classical Rome. But if the Romans invented it, the French perfected it. They added some flamboyance and a little chicness, because the charcuterie shops that sprang up in every village across France needed to attract the customer by every sense, so the aromas, the texture, the look and the taste made it virtually impossible for any 'foodie' to walk past the charcuterie without popping in to see what was available.

Curing is simply mixing salt, sugar and nitrates together and either rubbing the mixture dry into the meat ('dry curing') or dissolving it in a bath of water and dropping the meat into it to soak ('wet curing'). As a general rule, most gammons are wet cured, and then either cooked by boiling and then baked as ham, or sliced and pan-fried straight off. Bacon, on the other hand, lends itself beautifully to dry curing, which gives it a taste and a smell that's just incredible (most commercial bacon is wet cured). Of course, there are exceptions (most notably Parma-style ham, which is dry cured for 3–4 weeks and then air dried), but on the whole the wet- and dry-cured general rule works for most things produced in a home-kitchen environment.

EQUIPMENT

Large bowl

Large saucepan

For sausage-making: a method of stuffing the sausages (see the recipe on page 223–4)

Basic ingredients

There are not many ingredients for curing: just salt, pepper, sugar and nitrates (and the latter are optional). The salt should be sea salt, as it contains a certain amount of natural nitrates and tastes so much better than table salt. The sugar will differ with different recipes, but granulated, Demerara and brown are all popular.

As for the nitrates, potassium nitrate (saltpetre) has traditionally been used in much of the curing process, although in recent years awareness has been developing surrounding the use of nitrates and a possible carcinogenic link. In the light of this new information, the United States has limited the use of potassium nitrate to a maximum of 200 parts per million. In some EU countries other than the UK, it has been banned completely, but in the UK it is still commonly used, though reasonably difficult to get hold of for home use because it is also the primary ingredient in gunpowder.

The arguments for and against the use of nitrates go like this: in cured raw pork products such as chorizo and pancetta, use of the nitrates is essential because they help to fight the risk of illnesses such as botulism and E. coli. Yet in cooked products, such as ham, bacon, gammon and sausages, all the food has been or will be (depending on how it is sold) cooked thoroughly before it is eaten, so it could be argued that the use of nitrates as a preventative in these cases is less important, and all it really does is keep the colour pink.

Personally, I don't mind my bacon looking like meat (pink is such an odd colour for it anyway), and if I'm going to all the trouble of making something myself from scratch, I feel that using unnecessary additives is defeating the object, so while I do use nitrates in raw products, I don't include them in anything that will be cooked. However, that is only my opinion, and anyone setting out to cure their own meat should be encouraged to draw their own conclusions. For more information on the use of nitrates in meat, contact the Food Standards Agency, which is an independent watchdog, or go online at www. food.gov.uk.

Bacon

The simplest and most impressive of all the home-cured meats, home-made bacon is the one thing guaranteed to cause a sensation around the kitchen table. In the 11th century, a tiny English church declared that if any man could stand before the congregation and God, and swear that he had not had a cross word with his wife for a year and a day, he would be presented (if he were believed) with a whole side of bacon. Some people believe that this gave rise to the phrase, 'bringing home the bacon' (meaning to earn a living for the family or to have success). This became a well-known tradition that is still practised today. Chaucer made reference to it in his *Canterbury Tales*, and so did many other writers.

Cuts

To make really great back bacon you will need a boneless loin of pork, and for streaky bacon you need a belly. However, if you tell your local butcher what you are going to do, he is bound to steer you in the right direction.

Dry-cured bacon

To dry cure at home you will need a mixture of two parts fine sea salt to one part sugar (white, Demerara or brown – or a mixture if you like). The salt is a preservative and the sugar keeps the meat soft and moist while also helping to counteract the saltiness. Use 150g/5½oz cure to each 1kg/2¼lb boned meat. Spread the cure all over the meat and rub it in thoroughly. Put the meat in a lidded plastic container (never metal, as metal reacts with the cure) and leave for 3 days for streaky bacon or 5 days for back bacon, turning the meat and pouring off the resulting liquid each day. This will give you perfect breakfast-style bacon.

For harder, Pancetta-style, bacon, use 100g/3½oz cure to which you add an additional 50g/2oz fine sea salt to bring it up to the

150g/5½oz total amount you need for 1kg/2¼lb meat. Again, apply once and leave for 5–10 days depending how strong you want the cure to be. This bacon does not really lend itself to frying and eating, and is more for adding flavour to soups and stews, and will hot-smoke (see page 243) really well.

When the bacon has finished curing, wash it well, slice it and enjoy, remembering never to wrap it in aluminium foil or allow it to come into contact with metal. Before slicing the bacon, freeze it for 1 hour to firm up the meat, as this will give you much better rashers.

Wet-cured bacon

Make up a basic brine of 500g/1lb 2oz fine sea salt to about 6 litres/10½ pints water, and add 3 tbsp sugar to keep the meat soft and prevent it firming up too much. For a variation, replace the sugar with honey or maple syrup.

This works really well for back bacon, and the perfect place to store it is in the salad tray at the bottom of most fridges. Simply clean it out, put your meat in and pour the brine over it, then forget about it for 3 days.

At the end of this time, simply rinse the bacon thoroughly in clean water, slice it and use it straight away, or wrap it and store it in the fridge, where it should last for up to 10 days.

Gammon and hams

There are dozens and dozens of different cures for hams and gammons that exist throughout the world, recipes that have been perfected right up to one's great grandmother and then cast in stone in the firm belief that they could not possibly get any better. Some, mainly the dry-cured ones, are highly complex and involve lots of skill, effort and very precise atmospheric conditions. Easier by far are the wet-cured recipes, which are what we will explore here.

Cuts

The classic ham comes from a leg of pork. In Roman times this would have been a leg of wild boar, from which they produced the famous hams of Gaul. Today, wild boar can be very difficult to source. If you are lucky enough to be producing your own pigs, then you have your own supply to hand, but, if not, ask your butcher for a leg of pork from a rare breed (non-commercial), traditional free-range pig. The taste will be far superior, as will the texture, and you will be far happier with the result. You will also be promoting good animal husbandry.

An alternative to the leg of pork is the hock. Pig hocks are the bottom part of the leg; they are very cheap and packed full of flavour. But for something completely different, the texture of lamb works really well when gammoned, as does venison, or brisket of beef for homemade corned beef, which is far superior to anything found in a tin.

Wet-cured hams and gammon

All wet curing of hams and gammons is based on a basic brine solution, as shown on page 220 in 'wet-cured bacon'. For a twist, replace the water with cider for a cider-cured ham or gammon, or with bitter and 900g/2lb black treacle (boiled together first with the salt, then cooled before being used) for a Wiltshire cure, but be warned: this is very strong and STINKS when you boil it! The sugar can be replaced with maple syrup in the normal brine cure, but, once again, you would have to boil and chill it before using. Note that if you are using alcohol as a base instead of water, more salt is needed to prevent the meat from spoiling, so for every 6 litres/10½ pints alcohol use 1kg/2¼lb fine sea salt.

For ham, once the curing is complete, remove the ham from the solution and rinse it well, then boil in water for 20 minutes per 450g/1lb plus 20 minutes, or according to your favourite recipe. Remove the ham from the heat and leave it to cool slightly in the pan for extra succulence, then rinse it and strip off the rind (leaving the fat) before scoring the top. Glaze with something like mustard powder and honey or brown sugar, and bake, uncovered, in a foil-lined roasting tin at 180°C/350°F/gas 4 for 15 minutes. Alternatively, soak overnight in water and bake without boiling first. Or for a really lovely flavour and a natural preserve, try smoking it (see page 241).

For gammon, soak overnight in water and cut into thick slices, which can be gently fried or grilled.

Sausages

The earliest-known mention of sausages was recorded in the epic poem *The Odyssey* by Homer, written at some point during the period 900–800 BC. Sausages, which were originally cured, were first used as a method to preserve and transport meat, but then sausages of both types – cured and fresh – soon became popular, and virtually every nation in the world developed their own variation, because the beauty of the sausage is that it is so versatile. It can be dry cured or fresh, plain or flavoured. It can contain pork, beef, chicken or any other meat you fancy, and if you're not a meat eater, there's still a sausage for you, with a vegetarian recipe made from tofu, or a Glamorgan sausage made from cheese, leeks and breadcrumbs. There are Madras sausages, marmalade sausages, even Marmite sausages. There are some packed with so much chilli your head could quite possibly explode, and at the other end of the spectrum there are flavours that are as delicate as lemon and thyme. Yet the best sausage ever made in the entire history of sausage-making will be the one you make yourself in your own kitchen.

A healthy dilemma

At their most basic, sausages are made by mincing meat, adding flavourings and piping the mixture into casings. In the days before we really understood about the dangers of fat in our diet, sausages would be made from 100 per cent meat, but *half* of that, 50 per cent, would have been fat to keep the sausage moist. Nowadays, I'm not sure many people would be comfortable eating a sausage that contained such a high level of fat, so we have devised other, healthier, ways of retaining moisture and preventing our sausages from drying out. One solution is to include a small amount of pinhead rusk (unleavened bread, also known as cereal) and water. In the recipes that follow, I have used this method. The results are wonderful, the sausages are guaranteed not to be dry, and health-wise they are far better for you; but if you want to include more meat, the choice is yours, of course.

Cuts

In ancient Greece around the time of Homer, sausages were a way of preserving the off-cuts of pork in neat little packages. Nearly 3,000 years later, we're still doing exactly the same thing. If you are butchering your own pig, any scraps can and should be put in the sausage pile, but for the rest of us, the cuts of pork to use are belly and shoulder.

There are two kinds of sausages: cured ones, like salami and chorizo, and fresh sausages, for which I give a recipe here.

EQUIPMENT

Large bowl

You will need either a food mixer with a sausage-making attachment or a hand-cranked sausage-stuffer. Alternatively, if you don't have either of these, you'll have to go for the less specialist option of a large funnel and a wooden spoon

Ingredients

Pork belly and/or shoulder, finely minced (try to judge by eye that the mince carries at least 15 per cent fat)

Pinhead rusk (for a gluten-free alternative, polenta or rice flour can be used)

Seasoning

Natural casings (sheep casings for chipolatas, hog casings for sausages – ask your butcher or search online), soaked for 12–24 hours (depending on the casing) in water to remove the salt they are packed in.

Seven steps to a perfect breakfast sausage

1. Put the mince in a large bowl and add 10 per cent pinhead rusk plus 10 per cent water (by weight, or use cider or wine), and mix by hand. Don't worry about adding too much liquid, because any not absorbed as the sausage matures and increases in flavour will leach out overnight (a process butchers call 'blooming').

2. Season well with salt and pepper. This is the stage where you can leave the mixture plain for a good old traditional sausage, or add flavourings such as herbs and spices. Either way, mix well.

3. Now for a taste test: heat a little oil in a frying pan and cook a little ball of the mixture. Taste it and adjust the seasoning and flavours as necessary, then keep cooking and tasting and adjusting until you're happy.

4. Remove the casing from the soaking water, find one of the ends and slide it over your sausage-making attachment, followed by the rest of the casing until it's all concertinaed down and the end is hanging lose, untied, by about 2.5cm/1in.

5. Turn on the food mixer or start cranking the sausage stuffer (or grab your wooden spoon if you're doing it by hand), load with your

sausage meat and begin filling, though don't be tempted to pack the casing too tight or the sausages might burst during cooking.

6. Once your casing is filled, twist each sausage into length by simply pinching and twisting. Butchers twist sausages into bunches of three to hang and dry.

7. Leave in the fridge, uncovered, overnight to bloom (especially if you are going to freeze them). That's it: homemade sausages!

The spout, loaded with a casing ready to be filled

If the filling part seems to be a bit of a palaver, there is the option of making sausage meatballs or patties, which work almost as well, though for a little extra effort nothing excites quite like the real thing.

Flavourings

Once you have mastered the method of putting together a great sausage, then it's time to experiment and play with some mouth-watering variations.

Bold flavours:

- Madras – turmeric, chilli, coriander, cumin and desiccated coconut instead of rusk

- Cracked black pepper

- Garlic, red wine (instead of the water) and basil

- Chilli and sun-dried tomato

- Cider (instead of the water), apple and leek

- Garlic, red wine (instead of the water) and smoked paprika for a fresh chorizo-style sausage (without the high salt content of the dry-cured variety), ideal for the barbecue or as the base for a really great cassoulet or paella

Subtle flavours:

- Lemon and thyme

- Cranberry and rosemary – lovely Christmas variety

- Ground white pepper

PICKLES, CHUTNEYS AND SAUCES

It is no mistake that this section follows on after charcuterie, as the only thing that can possibly improve upon a homemade bacon or sausage sandwich is a spoonful of a sensational tomato sauce, a tangy marrow chutney or a really good pickle.

Finding quick and easy ways to preserve the summer glut from the kitchen garden or the allotment is a big part of the self-sufficient life. When Mother Nature is in full swing, the produce harvested from even a moderate veg patch can threaten to take over the kitchen, not to mention mealtimes. No matter how sweet and delicious a new crop of runner beans is, you can only eat them so many times before they become a bit samey. The trick is to store them in a preservative, such as vinegar.

Vinegar

The vast majority of recipes for chutneys, sauces and pickles are based on vinegar, so it is essential to select a good-quality vinegar with an acetic acid content of at least 5 per cent. Malt vinegar works well and has a good flavour, and this is fine for chutneys, but for pickled vegetables the distilled version, which is clear, presents a crisp, cleaner-looking finished product. Flavoured vinegars such as cider and white wine vinegars, rice, fruit and honey vinegars are now widely available, though beware of wasting your money if you venture down this more exotic and expensive route, as the flavours can be quite subtle and will be lost in a robust chutney.

Recycled jars

Before you start making your chutneys, pickles and sauces, you will need to assemble a good selection of jars to put them all in. Obviously you will have the empties from last year's jarred delights, and with luck friends and family will save their own empties for you so that you don't actually have to buy any. There is a staggering array of jars around – from pretty, petite ones to downright ugly ones via chunky, wide ones and tall, thin, narrow ones – but they are all needed (maybe with the exception of the ugly ones), and it's this lack of uniformity that makes everyone's pantry or store cupboard unique and personal.

Before you use any jars, make certain they have been sterilized. If you have a dishwasher, a normal wash cycle will sterilize them for you. Alternatively, set them on an ovenproof tray and pop them in a preheated oven at 75°C/170°F for 10 minutes, then remove and leave to cool.

The vinegar in these types of preserves will react with any metal in the lids, so always cover the preserve with a cut-out round of grease-proof paper to create a barrier before screwing on the top, unless it has a plastic coating on the inside. Coffee jars have tops made entirely from plastic, which is why you see lots of chutneys and pickles stored in them – though their chunky lids mean that they never look the prettiest of containers.

Pickles

From the vibrant crimson of a beetroot to the tanned brown of an onion or the emerald green of a cucumber, only the best produce is reserved for pickling because of the tendency to keep the pieces whole or nicely chopped into chunks, as opposed to chutneys and relishes, which are all mushed up. Pickling is the process of storing summer fruits and vegetables in a preserving solution, normally either vinegar, brine (salt water) or a stock syrup, and soft fruits do particularly well in alcohol and sugar. Pickles add a little panache to any meal, no matter what the season.

In America the best-known pickle is cucumber, in Germany it is sauerkraut (sour cabbage) and in the UK pickled onions, but so many more fruits and vegetables can be pickled (ginger, garlic, chillies, pears, rhubarb, walnuts…) that it's hard to know where to stop. In fact, if you have an idea to pickle something, no matter how way-out it might seem to be, the chances are you're not going to be the first person to try it.

EQUIPMENT

Stainless-steel preserving pan or large stainless-steel saucepan

Wooden spoon

Non-metallic bowl

Non-metallic colander

450g/1lb-capacity sterilized jars

Ingredients

Select only the freshest fruit and vegetables for your pickles. If you have your own vegetable plot, harvest quite early in the morning before the sun has a chance to wilt the produce, and make sure everything you pick is free from bruises and blemishes. If you are buying from a super-market or greengrocer, look for fresh produce and avoid anything that has been coated in wax.

Brining

Hard vegetables, such as cauliflower and asparagus, have a fairly low water content, which makes them ideal for pickles. Some soft fruit and vegetables, however, such as cucumber, pears and melon, present a problem because not only will their high water content dilute the pre-serving vinegar, but the vinegar itself will also struggle to penetrate the fruit in the first place, so it may not preserve at all. The solution is to remove the water, and for this you need salt, which can be used in two different ways: dry brining, which is simply layering the ingredients on a tray and sprinkling with salt to draw out the moisture (as in the cucumber recipe below), or wet brining, which involves making up a salt-water bath in which to soak the ingredients.

Quick and easy pickled cucumber

Perfect in the summer, but even better in the winter, pickled cucumber is a great way to store a glut from the garden and keep you going all year long. Keep for 1 month before using and store for up to 1 year.

    3 cucumbers, thinly sliced
    4 large onions, peeled and diced
    4 heaped tbsp coarse sea salt
    570ml/1 pint distilled malt vinegar
    175g/6oz granulated sugar
    1 tsp mustard seeds
    1 tsp celery seeds

Mix the cucumbers and onions in a large non-metallic bowl, sprinkle with the salt and leave to stand for 2–4 hours. Meanwhile, warm some large jars in a low oven. Rinse, drain and pat dry the vegetables with kitchen towel. Put the vinegar, sugar, mustard seeds and celery seeds in a saucepan and bring to the boil, then reduce the heat and simmer for 2–3 minutes. Spoon the cucumber and onions into the warm jars without packing them in too tightly, and cover with the spiced vinegar. Seal immediately.

Killer pickled onions

The trick of really great pickled onions is in the peeling. When you trim them, take off the barest bit of the root, as that's the part that holds the onion together. If you take off too much, the onions will just fall apart. These pickled onions will be ready to eat in 2 months, but the longer you leave them for, the better. The chillies are for flavouring only, and not to be eaten; add as few or as many as you wish.

pickling or baby onions, peeled and trimmed
malt vinegar
1 bay leaf
mixed peppercorns
whole chillies of whatever strength you like

Pack the onions as tightly as possible into the jar(s) you intend to use and fill with vinegar to give you an idea of how much you need. Now drain the vinegar off into a stainless-steel saucepan, adding a little extra to allow for evaporation, then add the bay leaf, 1 tsp mixed peppercorns per 1.2 litres/2 pints vinegar and some chillies. Bring to the boil, then remove from the heat and leave to cool thoroughly. Pour the spiced vinegar and chillies over the onions and seal tightly.

Mixed vegetable pickles

Arguably the most attractive and versatile jar of pickles is the mixed vegetable, with layers of different colours neatly packed one on top of another all in the same jar, for instance carrots above onions above green beans above red cabbage above cauliflower. Try to look out for not only different colours but also different shapes, so that you have round onions next to thin batons of carrot. Then, in the depths of winter when you're feeling drab, you can use them to add fantastic colour to a winter salad, serve them with a dip to accompany dinner-party aperitifs or nibble as a treat on a cold, grey winter's afternoon.

Chutneys

Sharp and sweet, aromatic, cool and tangy or hot and spicy, chutneys have become an indispensable partner to food such as cheese, meat, fish and, of course, curry. Thought to originate in India from the Hindu word *chatni*, meaning 'highly or strongly spiced', chutneys are the ideal way to use up and store any misshapen, bruised or imperfect fruit and vegetables – or at least that's how it started. These days chutneys are a much more serious business, and it's not at all frowned upon for people to dedicate whole sections of their vegetable and fruit gardens solely to produce for chutneys.

Although both pickles and chutneys use vinegar as their primary preserving agent, the main difference between them is the fact that the produce in chutneys is mushed as opposed to whole or sliced. The authentic way of mushing the ingredients down was using a pestle and mortar, though if you have a food processor you could use it on 'pulse' to give the texture and size of chunks you want. Not only will this method be faster and easier, but the end results will be far easier to replicate if you hit upon something that's especially good.

The idea of a chutney is to mix concoctions of fruits and vegetables with vinegar, sugar and spices, and then cook them long and slow (except for the cheat versions that I'm all in favour of, which are quick, practical and deliciously tasty, but take a fraction of the time – see below). Apart from that, anything goes. If it's edible and you can grow it or find it, you can make a chutney out of it, and a lot of the fun comes from mixing and matching combinations, because from a self-sufficient point of view, making chutney is all about using whatever is to hand. If you want to know if a combination is likely to work, take the primary ingredients, say a tomato and an apple, and cut a little from each, then pop them into your mouth at the same time and crunch into them while breathing in through your mouth (just in this case, it's OK to eat with your mouth open). If the flavours work together at this stage, then they're likely to work in a chutney. Note that chutneys are always left to cool before being covered, unlike jams, which are sealed when piping hot.

EQUIPMENT

Food processor with a pulse button, a hand mincer or a pestle and mortar (if you want to be authentic)

Stainless-steel preserving pan or large stainless-steel saucepan

Wooden spoon

Non-metallic colander

Ingredients

Any fruit and vegetables, or combinations of fruit and vegetables, that you want to use up, have bought cheap or just think will make a stunning chutney

Onions

Vinegar

Sugar

Spices, including turmeric – a truly incredible spice from the ginger family, which has many of the same healing and medicinal qualities as ginger, such as the ability to settle an upset stomach and even quell nausea, and can even be mixed with paint or lime wash for a natural colorant

Mustard powder

Seasoning

Cornflour – for the quick version

Runner-bean chutney

This is the ideal way to use up the glut of runner beans that every grower ends up with at the end of the season. It can be eaten within weeks or will keep for years, and works perfectly with sausages, robust cheeses such as Cheddar or as an alternative to tomato sauce on the side of a good old fry-up.

4–5 onions, peeled and diced
900g/2lb runner beans, diced
680g/1½lb granulated sugar
900ml/1½ pints vinegar of your choice, for example malt or cider
1½ tbsp turmeric
1½ tbsp mustard powder
1½ tbsp cornflour

Put the onions and beans in a stainless-steel pan of salted water and bring to the boil, then reduce the heat and simmer until tender. Strain through a non-metallic colander, allowing the mixture to drain well. Tip the mixture into a food processor and mince or pulse until it is chopped and mushed, but not a purée. Return to the pan and add the sugar and 720ml/1¼ pints of the vinegar. Bring to the boil and boil for 15 minutes. Meanwhile, mix the turmeric, mustard powder and cornflower in the remaining vinegar and add gradually to the beans over a low heat, stirring until the mixture has thickened. Return to the boil for another 15 minutes, then leave to cool thoroughly before pouring into cold jars and sealing.

Spicy marrow chutney

This is a good self-sufficient alternative to mango chutney, which will work fantastically well with your favourite curry and poppadoms. It will be ready to eat in 2 months but will also sit happily maturing and improving for years.

1.3kg/3lb marrow, peeled, deseeded and cut into 1cm/½in cubes
    (about 900g/2lb prepared weight)
450g/1lb tomatoes, skinned and quartered
450g/1lb onions, peeled and chopped
1 garlic clove, peeled and crushed
50g/2oz sultanas
1 tsp ground allspice
1 tsp salt
1 tsp ground black pepper
570ml/1 pint vinegar
680g/1½lb light soft brown sugar

Put the marrow, tomatoes, onions, garlic, sultanas, allspice and seasoning in a large stainless-steel pan and stir in 425ml/¾ pint of the vinegar. Bring to the boil, then cover and simmer until the marrow is tender. Remove the lid and continue simmering to reduce the liquid until no liquid pools in a furrow made by dragging a wooden spoon through the mixture to the bottom of the pan. Stir in the remaining vinegar and the sugar and return to the boil, then simmer until the chutney is thick, stirring gently occasionally just to ease the mixture around without breaking up the marrow. Remove from the heat and cool thoroughly before spooning into cold jars and sealing.

Christmas chutney

This chutney needs to be made around late September/early October to give it enough time to mature and mellow, and my advice is to pick a day when you're not likely to be interrupted, switch the phone off and put on a Christmas DVD, preferably *Miracle on 34th Street* (the version with Richard Attenborough as Father Christmas) or *It's a Wonderful Life*, turn the volume up and enjoy while you prep and stir!

The beauty of this recipe is that most of the ingredients can be grown in the garden or allotment or bought reasonably cheaply at the greengrocer or supermarket, and it really does taste of Christmas.

> 225g/8oz each of 2 of the following: plums, pears, rhubarb,
> greengage or quince, prepared as necessary, then chopped
> 2 cooking apples, peeled, cored and chopped
> 115g/4oz dried figs, chopped (optional)
> 225g/8oz onions, peeled and chopped
> 225g/8oz tomatoes, skinned and chopped
> 2 celery sticks, chopped
> 50g/2oz raisins
> ½ tbsp grated fresh root ginger
> 460ml/¾ pint cider vinegar
> 1 tbsp pickling spice
> 225g/8oz granulated sugar

Put all the ingredients except for the vinegar, spice and sugar into a stainless-steel pan and pour in half of the vinegar. Put the pickling spice in a muslin bag and tie the end before dropping it into the mixture. Bring to the boil, then reduce the heat and simmer for about 2 hours until everything is soft, stirring occasionally to stop it catching on the bottom. Add the remaining vinegar and the sugar and return to the boil, stirring to dissolve the sugar and avoid sticking, then boil until the mixture is thick enough to form a furrow that doesn't fill with liquid when a wooden spoon is dragged through it. Remove the muslin bag and leave the chutney to cool completely before spooning it into your best jars and sealing.

Sauces

What would life be like without tomato ketchup and brown sauce? What would happen to chips, hamburgers, egg sandwiches? The prospect is terrifying, but the solution (were it needed) is easy: make your own.

If pickling is for whole or chopped ingredients and chutneys for crushed or mushed ingredients, then sauces are the next step and should be blended until smooth and thick.

Red tomato sauce

900g/2lb ripe red tomatoes, peeled and deseeded
450g/1lb onions, peeled and chopped
2 red peppers, deseeded and chopped
1 tsp oil
75g/3oz granulated sugar
4 large garlic cloves, peeled and chopped
2 tbsp mustard powder
1 tbsp paprika
325ml/11fl oz white wine vinegar
pinch of ground cloves

Put the tomatoes in a stainless-steel saucepan and warm over a low heat. Add all the remaining ingredients and bring to the boil, then reduce the heat and simmer for about 2 hours, stirring occasionally to avoid sticking, until the whole thing becomes a thick red sauce. At the end of the cooking time, taste and adjust the seasoning, if necessary. When you're happy, blitz in a blender or food processor. Sterilize some preserving jars, and fill when hot, then seal the lids and carefully submerge each jar in a large pan of water over heat, so that when all the jars are standing in the water it comes half way up them. Bring the temperature up to 100°C/212°F and leave the jars in the hot water bath for 20 minutes to sterilize the sauce (see the bottling section on page 240).

Brilliant brown sauce

The story goes that HP Sauce was so named because the person who invented it heard that it was being served to members in a restaurant in the Houses of Parliament. To this day, the label on a bottle of HP Sauce carries a picture of the Houses of Parliament. This recipe is not for HP Sauce, but it is for a very similar brown sauce that has all the main tangy, brown, rich attributes that a really great brown sauce should have.

1.8kg/4lb apples, peeled, cored and chopped
450g/1lb pitted prunes, chopped
2 large onions, peeled and chopped
1.7 litres/3 pints malt vinegar
2 tsp ground ginger
1 tsp freshly grated nutmeg
1 tsp allspice
1 tsp cayenne pepper
125g/4½oz table salt
900g/2lb granulated sugar

Put the apples, prunes and onions in a large stainless-steel pan and cover with water. Bring to the boil, then reduce the heat and simmer until tender. Pass the mixture through a non-metallic sieve and return it to the pan. Add the remaining ingredients and stir well. Bring to the boil, then reduce the heat and simmer until it has reduced to that lovely gloopy sauce consistency. Pour into jars and sterilize as for the tomato sauce above. Alternatively, it will keep in the fridge indefinitely.

BOTTLING

Preserving food is all about the battle between you and the billions and billions of micro-organisms in the shape of yeasts, enzymes, moulds and bacteria that are hell-bent on infiltrating and destroying your produce. One of the weapons at your disposal is heat. Known as bottling, this way of preserving tackles the micro-organisms by first heating the glass jar (Mason and Kilner jars are both designed for the process; any other jar should not be used as they are not designed to be heated to such high temperatures) and the produce inside to kill off any nasties, and then cooling them to make a vacuum of the lid, thus preventing anything else getting in.

If this sounds complicated, it's not. If you made the tomato sauce or the brown sauce above, you have already done some bottling, as that's exactly the method used to sterilize at the end there.

Acidity

There are two types of bottling and the difference between them depends on the acidity of the produce you want to preserve. All food has a pH ranging from 1 to 14. In chemistry, the neutral point in the pH scale is 7. In food, it's 4.6. Anything with a pH of 4.6 and below is classed as a low-acid food, and anything above as a high-acid food, but pretty much all fruits, jams, vinegars, chutneys, etc. are high acid, and all vegetables, meats, fish and mushrooms are low acid. The reason it's important to have a little working knowledge of high and low acidity is because different micro-organisms thrive in each of the two environments, and the process of getting rid of them differs.

High-acid foods such as the fruits in jams and chutneys (and our tomato and brown sauces) harbour nasties that can be destroyed at boiling point (100°C/212°F) and so can be safely processed in a water bath.

Water bath

Prepare your high-acid produce, fruit in syrup, or relish. Meanwhile, sterilize some Mason or Kilner jars in the dishwasher or oven. Bring your water bath up to the boil and put your hot produce into your hot jars, seal the lids and place them in the simmering water until they are completely submerged. Leave in the water bath for as long as the recipe you are using states, or follow this chart if you are making the recipe up yourself: www.allotment.org.uk/allotment_foods/bottling-canning/Bottling-Canning-Time-Charts.php

Pressure canner

By contrast, the micro-organisms that prey on low-acid food, such as vegetables and so on, are much more resilient and need a higher temperature (116–130°C/240–266°F), and therefore require a specialized pressure canner – not to be confused with a pressure cooker: the two are *not* interchangeable.

In the introduction to this chapter I explained that, in the spirit of self-sufficiency, wherever possible I would include homemade alternatives to specialized equipment. Well this is one of those rare occasions where there is no alternative. Some of the micro-organisms that attack preserved food over a long period of time are really very nasty, and if you get it wrong the result can be life-threateningly dangerous. When it comes to the health of you, your family and your friends, it's just not worth taking a risk, so I'm afraid it's the proper kit or nothing at all. You may end up having to import one from the States, as they are very expensive in Britain. However, it's worth checking out the auction sites like eBay, as well as car-boot sales or large high-street discount stores, to see if you can find one at reduced cost.

Prepare some low-acid food – things like Bolognese mince for a busy person's quick-and-easy during-the-week spag bol, vegetables or even a curry all work well. Bottle as above and then follow the instructions on your pressure canner.

SMOKING

Arguably the oldest form of food preservation, smoking probably dates back to around the time humans first woke up to the idea of cooking meat and fish over an open fire. Anything not eaten straight away would have received a crude smoking, and we can guess that our fore-fathers recognized that the meat and fish that had spent time in the fire smoke lasted longer than food that hadn't. But it's for the flavour that we smoke food today. Chicken, ham, sausages, salmon, mackerel, garlic, cheese … just about anything can be smoked by anyone with no more than a patio.

Home smoking is a complete hobby in itself, with enthusiasts ranging from fishermen to smallholders and homesteaders, from chefs to cooks, families and keen barbecuers to full- and part-time profes-sionals selling to the trade and public at farmers' markets.

One of the reasons why it is so popular is that it's so incredibly cre-ative. There's a fire to build in the fire box, a slow and steady one that produces plenty of smoke. Most hardwoods are fine to use, but do avoid resinous softwood, as the resin can come through in the smoke and taint the food. Oak is a safe bet, as are ash, beech and elm. Without encouraging anyone into pyromania, playing with fire in this instance is embarrassingly good fun, and if you experiment close to the end of the smoking process by adding branches such as gorse, hawthorn, damson or similar to the fire, subtly unique flavours can be achieved that are as distinct and individual as a signature at the bottom of a canvas.

Then there is the issue of hot or cold smoking. Hot smoking will cook the food and impart a light smoky flavour, such as hot-smoked chicken, whereas cold smoking smokes without cooking (think of smoked salmon or smoked cheese – although if you hot-smoke a slab of Cheddar in an aluminium foil parcel just until it melts, and then treat it as a fondue, it is to die for!). Then there is the building of the smoker … and all this before you get anywhere near deciding what food you actually want to smoke.

EQUIPMENT

Commercial smokers are available from companies such as Bradley, which have stockists throughout Europe, America and Canada; they can easily be found online. Commercial smokers are typically cabinets about the size of a standard fridge. Inside they have metal plates that heat flavoured briquettes of compressed sawdust to produce the smoke. These units are ideal if you do not have the space to build a fire or have children and are concerned about the safety issue, or need to have guaranteed consistency in your smoked produce and prefer low-maintenance smoking. Smaller and cheaper alternatives are stove-top smokers and campfire smokers, which produce excellent results on a much smaller scale.

Homemade smokers vary in size and shape from something about as big as a double garage right down to just a wok on the hob. I use something in between these two extremes, namely converted filing cabinets, which are very effective. These work as follows:

- For the hot smoker, there is a fire box in the form of a tray with sides in the bottom drawer (with air vents on either side to allow it to draw) in which you build a slow-burning fire. From here the heat and smoke pass up through holes into the drawers above, the first of which (the one directly above the fire) contains a bowl of sand. Above this are more drawers, with mesh bottoms, containing whatever is to be smoked. At the top is a chimney with an adjustable cap.

- As for the cold smoker, the fire box, which is an enclosed box here, is outside the cabinet to reduce the heat, and a pipe conducts the smoke into the lowest drawer (no air vents are needed), above which are different foods on mesh layers (as for the hot smoker), and finally the chimney. For both smokers, you will need to keep tending the fires to ensure they keep burning.

Hot smoking

This is the process of cooking meat and fish in heat and smoke so they take on some of the smoky flavour. Meat is easier to hot smoke than fish, which can dry out and even shrivel if the temperature is not regulated closely enough. One trick for fish is to part cold smoke it first so it has a chance to take on the delicious taste and texture, and then finish it off by turning up the heat.

Poultry and game are particularly good hot smoked, and hot-smoked salmon is stunning, with a very different flavour to the cold-smoked version. Hot-smoked hams and gammons are fantastic, and of course you don't need to cook them afterwards.

But a word of warning – hot smoking, which is very similar to cooking over a barbecue, can be deceptive because the smoke darkens the produce and makes it appear cooked when it actually may not be. Unless you are really experienced, never trust your eyes; instead buy a meat thermometer. They are invaluable, especially with chicken and game, which, if underdone, can give food poisoning. For meat to be cooked properly, the inside should reach 78°C/172°F.

For a fun, quick-and-easy hot-smoked salmon dish that needs nothing more inventive than a wok on the hob, line your wok with foil and mix together some uncooked rice, brown sugar and a couple of split-open tea bags in the bottom (lapsang souchong works well because it already has a smoky flavour). Place a steaming grid across it so the food does not come into direct contact with the mixture, put the salmon on the grid, place the lid on top and cook. When the food is cooked, it's done.

A hot smoker made from an old five-drawer steel filing cabinet

A homemade cold smoker using a metal dustbin as a fire box

Cold smoking

Now this is where it becomes an art. Cold smoking has nothing to do with cooking and everything to do with imparting flavour, and the reason it's an art form is that you have to be able to make a fire that gives off very little, if any, heat, with temperatures no greater than 10–29°C/50–84°F, often with just a trickle of smoke rising into the produce, and maintain it for days.

The smoke and slight temperature dry out the produce and coat the surface of the food with particles of smoke. These particles have antiseptic qualities, which, when combined with the moisture loss and salt (see 'Salt before smoking', page 246), help to preserve the produce for weeks, if not months.

Cold smoking is more delicate than hot smoking. The flavours, although deep, are mild and almost creamy. Smoked salmon is the classic, and if you catch your own fish, smoking some of it is the natural progression, though anything you catch will benefit from smoking. Homemade cheese also takes on a fantastic new flavour, and hams and gammons, sausages and chicken, even eggs change completely when they've been smoked.

Salt before smoking

If you salt meat and fish (both of which have a high water content) before smoking, the salt will act as a dehydrator to draw out some of the liquid, leaving behind a residue of the cure along with any sugar (which helps to keep the meat soft) and spices you might have included in the cure. This means that the smoke will be able to penetrate much more easily now that much of the liquid has been removed, and it can linger for longer, which improves the flavour. Actually, very little of the salt penetrates the meat/fish at all, and most of it is rinsed off afterwards before the meat/fish is patted dry, ready for smoking.

There are two methods of salting, as for curing: dry salting or wet salting (soaking in a brine solution). It may seem strange to think of soaking fish that have spent their entire life living in the biggest brine solution there is (the sea) in a homemade brine solution with some brown sugar for 3–4 hours prior to smoking, but this will still lift the flavour of the fish way beyond its pre-salted state.

The longer you salt food for, the more into curing territory you encroach, so a leg of pork you want to turn into ham should sit in a brine of salt, sugar and spices for 2–4 days per 450g/1lb, which means leaving a 4.5kg/10lb ham salting for 20–40 days before smoking it. On the other hand, if you had only a couple of small pieces of fish, or a small cut of meat, you might salt for only 1 hour.

DRYING

By now you will have realized that the recurring theme of preserving food is to remove the moisture, because this is where bacteria breed. This means that the most natural, labour-saving and cheap form of preserving must surely be drying. The three types of food that work well when dried are: those that can be coaxed back from their shrivelled shell by immersing them in a bath of boiling water for a couple of minutes, such as mushrooms; those that can be used dried, such as herbs; and those that can be eaten as they are, like biltong (South African beef jerky).

EQUIPMENT

Long Caribbean days of glorious hot sunshine to sun dry the food would be perfect, but if this isn't possible, the practical (though unimaginative) alternative is an airing cupboard or the bottom of a range cooker.

Drying mushrooms

String mushrooms on to a strong thread using a darning needle and hang the mushrooms in a warm room until they feel dry (usually about a couple of weeks). Once the mushrooms feel dry, pop them in a paper bag and sit them in an airing cupboard for up to 10 days. Then seal them in an airtight container, where they will last for years. To rehydrate, simply drop into boiling water for a couple of minutes, and they're as good as new – perfect for soups, stews or pasta dishes.

Drying herbs

Just about any herb can be dried. Pick a bunch of fresh mint, thyme or basil, tie it together by the stalks and hang it upside down in the kitchen or somewhere equally warm with a good airflow (so not the airing cupboard) for a couple of weeks or until they sound crunchy when you touch them. Take a large sheet of paper and lay the herbs across it, then just pat them until all the leaves break off. Now fold the paper in half so all the herbs fall into the centre crease and carefully pour them into a container, and seal. Don't forget to label the container, as there is nothing more annoying than sniffing your way through all the containers in your store cupboard for the mint while your roast lamb is waiting.

Biltong (South African jerky)

This South African snack is made of spicy dried beef, although it could be made of other red meats, such as lamb or venison. In South Africa they are lucky enough to have gorgeous weather, so air drying is easy. For the rest of us, it's down to improvisation, such as this method of box drying, the results of which are stunning. In just 4 days you can produce your own jerky, perfect for a snack, or why not be adventurous and use it as a pizza topping?

Building a biltong box

Take a largish cardboard box and cut a 2.5cm/1in deep lateral slit towards the bottom of each side: 5cm/2in up from the base and 5cm/2in in from each corner. In the lid, cut three slits about 2.5cm/1in wide and two-thirds the length of the lid. Next you need to secure a lightbulb fitting on the bottom so the bulb faces up. The ideal is a bathroom light fitting, one of the ones with a round outer bowl, as the wide base of the fitting gives it plenty of stability when sitting in the box – but don't forget to remove the bowl so the bulb is naked. Use a 50–75 watt bulb.

For the meat to hang, it needs something to hang from. Most of us have hanging files for a filing drawer or cabinet (and if not, they are easy to get hold of). Wrap an elastic band around each end of a file so the two metal strips are clamped together, and with a pair of scissors cut away the cardboard file. Push the metal strips through the sides of the box, so that the ends poke out and the strips are suspended across the box. To hang the meat, unfold a paper clip and wrap one end around the strips, and use the other end to form a hook on which to hang a strip of meat. Add as many hooks as you want and fashion as many hangers in this way as you need.

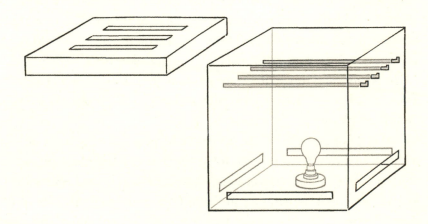

A homemade biltong box

Homemade jerky

Jerky (basically, cured and dried meat) is simple to make. Select a cut of meat that will lend itself to thin slicing, such as rump, silverside or porterhouse, and slice it thinly but not wafer thin. As an alternative to curing, the jerky can be smoked.

350g/12oz rump, silverside or porterhouse steak, thinly sliced

sea salt and white pepper

80ml/2½fl oz malt vinegar

80ml/2½fl oz distilled malt vinegar

115g/4oz raw cane sugar

2 tsp soy sauce

2 tsp Worcestershire sauce

1 tsp garlic powder

½ tsp ground black pepper

1 tsp onion powder

Rub both sides of the steak liberally with sea salt and white pepper. Meanwhile, in a bowl mix the malt and distilled malt vinegars together. Add the sugar and stir to dissolve as much of it into the mixture as you can without having a residue on the bottom. Add the soy sauce and Worcestershire sauce, garlic powder, black pepper and onion powder and mix well. Sit the steaks in the cure so they all receive a coating, then cover with cling film and put in the fridge for a day. Drain and pat dry.

At this point you have the option of leaving the jerky plain or of making up a powdered coating for it, such as cracked black pepper-corns, coriander, Cajun seasoning and cayenne pepper, and rolling the strips in it. Hang the jerky in the biltong box (see page 248) for 4–5 days. Remove and store in the fridge in a lidded container and eat within 2 days.

JAM

The beauty of jam – and its close cousins jellies, preserves and conserves – is that it answers 'yes' to many of the self-sufficient questions, such as: Is it cheap or free? Can I process it without buying any expensive equipment? Is it quick and easy to do? When it's done, will it last? And, of course, it will eliminate the other self-sufficient problem of what to do with excess fruit, because you can make all these types of preserves (in the wider sense of the word) from anything. Whether you have a glut of gooseberries or strawberries in the garden, a gift of apples or find a particularly full blackberry bush in the hedgerow, the answer to all the questions of what to do with them is 'jam'.

As to what the difference is between jams, jellies, preserves and conserves, they really are just variations on a theme:

- Jams are thick spreads made from crushed fruit and sugar.

- Jellies are typically clear and made with fruit juice, but are thicker than jam.

- Preserves are whole or sliced pieces of fruit in a clear syrup.

- Conserves are similar to jam but may contain mixed fruit and sometimes nuts and raisins.

The processes of producing them are all very similar, and consist of combining fresh fruit, sugar and water, and heating them until they reach a setting point. The setting point is reached when pectin, which is found in the cells of fruit, and in acid, is released and reacts with the sugar to produce a gel-like consistency. Without the pectin and acid, jam would just be runny juice.

All fruit has pectin, but in varying quantities. Fruits high in pectin, which give a really good set, include apples, blackcurrants and redcurrants, gooseberries and damsons, lemons and lime. Fruits with a medium set include raspberries and apricots, greengages and plums. Fruits that are low in pectin, and therefore require a little extra pectin to help them set (often by adding lemon juice, as it helps to enhance the flavour without becoming dominant itself), include strawberries, rhubarb, cherries and pears.

EQUIPMENT

Preserving pan or a large saucepan

Jam funnel – not essential until you have used one, then you will never want to fill jam jars again without one

Jam jars

Waxed discs

Cellophane tops

Jams

There are numerous different jam recipes, but the following are really good for self-sufficiency because they use up the standard things that are in the garden already. They are also a good introduction to jam-making because they give you a run through of the basic method involved. Once you understand the principles, simply substitute the fruit in the recipe with whatever you have available, though it will need to be in the same pectin 'group' for you to be assured of success.

Basic jam-making hints and tips

- Warm and sterilize jam jars as you would for chutney, but always fill *warm* jars with *hot* jam, never cold.

- If the recipe does not call for the fruit to be left in sugar overnight, then warm the sugar in the oven with the jam jars before adding it to the fruit, to give a better, faster-made jam.

- Add a knob of butter before boiling point is reached to reduce scum and virtually eliminate the need for skimming – less wasteful.

- Test for the setting point by spreading a little jam on an ice-cold plate (remove the pan from the heat while you do this). When the jam has cooled slightly, prod the edge of it with your finger. If it crinkles under the pressure, then the setting point has been reached and you can pour the jam into the jars; if it doesn't crinkle, then return the pan to the heat and boil for a few minutes more before testing again.

- If you use a jam thermometer, make sure the thermometer is in the pan right from the start to avoid shattering – never put a thermometer into boiling jam.

- When jam has been transferred hot into jars, seal immediately with a waxed disc to exclude any air, then fit a damp cellophane top secured by an elastic band on top.

Rhubarb and ginger jam

  rhubarb, trimmed and chopped to give about 1kg/2¼lb
  1kg/2¼lb preserving or granulated sugar
  juice of 2 lemons
  25g/1oz piece root ginger

Put the rhubarb, sugar and lemon juice in a large bowl and scrunch it all together with your hands. Cover and leave overnight. The next day, crush or bruise the piece of root ginger with a rolling pin or something heavy, and tie it in a square of muslin. Put the rhubarb mixture in a stainless-steel preserving pan or saucepan with the muslin bag. Bring to the boil and boil for about 15 minutes, then remove the muslin bag.

Boil for another 5 minutes or until setting point has been reached (see tests above), then skim any scum from the surface with a slotted spoon. Pour the hot jam into warm sterilized jars (see page 240), seal with a waxed disc and cover in the usual way.

Gooseberry and orange jam

A good substitute for marmalade, this jam works because everyone can grow, barter for or buy gooseberries, thereby reducing the need to buy tons of Seville oranges, which makes it more cost-effective and self-sufficient than marmalade.

2 oranges
1.3kg/3lb gooseberries, topped and tailed
1.6kg/3lb 8oz granulated sugar

Squeeze the juice out of the oranges and either slice the peel thinly or pulse it in a food processor. Put the orange juice and peel in a large saucepan with the gooseberries and 450ml/¾ pint water. Bring to the boil, then reduce the heat and simmer until the fruit is tender. Meanwhile, warm the sugar and the jam jars in a low oven. Add the warmed sugar to the pan and stir until it has dissolved – do not let the jam boil until all the sugar has dissolved. Bring to a rolling boil and retain this heat for about 10 minutes until setting point has been reached. Fill the warmed jars to the brim and cover with waxed discs immediately.

FREEZING

The rule of thumb in food preservation is, if all else fails or you have run out of time, freeze it!

Pretty much everyone who is interested in a self-sufficient lifestyle will have access to a freezer and will be well used to freezing both prepared and raw food. Of all the ways to preserve food, freezing is about the simplest, though there is a danger that it can be a little too convenient at times, which means that getting the door shut can involve all the tricks you would normally associate with closing the lid on a holiday suitcase.

Freezer bags are a great time and space saver, but one of the most underused bits of kit for freezing is the ice tray. This is perfect for freezing individual portions of things like stock or chopped fresh herbs: chop them fresh and half-fill each compartment in the ice tray, then top up with water and freeze. When they're frozen, turn them out into a bag (don't forget to label), and next time you need fresh herbs to top a dish like pasta or a curry, simply pop in an individual cube.

Freezing in portions also works well for eggs. Many people find that either their chickens are in full lay and they're sinking under the weight of all the eggs, or they have no eggs at all. You can't freeze them whole, as they just crack and spoil, but you can freeze them beaten.

If you have got a dozen eggs to freeze, line the cups of a 12-hole muffin tin with cling film. Beat each egg separately in a cup or ramekin, adding a pinch of sugar for sweet recipes (cakes, biscuits, pancakes, scones) or a pinch of salt for savoury recipes (Yorkshire puddings, scrambled eggs, omelettes, glazes), and pour them into the muffin cups, then you'll know that each one holds one egg. Freeze them, and when they are frozen, bag them up. To use, take out however many eggs you need and defrost. If you have fewer than a dozen eggs to freeze, scale down the operation accordingly.

·

CHAPTER TEN

Foraging

Self-sufficiency isn't just about changing your lifestyle, it's also about changing your attitude to the world around you and becoming more attuned to the natural rhythms of life. Picking and eating wild foods that are in season, or foraging, is one of the most pleasurable ways of connecting with the land and the environment. Not only are you eating food that is fresh, seasonal, local and free but you can be more confident that it will be uncontaminated by toxins and chemicals. Foraging is something that almost everyone can do – if you can spot an apple in an apple tree or a blackberry between the thorns, then you can forage. And at the end of it all you can come away with anything from a complete three-course meal to a simple punnet of berries.

Whether kicking along the seashore in search of edible seaweed, rummaging about in the hedgerows for berries or searching out mushrooms in the woods, vital to any foraging expedition are your senses of sight, smell, touch, hearing and, of course, taste. And it's always a good idea to carry a specialized field reference guide to help in accurate identification, some gloves, a pair of scissors, water, a camera (to have a record of plants *in situ*), a mobile phone and a container in which to collect your goodies. There are some important 'do's and don'ts' while foraging:

Be legal

- Under the law of trespass it is illegal to wander on to another person's land uninvited.

- In many places it is illegal to take a whole plant without the owner's permission.

- Endangered or protected plant species that are covered by law can carry huge penalties if disturbed. They should always be left in peace.

Be ethical

- Only harvest a small amount of what is available. Remember: one for you, one for the plant and one for the wildlife – in other words, ensure there's enough for wild animals to eat and for the species to be preserved.

- Respect wildlife and avoid upsetting their homes and nests in hedgerows, fields and trees, especially around springtime.

Be safe

- Be aware of your surroundings and steer clear of foraging close to heavy industry, stagnant water, landfill sites, main roads and any-where that may have been sprayed with chemicals.

- Only harvest from healthy, strong-looking plants.

- Always wash produce before eating.

The golden rule

- Be absolutely certain that you have identified a plant correctly before you consider eating it.

WHEN AND WHERE TO FORAGE

Wild food grows everywhere: on the seashore, the sides of roads, in bushes, hedgerows, the middle of fields, on trees and sometimes even in your own back garden. It's always a good idea to find out about the plants that may be growing and readily available in your area. Understanding what is available to eat, and when, is a life skill anyone interested in foraging can learn and from this will come the ability to eat a gourmet banquet for free almost any day of the year.

Tastes of the seasons

Spring: This is a fantastic season for the forager – a period of growth and abundance when everything is fresh and bright. It's a perfect time to gather young, tender shoots and leaves and flowers that have a distinctly crisp, clean taste.

Summer: The warmest and most humid of the seasons, this is a period of ripening and of maturing tastes and textures. Summer food is simply bursting with flavour: rich and juicy, with a multitude of berries, fruits and fragrant herbs.

Autumn: The contemplative season, but also one of preparation, gathering and storing for the cold months to come. The autumn harvest is full of woody, musky, earthy flavours, with fruit, nuts and mushrooms dominating.

Winter: The short days and long, cold nights of winter mean that foragers have to work hard for their dinner. This is the season for soups, casseroles, slow-cooked recipes and the strong, rich flavours of hardy mushrooms, garlic and herbs.

The forager's favourite haunts

Hedges: Hedgerows are often teeming with delicious edibles such as blackberries, raspberries, redcurrants, blackcurrants, gooseberries, sloes, wild cherries, elderberries and damsons, as well as wild garlic, elderflowers and rose hips.

Pastures and open fields: These sites offer an abundance of wild herbs, including thyme, marjoram, sorrel, chicory, pignut and, in damp areas, mint. They are also host to other wonderful favourites such as field mushrooms, St George's mushrooms and giant puffballs.

Roadsides: Although it's always best to avoid roads with heavy traffic, roadsides are surprisingly abundant with food and often contain wild cabbage, fennel, horseradish, asparagus, berries and even common lime.

The seashore: This is a seriously good site for the forager. Seawater contains almost the same minerals and trace elements as blood, which means that seaweed is incredibly good for you. Some types of seaweed, laver in particular, are eaten in pies, bread and sausages. Other edible seaweeds include carragheen, sea lettuce and sweet oar weed. Some of the shellfish along Britain's coastal areas will equal any around the world. Clams, razor clams, cockles, mussels and limpets are particularly good.

Woodlands: These are great places to go in search of the foraging well-knowns, including hawthorn leaves (best eaten in April and known to many as 'bread and cheese') and pine needles for pine-needle tea, as well as for more adventurous plant foods, such as stinging nettles. In late summer and autumn the woodlands are bursting with mushrooms such as chanterelle, beefsteak, cep, horn of plenty and chicken of the woods.

WILD FOOD

There are six main categories of wild food: fruits (including berries), herbs, leaves, mushrooms, nuts and food from the seashore. The variety within each category is staggering and has led some of the world's most innovative chefs to now consider the great outdoors as an extension of their larder. This chapter gives just a sample of some of the most common and easily obtainable wild foods that can be used in the kitchen to add tremendous flavour, texture and character to your meals. Mushrooms offer a particularly rich and plentiful source of food for the forager and can also be preserved quite easily, which is great news for self-sufficiency. Some of the plants and foods in the sections that follow have been highlighted as 'special features'. The criteria for selection are unashamedly personal – these foods are favourites of mine and are either versatile or simple to find, easy to identify or fantastic fun at mealtimes, or maybe even a combination of all of these things!

Fruits and berries

What could be more pleasurable than blackberrying with the children on a glorious Sunday afternoon in late summer and then sitting down to enjoy a mouthwatering apple and blackberry crumble? Fruits and berries are common from mid-summer through to autumn and can be found anywhere from hedgerows to trees, bushes to roadsides. Be gentle when handling them as they are easily bruised or squashed. Also avoid picking from low down on hedges that are growing on or near well-walked paths and tracks – you probably won't be the first person to have walked there that day and the thought that a dog may have lifted its leg on your fruit may take some of the joy out of your foraging experience!

Among the most mouthwatering wild fruits are cherries, plums and, if you can find them, apples and pears. But it's the berries that in late summer and autumn are most prevalent: blackberries, raspberries, gooseberries, whortleberries, junipers, dewberries, rowan berries, red-currants, blackcurrants and wild strawberries. An abundance of these delicious, plump berries fills our bushes, hedgerows and woodlands in band after band of vibrant colour. Many of the wild berries are rich in antioxidants, fibre, vitamins C and B, folic acid, magnesium, copper and iron and are therefore a tremendous source of natural goodness and are believed to help combat a number of ailments, including (among many other things) general aches and pains, inflammation and allergies (although no definitive medical evidence yet exists to support these claims). The real treat after a superb day's foraging comes the following morning, when you mix equal portions of your fruit, berries and nuts with raw oatmeal and a splash of ice-cold milk for the perfect forager's breakfast that will literally ping your body awake and make you feel good for the rest of the day.

Rose hip, *Rosa canina*

The rose hip is one of the most common wild fruits and should be picked soon after the first frost of the year. An extremely rich source of vitamin C, its ripe, red fruits are famously used to produce a syrup. One traditional recipe (still in use to this day) dates to the Second World War, when the Ministry of Health requested volunteers to forage and gather hips. A staggering 120 tons were collected, boiled at length and turned into rose-hip syrup, which was then used to help prevent the onset of scurvy. Rose hips can be combined with crab-apples (another good foraging fruit) to make a delicious crabapple and rose-hip jelly. The juice from this fruit should always be strained before use – the tiny fibres in the hips used to be dried to produce 'itching powder'!

Elder, *Sambucus nigra*

This has to be one of the most exciting and versatile plants on the forager's wish-list. The deciduous shrub produces off-white to cream-coloured clusters of flowers in late June and small, shiny berries of darkest blue to black in late August through to October (avoid the later berries if they appear dull or wrinkled). The flowers as well as the berries can be used. Elder is steeped in folklore and has strong associations with witchcraft. Legend has it, for example, that when a witch needed to change identity she would turn herself into an elder bush – the proof of this transformation was to cut into the elder to see if it bled.

Elderberries make a great addition to blackberry and apple pie or fruit jam because of their high level of pectin, a gelling agent. Most famously they are used to produce elderberry wine, with its wonderful deep velvety red colour (it is thought that some of the most sought-after French wines, including certain Bordeaux and clarets, were first based on English elderberry wine). The honey-scented flowers can be deep fried as fritters or turned into a refreshing sparkling wine or cordial. Elderflower also has some exciting medicinal qualities – if infused with water, it can be helpful in treating various ailments, including bronchitis, coughs, colds and sore throats. When harvesting, cut the complete cluster of flowers or berries where they join the stem of the shrub. Pick the flowers from high on the bush as washing them will destroy their fragrance; use them straight away.

Herbs

Wild herbs are more delicate and have a milder flavour than their domestic cousins because they are natural and have not been intensified (selectively bred to produce hybrids). They should be harvested from heaths, grassland and pastureland early in the morning on a dry spring day, just as they are beginning to flower (the flowers will help you with identification). Always cut a little of what's available, never tear, and either use the herbs the same day or put them down to dry as soon as possible.

Not to be confused with garden thyme, wild thyme is available throughout the year. It has a subtle flavour that can be added to many soups and stews. Many varieties of wild mint can be found all through the summer, including hybrids of the cultivated and wild types that produce a range of different flavours. But beware of water mint, which is all too common in the waterways and ditches of Britain – it has a watery, muddy smell and tastes horrible when used with any food! Bergamot is a perennial herb with showy, scarlet flowers. It is a summer herb that is often used in teas. But it is also wonderful in salads and can be made into herb butter for use on poultry and game. Wild fennel, with its gorgeous smell and aniseed taste, is increasingly easy to find. It makes a perfect accompaniment to fish in a cream or crème fraiche sauce, and is a pleasant alternative to dill.

Common comfrey is a perennial, stout, coarse-looking herb that flowers from late spring right through the summer. When made with young leaves, comfrey soup is delicious and wholesome. Comfrey is also excellent when cooked as a vegetable – the leaves are softer and more tender than spinach. Although strong in flavour this herb will add a lift and intensity to any cream sauce or white sauce.

Meadowsweet is an elegant plant that grows in damp areas and is available throughout the summer. Its distinct honey flavour was once used to enhance the taste of mead, beer and wine. The flowers combine well with crabapples – when cooked together the apples taste as though they have been sweetened with honey. Meadowsweet flowers can also be cooked with rhubarb or made into a syrup and used as a cordial.

Sorrel, *Rumex acetosa*

Sorrel is a perennial herb and one of the earliest, flowering between May and August, although the leaves can be picked at the beginning of March if the tail-end of winter is mild. The leaves are green, slim and arrow shaped with tiny flowers that bloom a purply red in summer. Sorrel was traditionally used and prepared in much the same way as we prepare mint sauce today, by chopping finely or grinding into a paste, adding sugar and vinegar and serving as an accompaniment to meat. But most people are familiar with it in a soup and occasionally as an addition to an early summer salad. When preparing sorrel, take care not to use any pots, pans or utensils made from iron as the natural chemicals in the plant can react to it. Sorrel contains vitamin C and is thought to enhance the haemoglobin content of the blood. Avoid eating large quantities as sorrel contains small amounts of oxalic acid.

Stinging nettle, *Urtica dioica*

The nettles of this perennial herb taste fantastic and are incredibly healthy, containing vitamins A, C, D, iron, potassium, manganese, calcium and even protein. They are also known to help with rheumatism, increase haemoglobin in the blood and improve circulation.

Pick the nettle tops when they are young using scissors and gloves to protect against the sting (cooking removes the sting, making them safe to eat). Avoid picking after June, when they turn bitter and gritty. After washing, the leaves can be used for soup, pesto, purée, paté or fried to make crisps. But in my opinion the best way to cook them is as a vegetable: simply simmer in a saucepan with a splash of water, some chopped onion, plenty of seasoning and a little nutmeg for about 10 minutes; then fold them into cold mashed potato and fry as a bubble and squeak.

Bannock bread

Any discussion of foraging and herbs would not be complete without at least a brief mention of bannock bread, a recipe that is thought to have originated in Scotland and northern England around the 5th century AD. In its simplest form, bannock bread consists of 1 mug of plain flour, 1 teaspoon of baking powder, 4 teaspoons of oil, half a teaspoon of salt, then enough water to make a stiff dough (the quantity of water will depend on the type of flour used). Delicious and simple to make, it's an ideal family treat on a summer evening, flavoured with virtually anything you can forage. Pre-mix the dough and seal it in an air-tight container before setting out. Then search for wild herbs to make a savoury bread or berries to make a sweet one – take a bottle of water so that you can clean anything you pick. Build a small fire (check beforehand that it is safe and legal to do so). Break off a small round of dough and press some of your goodies firmly into it. Shape it around the end of a stick, lean it into the heat of the fire to cook and enjoy!

Leaves

Leaves can be found almost everywhere, from waste ground and hedgerows to woods and roadsides. They generally benefit from being picked and eaten while young, in late spring and early summer, so that they retain most of their nutrition. Always cut a little of what's available and as low down on the leaf blade or stem as possible.

Dried or fresh rose leaves make excellent tea, as do raspberry and ground-ivy leaves. Pine needles were also used for tea in days gone by because of their high vitamin C content, which helped to prevent scurvy (I can't vouch for the taste however!). Beech leaves can be used as a flavouring for gin and oak leaves make wonderful wine. Wild garlic or ramson leaves make a great addition to any spring salad and are ideal thinly shredded and used as a final addition to soups and stews. (Always be sure that you have identified the plant correctly as garlic leaves are similar to the leaves of some poisonous plants. At the very least you should rub the leaves to see if they have a definite smell of garlic.) The leaves of some members of the daisy family (chicory, nipplewort and wall lettuce, for example) also make welcome additions to a wild leaf salad (see page 267).

Fat hen, *Chenopodium album*

Pick the young, tender leaves of this plant in the spring and wash and cook them as you would spinach. They make a wonderful green vegetable. There is evidence to suggest that *Chenopodium album* may have featured quite heavily in the diet of prehistoric man. Traces of the plant were found in the stomach of the astonishingly well-preserved 'Tollund Man', whose body was found in a bog in Denmark in 1950 and was later carbon dated to the 4th century BC. This hardy plant flourishes everywhere, even along the most well-worn paths.

Dandelion, *Taraxacum officinale*

With its vibrant yellow flower and green leaves, the dandelion can be found in fields and pastures from spring right though to winter, only dying off during the very coldest few weeks of the year. If you can find enough leaves, wash, chop and sauté them in a hot saucepan for 2–3 minutes, adding a knob of butter for the last 30 seconds, drain and turn on to a plate. Season with a little salt and pepper and sprinkle with some crushed or roughly grated nuts and serve with wild meat and game, such as rabbit, pheasant, wood pigeon or venison. The flowering heads of the dandelion can be collected and made into dandelion wine, the roots can be used to make beer or dandelion coffee and the younger, tender leaves can be used in a mixed salad.

Forager's wild leaf salad

Looking into a bowl of salad should be like looking into a box of jewels. If it hasn't got lots and lots of colour, then it's not a true forager's salad. Put a selection of sorrel leaves, dandelion leaves, wild garlic, pansy petals, nasturtium flowers, mint, chive flowers, apples, pears, strawberries, other berries, nuts, lettuce, cucumbers and cherry tomatoes in a bowl, chopping first where necessary, and make it look pretty. Use a light dressing of a delicately smoked extra virgin olive oil if you have access to a smoker; otherwise use an olive oil or nut oil and lemon juice dressing. Toss and serve.

Mushrooms

From early autumn to the first frost of winter wild mushrooms are on the menu in every forager's home. If you know where to look, certain types are available all year round, although it's in the chilly, damp autumn mornings that they are most prolific. Found mainly in fields and wooded areas, there are thousands of known species of mushroom (and no doubt thousands more yet to be discovered). Yet of this vast quantity only relatively few are safe to eat. Most of the rest will simply make you feel unwell but some are deadly. It is therefore essential to determine that the varieties you have picked are not poisonous. *Always* harvest *all* of the mushroom, as some toxic and poisonous varieties look incredibly similar to the edible ones and positive identification can only be made if you have the entire plant. A definitive guide, preferably in the shape of an experienced forager standing by your side, should always be used. There are some fantastic and reliable online sites that give photographs and detailed descriptions of just about every type of fungus you're likely to stumble across. However, if you're new to foraging and fancy adding an adventurous twist to your morning stroll with the dog, consider going on a guided mushroom walk with an expert before launching out on your own (they are often advertised in the local press).

Mushrooms grow up overnight, so it's important to venture out at dawn and be the first on the scene before the insects and flies discover them. The rewards for your early start can be staggering. For anyone who loves food and enjoys cooking, a basket of freshly picked wild mushrooms is enough to make you gasp. The prospect of the different flavours, textures and scents is quite irresistible. Rich in vitamin B2 (riboflavin) and copper and with virtually no fat, sugar or salt, they're not only good for you but are also non-fattening.

If you find a beefsteak mushroom, *Fistulina hepatica*, growing on a chestnut or an old oak tree, count yourself very fortunate, though expect a reddish juice to leach during cooking (this adds incredible flavour and colour to the sauce). Another good find is St George's mushroom, *Tricholoma gambosum*, which, according to legend, is said to appear every year on 23 April, St George's Day (and also my horse's birthday – hence her name, Georgie Girl). If you happen to stumble across a giant puffball, *Langermannia gigantea*, you probably won't know what to do with yourself or with all of the mushroom – some of them can grow larger than a football!

Field or meadow mushroom, *Agaricus campestris*

Most common of all the mushrooms, and the wild relative of the cultivated button mushroom, these are found from July to November in fields and meadows. Although they are common, this doesn't mean they are easy to identify: a couple of poisonous fungi look very similar, including Destroying Angel, *Amanita virosa*, and Yellow Stainer, *Agaricus xanthodermus*. If you are at all uncertain about the safety of the plant, cut the mushroom in half vertically and avoid any that stain an orangey yellow or have white gills (in addition to this, always consult a reputable field guide). But otherwise, field or meadow mushrooms are delicious eaten raw, sliced into a salad, cooked on their own in a little butter and oil or mixed into a sauce to help bulk out and add depth of flavour to a meat dish.

Cep or porcini or penny bun, *Boletus edulis*

The distinctive chocolate brown cap of this mushroom gives it the appearance of a freshly toasted bun (hence penny bun, one of its common names). It is found in woods and clearings during September, October and November. Unfortunately it's not just humans who find these mushrooms appetizing. Insects are also attracted to them – the trick is to cut into them before you cook and discard anything that looks infested. Small, tight ceps can be eaten raw and taste creamy and leafy, nutty and rich. The older and larger ceps are better sautéed with a little fresh thyme, a hint of garlic and a tiny squeeze of lemon (the lemon will bring out the flavour of the mushroom without being an identifiable taste itself) and are best served on hot, toasted brioche.

Chanterelle, *Cantharellus cibarius*

These gorgeous corn-yellow mushrooms with their distinctive trumpet shape and slightly citrus smell are common, and often grow near birch and beech trees. They can be found from July right the way through to the first frost of winter. However, take care not to confuse them with the highly hallucinogenic false chanterelle, *Hygrophoropsis aurantiaca*. Unlike the cep, chanterelles are not a target for insects and maggots. However, they do have their quirks when it comes to cooking and preparation. Chanterelles are not good eaten raw and need to be cooked reasonably slowly and carefully by either poaching in milk or frying in butter. They complement eggs beautifully and work well in omelets or with scrambled egg.

Chicken of the woods or sulphur polypore, *Laetiporus sulphureus*

A wood fungus that is found growing in clusters attached to old trees in the summer and autumn before the cold of winter sets in, this mushroom is an exciting find. The more vibrant and yellow the colour, the younger the mushroom (older ones tend to go tough and can taste bitter). They have a definite smell, taste and even texture of roast chicken, which makes them perfect for casseroles and stews (wash, cube and fry them lightly in butter and add to the pot about half an hour before serving), or for breakfast (part boil before frying in the same pan as some fatty bacon).

Wild mushroom risotto

Like all risottos, this is a little work, but the delicious, creamy result is well worth the effort!

250g/9oz mixed wild mushrooms, sliced or torn
4 tbsp olive oil
small handful chopped thyme
squeeze of lemon juice
2 onions, finely chopped
2 garlic cloves, finely chopped
400g/14oz risotto rice
125ml/4fl oz dry white wine

1.2 litres/2 pints hot chicken or vegetable stock
75g/3oz butter
115g/4oz hard cheese, such as Parmesan, finely grated
sea salt and freshly ground black pepper

Sauté the mushrooms in 3 tbsp of the oil in a frying pan until just cooked. Season, and add the thyme and lemon juice. Set to one side. In a large saucepan, heat the remaining oil and sweat the chopped onions and garlic until softened. Turn the heat up, add the rice and stir continuously for 2–3 minutes until beginning to look translucent. Add the wine, and keep stirring so that any harsh alcohol flavours are evaporated. Once nearly all the wine has evaporated, add a ladleful of hot stock and a pinch of salt. Turn the heat down to a simmer, chop half of the cooked mushrooms and add to the pan. Keep adding ladlefuls of stock while stirring, allowing each addition to be absorbed before adding the next. This should take about 15 minutes. Test the rice to make sure it is cooked. Remove from the heat, add the butter, the Parmesan and the remaining mushrooms. Stir gently, then serve as soon as possible.

Variation

Use cultivated mushrooms and 25g/1oz dried mushrooms, reconstituted in a little hot water (add the strained soaking liquid to your stock). Add the dried mushrooms when you add the first half of the fresh mushrooms.

Preserving mushrooms

The drawback to developing a taste for wild mushrooms comes around the time of the first hard frost – they seem to simply disappear overnight with the onset of winter. The answer is to preserve some of your gatherings in the autumn to use later in the year.

Chanterelle vodka: Not for the faint-hearted! Clean the chanterelles and pop them into a Kilner jar before adding the vodka (85g/3oz of mushrooms to 350ml/12fl oz of vodka). When all the mushrooms are lying on the bottom, the vodka is ready to drink. Chill well and serve as an aperitif.

Drying: Slice the mushrooms thinly and either lay them flat on a baking tray lined with greaseproof paper or thread them on a needle and cotton. Leave to dry for about two days then store in a jar, bag or plastic container.

Duxelle: This classic French method of preparing mushrooms involves chopping them finely with some shallots and frying both ingredients gently in butter without browning. Add some herbs (thyme works well) and a little white wine and continue cooking on a low heat until all the moisture has evaporated. Then cool and refrigerate them or freeze them in an ice tray for easy portioning.

Freezing: Boil the mushrooms in salted water briefly, drain and allow to cool. Then freeze them separately on a tray before bagging and returning to the freezer.

Powder: Dry the mushrooms before putting them through a clean coffee grinder. Store in a Kilner jar. Perfect for flavouring winter curries, but use sparingly.

Purée: Preparation is as for duxelles but instead of refrigerating or freezing, whiz them in a blender until smooth. Then store the mixture in a Kilner jar or similar (or freeze) and use in soups and casseroles or in sauces for red meats such as beef or game.

Salting: Slice the mushrooms thickly and layer in a tall, air-tight jar, first with salt, then a layer of mushroom slices, salt, mushrooms, and so on, repeating the process until all the mushrooms are used up. Always use a good quality sea or rock salt. The mushrooms will need soaking before use.

Wild mushroom butter: Close chop and lightly fry the mushrooms before adding the butter (unsalted works best). Simmer for a couple of minutes, then pour into a suitable tub. Perfect with pasta or simply melted over meat or fish. The butter can be frozen.

Note: This section is not intended as a definitive guide to mushrooms and should not be used as one. Before trying any of the mushrooms or recipes described in it, always verify with other reliable sources that a correct identification of the fungus has been made and that it is safe to eat.

Nuts

Take a stout stick and a wicker basket and spend a late summer or early autumn afternoon hunting through the woods, hedgerows and scrubland and you'll be amazed not only at the quantity and variety of nuts but also how easy they are to gather. In September, October and November look out for sweet chestnuts, hazelnuts and beech nuts. Packed with nutrients and often rich in protein, unsaturated fat, vitamins (including B6 and E) and carbohydrates, nuts are a staple food in some Mediterranean countries and for many vegetarians. They are thought to help prevent coronary heart disease.

Avoid picking nuts before they are ripe as they will taste bitter and discard any that smell musty. Use gloves and a hooked stick to get to any that are out of reach, but remember – you are sharing this important food with wildlife that doesn't have the option of nipping out to the supermarket if stocks run out, so only pick a little of what's available.

Beech nuts can be pressed to make oil or beech mast butter. (Beech trees only produce good mast, or encased nuts, every 5 to 8 years, depending on growing conditions.) The nuts are very small and must be gathered as soon as they fall, so some people think they're too much effort. Although time-consuming to gather they are excellent when roasted. Keep the nuts indoors for 12 to 24 hours after collecting to allow the husks to burst open so that you can shake out the 3 little nuts inside. Remove the leathery outer skins from the nuts and place them on a baking tray in a single layer. Roast in a hot oven for 5–10 minutes, checking that they don't burn, shake on a little salt and eat warm.

One of the most traditional wild food recipes is for acorn 'coffee'. It is a bitter drink but boiling the acorns whole for 20 minutes or so before peeling can help reduce this. Then treat them as you would coffee beans – simply grind and filter before drinking.

Sweet chestnut, *Castanea sativa*

A delicious and traditional way to eat sweet chestnuts is simply to roast them. Prick the skins first to avoid explosion. Fresh chestnuts also make an excellent stuffing for poultry and the French marrons glacés are a Christmas treat not to be missed. To make marrons glacés, split the fresh chestnut skins (with the chestnuts still inside) and boil them for a few minutes so that the skins are easier to remove. Take off the skins and the membrane and boil the chestnuts for an additional 20 minutes to soften them. Make a sugar syrup by boiling together equal quantities of sugar and water. Add the drained chestnuts to the syrup and simmer gently for one hour, ensuring that they do not boil over or catch the bottom of the pan. Remove from the syrup, place on a baking tray and coat with granulated sugar. Bake in the oven for a few minutes or until the sugar has glazed the nuts. Take out of the oven, sprinkle with a little caster sugar and allow to cool. Heavenly!

Hazelnut, *Corylus avellana*

Fight off the birds and squirrels and you can pick hazelnuts (also known as cobnuts) from September until November. Eat them raw or roasted in the top of a medium oven for about 10 minutes. Add salt and eat them hot, served in a paper cone, preferably in front of an open fire. For the slightly more adventurous, they also make an excellent addition to a nut and berry praline.

Nut and mixed berry praline

This is a really quick solution to satisfy a sweet craving using a selection of foraged nuts and berries. It is absolutely delicious.

butter, for greasing
280g/10oz granulated sugar
2 tbsp honey
2 handfuls mixed nuts, such as chestnuts, walnuts and hazelnuts
½ handful mixed berries

Grease a 30 × 25cm/12 × 10in baking tray. Put the sugar and 125ml/4fl oz water in a saucepan and heat over a low heat until the sugar has dissolved, then increase to a moderate heat until the liquid takes on a dazzling golden colour. Stir in the honey, nuts and berries, then pour into the baking tray. Leave until cold, then break up into pieces. Absolutely delicious!

Plants and seafood from the seashore

There is something quite magical about standing on a beach, smelling the salt in the air and hearing the waves either gently lapping back and forth or crashing in and out, depending on the weather. The same stretch of coastline can be tranquil and romantic one day yet dark and foreboding the next. But look past the drama and there is food everywhere.

Seaweed is ridiculously underrated and it baffles me why more people don't eat it. High in minerals, trace elements, proteins and vitamins (A, B, B12, C and D), not only is it good for humans and used in many medicines, but if washed and hung up to dry it makes a wonderful winter supplement crumbled into animal feed. It is also a fantastic organic fertilizer. It is best picked in late spring from shingle and rocky beaches and most shores. Seaweed should not be cut too close to the base of the plant so that it won't be killed off completely and will be able to regrow. Always wash in clean, fresh water before cooking.

Forage along the seashore for shellfish whenever there's an 'r' in the month (September to April) as these tend to be the cooler, non-breeding months when there's less chance of picking up a bad one. Work at low tide, bearing in mind that the water can turn within minutes. Always learn the tide times before venturing out. An hour either side of low tide is ideal (if you plan on working a mud flat, be especially vigilant, and if in doubt, take a local guide). Another essential is to check out the cleanliness of the beach you intend to comb – it's well worth spending an hour or so researching this on the Internet before setting out.

Cockles, clams and razor clams

When molluscs are good, they are incredibly good. But for every person who raves about them, there's always someone else with a horror story about food poisoning or similar. But a little knowledge and attention to detail can eliminate most of the risk concerned with eating bad shellfish. Always collect from 'clean' beaches with a good reputation for its shellfish (again, check online). And at the point of cooking, make sure the shellfish is clean, healthy looking and, most important, alive.

Cockling is incredible fun but it pays to go prepared as cockles tend to hide just beneath the surface of the sand around the low-water mark. A garden rake is therefore the ideal tool with which to trawl back and forth to bring them to the surface. Find a good patch of cockles and you can drag up dozens in no time at all – but the art certainly is in finding a good patch. If you don't have time to speculate, head for well-known cockling sites, but expect some friendly competition.

Some clams can be harvested with a rake in much the same way as cockles. The alternative is to walk along the top of the beach where the high tide reaches and look out for two small dips in the sand, about a finger's width apart, and then start digging down.

Mostly found along the furthest low-water mark, razor clams hide just beneath the surface of the sand waiting for the sea to come back in, which is when they will pop up and head off. So the best trick I've found is to fool them into thinking that the tide has turned by pouring a little seawater down their holes and grabbing them when they make an appearance. An alternative is to pour salt into the holes, which is said to irritate them. Razor clams can be a bit gritty but are good to eat after having been washed properly and soaked for a couple of hours in clean, slightly saline water.

Limpets

There are many different ways of prizing a limpet from a rock but I have always found the most effective is to run the edge of a palette knife between the limpet and the stone. Once they are free, treat them as mussels (see below).

Mussels

The first time I ever tried mussels was along the Champs-Elysées in Paris. Moules and frites – all those mussels, all that sauce, all that garlic! Sensational! It may be difficult to recreate the atmosphere of down-town Paris but it's not hard to recreate the dish. Mussels are incredibly common along the coastline and tend to attach themselves in clumps, which makes life a little easier! As with all shellfish, make certain they are alive before you cook them, clean them well and debeard them with a pair of tweezers (well worth the extra effort).

Marsh samphire, *Salicornia europaea*

Samphire is a seashore plant, not a seaweed, and can be gathered along the coastline. Also known as glasswort (it was once used in the glass-making process), it is traditionally picked on 21 June, the longest day of the year, but can also be found throughout July and August. When young and sweet it can be eaten raw; if slightly older and larger it will benefit from cooking in a little salt water. Samphire goes particularly well with fish.

Sea lettuce, *Ulva lactuca*

Famous for containing more vitamin A (the growth vitamin) than butter, sea lettuce is one of the most common seaweeds and can be found all along the shoreline among the rocks and rock pools. The best time to gather it is just as the sea is turning from high to low tide. As the water retreats you can pick up clumps of it – fresh, still wet and very green. Wash and use in a salad or, if you are feeling particularly daring, add a small amount to a seafood stir-fry.

CHAPTER ELEVEN

Reduce, Reuse, Recycle

'REDUCE, REUSE, RECYCLE' is the eco-enthusiast's mantra and a useful rule of thumb in self-sufficiency too. Reduce the amount you consume (and the amount you throw away), reuse as much as you can and recycle what is left over. A useful way to think about this is to imagine that you aren't allowed to buy anything new (except food) for six months. You can get new things for your home, but only if you buy them second-hand, or swap them for something else, or are given them. This may sound a terrifying prospect, but by looking in detail at what you buy, you are forced to consider what are essentials and what, in reality, you can do without – those cute new shoes, that mobile phone upgrade, the iPod in a shiny new colour. So much of what we think we 'need' is really just advertising-fuelled, short-lived desire. Once we step out of that loop and consider our needs from a wider perspective, things look very different.

And more interesting, too. We throw away so much stuff. In 2005 the United States generated 246 million tons of Municipal Solid Waste, better known as trash. In the UK, the average adult throws away his or her own body weight in rubbish every six to seven weeks. These are big numbers. However, recycling is gradually improving, and now more than 30 per cent of all waste in both countries is composted or recycled, and 50 per cent of paper recycled. But more could be done – perhaps we are just not aware of quite how much more. In fact, approximately 50 per cent of the contents of an average household bin could be recycled. And a whole lot of it probably didn't need to be thrown away in the first place.

The concept of reducing consumption is a basic one in self-sufficiency, and goes hand in hand with reuse and recycling. This chapter offers some tips on how to set about it.

SECOND TIME AROUND

'Reuse' can mean two things. It can mean being creative with your own once-used items and reusing them for things other than what they were designed for; and it can mean taking something that someone else was throwing out and giving it a new lease of life – put simply, buying second-hand rather than new.

Reusing within the home and garden

Our grandparents and great-grandparents were thrifty, reusing and mending whatever they could. And goods tended to be well made, built to last. Today's mass-manufactured products are all too often shoddily constructed out of poor-quality materials and quick to fall apart. But more and more people no longer wish to live in a completely disposable world, and, in recent years, some manufacturers have responded to the growing sensibility among consumers that goods should last and not break a few days after the warranty runs out.

The really enjoyable, creative part of reusing goods in self-sufficiency is looking for alternative uses for things that otherwise might have been thrown out. Use that old handbag as a clothes-peg holder; empty cereal-packet liners as freezer-bags; old, washed tin cans as stylish pen-holders or cutlery containers. If you have left-over tiles after tiling the kitchen or bathroom, they make original coasters. Interestingly shaped jam jars or small glass yoghurt pots can be used as tea-light holders in the garden on summer evenings. The possibilities are endless.

If you have a garden, cardboard loo-roll tubes and empty yoghurt pots can be used as seed propagators (cardboard can be buried directly in the ground, where it will decompose naturally); cut-down plastic bottles can serve as cloches to protect delicate young seedlings. Old tyres can be filled with earth and used as planters. Old CDs can be strung together and hung up among your runner beans and tomatoes as bird-scarers. (See pages 33, 44.)

If you have a smallholding or livestock, numerous items can be given a new life as something different. Old freezers make excellent feed stores that are rodent- and weather-proof. Old bits of carpet are ideal to lay over a vegetable bed to keep weeds at bay, or as insulation tacked under the roof of a chicken- or pig-house. Old pallets have myriad uses, including as gates, temporary fence-pluggers, and (nailed together to form three sides of a square) compost-heap containers. Old paint buckets can be used as plant pots, feed containers or – buckets. Old scaffolding planks make great heavy-duty shelving.

Reuse is a habit of mind. All you need is a little ingenuity and some imagination.

Reusing other people's goods

Buying second-hand is ethical and saves resources. If you buy from a charity shop, your money is going directly to a good cause. If you buy from an individual, you are helping him or her recoup the original expense. If you buy locally, you are keeping the money within the local economy. Some people even give away their unwanted items rather than selling them.

Online buying and selling

You can find practically anything you'll ever need on the Internet. For online buying and selling, many people's first port of call is the online auction site eBay (www.ebay.co.uk), where you can find both new and second-hand goods. Using this site is like walking through the biggest department store in the world while sitting comfortably in front of your computer, and you can lose yourself for hours just browsing. There are many genuine bargains to be had.

A slightly different take on passing on unwanted goods is offered by the Freecycle network (www.freecycle.org). This is a neat concept, by which local groups of people offer their unwanted items online for free, or you can also advertise for something you need. Freecycle is a non-profit movement and its stated aim is to help keep material out of landfill; by clicking on their main site you can find out if there is a community in your local area – and if not, you can always start one.

These are just two examples of sites dedicated to selling and gifting goods on the net, but there are many others, and it is worthwhile sifting through the results of a search engine to see what's available in your area. For example, Amazon (www.amazon.co.uk) now offers second-hand goods via its Marketplace section; and the Oxfam shop also has an online presence where you can pick up second-hand clothes and books just as if you were browsing in one of their physical shops (www.oxfam.org.uk/shop/).

Sourcing locally

In the UK there are many sources of second-hand goods. First of all, of course – once you've asked around all your friends and relatives – there are the classified ads in the local paper and the traditional cards in the newsagent's window or on the supermarket noticeboard, in which people try to give away or sell anything from their old fridge or superseded laptop to their unwanted kittens or a hundredweight of logs. Then you can have fun trawling round boot fairs on a Sunday afternoon, or visiting recycling centres and reclamation or architectural salvage yards. Charity shops often yield good bargains, especially clothes and books, and are clearly a particularly ethical method of obtaining goods.

For the smallholder aiming to be as self-sufficient as possible, if you had to buy everything new, life would be a great deal harder. Chicken houses, feed stores, pig arcs; wood, wire, tools, fence posts… The list goes on. Being able to pick items up second-hand is often the only way to keep it all ticking over.

A good place to find items for the smallholding is the farm clearance sale, generally held when a farm needs to be disposed of after a farmer has died, retired or moved away. Farm sales tend to be auctions and you can often find anything from a set of gardening tools to a nearly-new tractor, all being sold to the highest bidder. Keep an eye on local newspapers, rural estate agents and country auctioneer's brochures for notices of upcoming farm clearance sales.

The other side of the coin

It may sound obvious, but the second-hand system only works if people are putting in as well as taking out. So, online or offline, do join reuse communities, and join in! Such forums will give you inspiration and energy. It may be a challenge for you to overcome the smallholder's or homesteader's natural urge to hoard. 'That'll come in handy one day…' Sound familiar? When you're having a clear-out, look at everything with a dispassionate eye and consider whether you really still need it. A good rule of thumb is, if it hasn't been used in a year, pass it on to someone else.

RECYCLING AND WASTE REDUCTION

First reduce consumption, then reduce waste, and finally recycle what's left over.

Reduce your waste at source

Reducing your waste begins while you shop. The packaging around food is the biggest culprit in waste and is all too often way over the top for the size of the item inside. As much as 16 per cent of the price you pay can be for the packaging, which is simply tossed in the bin. Where possible, buy concentrates or loose goods. For example, normal washing-up liquid is about 95 per cent water and thickened with hefty amounts of salt: in its concentrated form, the active ingredients are doubled, and the bottle costs less because there is less packaging. Remember to use correspondingly less of the concentrated product. (If you tend to forget, tip half the concentrate into another bottle and top both up with water.)

When selecting what to buy in shops, avoid individually wrapped portions where you can, and all products with excessive packaging.

Many shops nowadays, especially independently owned local stores, sell loose goods by weight, so that you can choose the exact amount that you want and scoop it into a paper bag – muesli, nuts and grains are some examples of products that work well sold in this way. Some shops operate a refill system where you can take back your old liquid container and have it refilled with washing liquid, conditioner, shampoo or whatever it may have been.

Compost

All your organic waste can be composted (the bits that you don't feed to the chickens, the cats and the dogs, that is), although it's best not to put cheese or meat on the compost heap as this is likely to attract rats. If you don't have a garden, investigate whether your local council runs a composting scheme; organic waste now often forms part of kerbside collections. If you do have a garden, then well-worked and rotted compost is worth its weight in gold. If you make too much compost for your needs, try selling or giving away the remainder (put it on Freecycle and you will have people knocking down the front door). For a gardening friend, a big bag of compost would be a perfect birthday present (though probably only for someone you know very, very well).

Recycling

Can your waste be turned into something else? The biggest impact on reducing your household waste is through recycling. Pretty much everyone is aware that aluminium cans, paper, glass and plastic can be recycled. Contact your local council to find out what else they will accept – some recycling plants, for example, can now recycle the dreaded Tetrapaks, a great step forward. Batteries should never be thrown away into landfill as they contain poisonous metals and chemicals that will leach out into the environment, and the same goes for old mobile phones, computers and other technological items: shops will sometimes take these back, or your council will tell you how to dispose of them safely. You might even be able to get cash for some of them.

People are recycling things in ever more interesting and creative ways. Wool is reclaimed from old sweaters and knitted into funky new garments. Beer bottles are cut down to make attractive drinking-glasses. Circuit boards become mouse-mats and book-covers. Plastic bottles are melted down, spun into thread and woven into strong ruck-sacks or soft fleece jackets; plastic cups become pencils. Elephant dung is made into paper. Rubber car tyres are made into sandals, pencil cases and satchels. Old floorboards have even been made into guitars and violins. Truly, one person's waste is another's goldmine. In the world of self-sufficiency, this is inspirational.

CHAPTER TWELVE

Harnessing Renewable Energy

O UR PLANET IS FULL OF energy. Sunlight, wind, tides, waves, weather – we could power our energy needs cleanly and for ever, if only we could overcome the problems of collection and storage. Almost everyone is aware that fossil fuels, while providing us with an easily accessible store of energy, also produce the CO_2 emissions, along with other pollutants, that are responsible for heating up the planet. Scientists and governments now agree that CO_2 levels in the atmosphere are reaching dangerous levels and that our reliance on fossil fuels must diminish drastically. Renewable energy (once it has been installed) does not pollute and will not run out. On a large scale, it will undoubtedly have to form part of the way forward for human beings across the planet; but on a small scale, renewables can play an important and rewarding part in a self-sufficient lifestyle.

With the technology available today, 'renewables' refers principally to solar, wind and hydro (water) power. The main problem – on any scale – with renewables is their sporadic nature. At night the sun doesn't shine; at times the wind doesn't blow. Whether we're talking on a country-wide level or in terms of a smallholding, it's no good if the electricity cuts out at midday because the wind suddenly drops. Some energy can be stored in batteries for use when the source quits, but energy storage is inefficient and difficult on a large scale. For this reason, the best way to make the most of renewable energy is to combine various sources rather than relying on any one source. This means more solar in the summer for obvious reasons, more wind in the winter, some hydro thrown into the mix too if you live near a water source. A household with a good bank of batteries could live off-grid in this way; a whole country could go some way to meeting its power needs provided it didn't switch off its fossil-fuel power stations altogether: some reliable source of power is almost always going to be needed there in the background for when the renewables don't produce enough.

This chapter isn't going to tell you how to go off-grid; there's simply not enough space. Instead it aims to give you a basic idea of how you can use renewable energy in a pick-and-mix way to boost your self-sufficiency, using what works for you on your site and according to your needs, whether you have a small urban back garden, an allotment or a rural smallholding.

Essentially, renewables are used for two purposes: electricity and heat. Solar energy provides both, but by different means – photovoltaic cells for electricity and thermal panels for hot water. Wind turbines produce electricity, as does hydro power. For the smallholder, wood can be (but isn't always) a sustainable source of heat.

ELECTRICITY

A few points before we get going. First, don't think only about *generating* your own electricity: think about *saving* it. Turn lights off, fit low-energy bulbs, never leave appliances on standby, don't over-fill the kettle, use energy-efficient appliances, and don't run the washing machine half-empty. Secondly, if you are inspired by some of the ideas in this chapter to generate your own electricity, remember to be safe: care should always be used when handling electricity and electrical equipment. And if you plan to erect anything such as solar panels on your roof or a wind turbine in your field, check first with your local council to see if planning permission is need or any other regulation needs satisfying.

Solar

If money were no object, or if the UK government offered the kind of incentives available in a number of other European countries, then installing an array of photovoltaic (PV) panels on your south-facing roof to generate all the electricity your household required would be an attractive option, either to take you off-grid entirely (using batteries to store the energy your panels generated, so your lights didn't go out when the sun went down) or to remain connected and sell your surplus energy production back into the grid. Sadly, for most people money is an obstacle and this set-up is probably not going to be a serious option, although the costs of photovoltaics are coming down all the time. There are some grants available, though, so it could be worth checking for them in your area.

Small-scale solar energy is very useful in self-sufficiency when it is used to power a range of standalone devices. Low-power PV panels can be bought relatively cheaply and a single small panel measuring around 40 × 30cm/16 × 12in will trickle-feed the 12V car battery with which you run your electric livestock fencing – constantly replenishing the energy store and freeing you from the daily fear that the battery will die on you. No more living with that constant niggling worry that the pigs will get into the hen run, the ram in amongst the sheep, or the goats into the veg patch!

Photovoltaic cells are also used in solar lighting. Solar garden lights are widely available in many different shapes and sizes. A small PV panel collects the solar energy during the day, which is stored in rechargeable (often AA) batteries and then used to run the light at night time; a sensor detects the light level dropping as dusk approaches and switches the light on automatically. These garden lights tend to be useful as path markers but don't give a huge amount of light. More useful, as more powerful, are shed lights, in which a small solar panel is fixed to the side or roof of a shed – or barn or stable or greenhouse – and the energy generated runs a bulb inside the shed, or wherever needed. These are useful as lights, of course, but perhaps of even more interest in a self-sufficiency context is their potential as a source of heat. Such a bulb can be used to provide warmth for egg incubation and for just-hatched chicks; homemade wine can be started off and its temperature kept constant; in the potting shed seeds can be encouraged to germinate and seedlings to grow; and orphan lambs, kittens or puppies can be kept warm and cosy at night.

Wind

As with solar energy, to power your entire house you would need a large-scale, expensive installation, in this case a wind turbine mounted on a very tall pole, preferably on your own rural plot. Not impossible, but not practical for the majority of people, and certainly not for those living in towns. The fad for individual small wind turbines on residential streets that sprang up a few years ago, however well intentioned, was misplaced, because the wind down at house level is gusty and turbulent, making it hard to harness and next to useless for the purpose of electricity generation.

Small wind turbines are available to buy that can charge a 12V battery in the same way as solar, but these are more expensive than PV panels and less efficient.

Micro-hydro

This is obviously very site-specific, but many smallholdings do have a stream or river running through the property – and this can be used not only for watering livestock and the land but as a source of power. To generate a serious amount of electricity you need a 'head' of water – a good 10m/33ft drop – but properties with their own waterfall are even more rare and sought-after than those with their own stream. For our purposes, we can confine ourselves to using the simple flow of the stream to generate energy to trickle-charge our usual hard-working 12V battery.

In fact there are two ways of using the power of water: to generate electricity, or as a source of mechanical power. Traditional watermills used mechanical power, harnessing the vast, slow strength of a river flow to turn a millwheel, the power from which would be transferred by means of a system of gears, shafts and cogs to turn the grindstones. Nowadays water is more usually used to generate electricity (hydro-electric power).

Hydro-electric power is satisfyingly simple in principle: blades are made to spin by being dipped into running or falling water (think of turning a windmill upside down and putting the sails into the stream); the blades spin a rod; the rod is connected to a generator to make power. Making electricity in this way is clean and efficient, once the power plant has been built (bearing in mind flooded valleys and diverted and overused watercourses), and hydro-electric power represents about 20 per cent of the world's electrical output.

On a self-sufficiency level, it's not difficult to home-make a simple turbine to harness the power of a stream and turn it into electricity. All you need is a largish propeller (fairly simple to make out of wood), a rod, an alternator from a car (breakers are a good place to look, as are second-hand parts stockists online or the back of the local paper), a switch (again you can salvage the ignition switch from a broken car) and a small light or gauge. The propeller is mounted on a frame in the stream so that the fins touch the surface and spin. The rod is connected to the propeller and comes to the bank, where it slots into the alternator. The switch is to turn it on and off, and the light or gauge to make sure it's charging. In a car, the alternator's job is to generate the power that recharges the battery, so this is what we'll use it for here, connecting it to our 12V battery – free power for your electric fencing! (There are plenty of online sources available for any-one interested in pursuing the idea of a homemade turbine.)

HEAT

Renewables can be used in two ways for heat generation: for heating water (solar) and for heating space (wood). The two can also be combined in a neat and satisfying way.

Solar

Solar thermal panels for hot water are what most people think of when they think of solar power, and are a very different – a simpler and cheaper – kind of technology than photovoltaics. Have you ever picked up a hose that's been lying on the ground in the sun all day and felt the temperature of the water that trickles out of it? Hot! And that's exactly what solar collectors are: insulated panels containing tubes full of water (or water plus anti-freeze) that absorb the heat from the sun. Set them up on a south-facing roof or piece of ground, and let the sun do its work: in Britain, a solar panel system can provide 80–90 per cent of a household's hot water in summer, 40–50 per cent in spring and autumn, and 10–15 per cent in winter. Over a year that can add up to about half your hot water needs.

There are two principal types of solar hot-water systems, passive and active. In a passive system there are no moving parts (and there-fore less can go wrong): a storage tank and a solar panel are mounted on the roof, and the water heated by the panel moves round the system naturally (because heat rises), being gravity-fed into the house. An active system is slightly more complex, with the fluid being circulated through the panel by a pump; the storage tank can therefore be inside the house rather than on the roof, with obvious advantages. This system often uses a heat exchanger (a copper coil inside the hot-water cylinder) to transfer heat from the solar-heated water to the domestic hot water, and this allows the circulating fluid to be a mixture of water and anti-freeze, meaning that these panels can be used even when tem-peratures go below freezing. In very cold areas, panels containing only water will need to be drained every winter. Needless to say, there are many variations on these themes, depending on such factors as climate, existing hot-water systems, roof design, and aesthetic priorities.

As for the solar collectors themselves, there are two main types: the traditional flat plate variety, comprising tubes embedded in a black sheet of metal, while the newer (and more expensive) evacuated tube collectors use water pipes encased in glass tubes with a vacuum between them, reducing heat loss and making them considerably more efficient.

For a self-sufficient home, solar thermal panels make a lot of sense. Numerous commercial systems exist and grants are often available for them. Payback time is generally well within the system's lifetime and solar thermal is certainly more financially viable than photovoltaic. Costs can be hugely reduced, however, by anyone with a bit of DIY experience – a solar collector is not that hard to build and even install, and can be an interesting project. The Internet abounds with detailed instructions, tales of personal experience, discussion forums and advice on how to use salvaged materials and so on. For example, the most basic homemade panel consists of an old radiator painted black and fitted in an insulated, glass-covered frame.

Because solar power can't supply all your hot water outside of summer time, you need to have a conventional water-heating system too – a gas- or oil-fired boiler, a wood-burner, or even an electric immersion heater. The pre-heated water from your solar panels will feed into your boiler, meaning that it has to work less hard to raise the water to the desired temperature, and reducing your energy bills. Solar power can be fitted easily into most existing hot-water systems, though it works better with a condensing boiler than a combi boiler and you may need to add a new hot-water cylinder for storage.

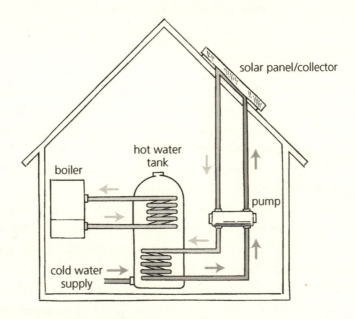

Domestic hot-water system using energy from a solar panel

If you don't want to go the whole hog and install solar panels, you can still use solar power during periods of hot weather in a way that's both fun and a footstep towards self-sufficiency – by making an outdoor solar shower. Camping and outdoor equipment suppliers sell camping showers, which are essentially thick black plastic bags with a tube and shower head attached; you lay or hang one of these in the sun and after a couple of hours you have hot water for a good shower. You can improve on this, with as many degrees of sophistication as you like, by fixing a long coil of black hosepipe to your roof (or run it up and down the side of your house), with one end attached to the outside tap and a shower head fixed to the other end. The variations on this are endless. Depending on your plumbing skills, you may want to think about mixing in a cold-water supply for those days when the sun is really hot. You may also want to construct a shower cabin for privacy, or you'll risk giving the neighbours something to talk about!

Wood

A blazing open fire on your living-room hearth may be unbeatably welcoming and attractive, but as a means of heating your home, it's a non-starter. Instead, consider a wood-burning stove, which is a far more efficient way of utilizing fire for warmth. Many wood-burners have glass fronts, meaning that you do get a chance to get lost in contemplation of the flickering flames.

Wood releases the same amount of CO_2 when it burns as it absorbed during its growth. For this reason, wood is considered a renewable fuel, and all the better if it comes from sustainable sources such as managed forests, or, of course, if it is wood that you yourself have coppiced – the ideal from a self-sufficiency point of view. For a clean burn, always use logs that are dry, well seasoned and preferably split.

A wood-burning stove with a back boiler will heat water that can be used for radiators in other rooms, meaning that a whole house can be heated with a single wood-burner. Highly efficient systems are now available, including built-in glass-fronted fireplaces with thermostatic controls. Stoves with flat tops can also of course be used for heating kettles and pans – and simmering that bean soup for three hours is less worryingly fuel-intensive once you pop it on top of your wood-burner. A system combining solar thermal panels with a wood-burner, using wood that you have sustainably harvested with your own hands from your own land, must be the ultimate in this area of self-sufficiency, and is a totally realizable dream. There are not many things you can say that about!

Resources

The following is a list of useful websites and published books that look in more detail at some of the topics covered in the book.

General

Fearnley-Whittingstall, Hugh, *The River Cottage Cookbook*, Collins, 2003

Friendly self-sufficient and countryside forums
  www.overthegate.co.uk and www.downsizer.net
Outdoor-lover's website, connecting people with the countryside
  www.countrylovers.co.uk
A great food website from the Good Food Channel
  www.uktv.co.uk/food
Recipes, support and opportunities from the Women's Institute
  www.thewi.org.uk

The Kitchen Garden

Buckingham, Alan, *Allotment Month by Month*, Dorling Kindersley, 2009
Diacono, Mark, *Veg Patch: River Cottage Handbook 4*, Bloomsbury, 2009
Flowerdew, Bob, *The No-work Garden: Getting the Most Out of Your Garden for the Least Amount of Work*, Kyle Cathie, 2004

Gear, Alan and Jackie, *Organic Gardening: The Whole Story*, Watkins, 2009

Guerra, Michael, *The Edible Container Garden: Fresh Food from Tiny Spaces*, Gaia, 2005

Liebreich, Karen, Jutta Wagner, Annette Wendland, *The Family Kitchen Garden*, Frances Lincoln, 2009

The perfect site for everything organic
www.OrganicCatalogue.com
Lively discussion forum about allotments and allotment holders
www.allotments4all.co.uk
Great site for seeds and gardening equipment
www.dobies.co.uk
Heirloom and heritage seeds
www.greenlivingtips.com/articles/130/1/Heirloom-and-heritage-seeds.html

The Home Baker

Miles, Hannah, *The Big Book of Cakes and Cookies*, Duncan Baird, 2009

Hand-cranked flour mill and wheat direct from the farm
www.browfarmwheatproducts.co.uk

The Home Dairy

Carroll, Ricki, *Home Cheese Making*, Storey, 2003

The Home Brewer

Berry, CJJ, *First Steps in Winemaking*, Special Interest Model Books, 2002

Nachel, Marty, *Homebrewing for Dummies*, John Wiley & Sons, 2008

Natural Solutions: Health, Beauty and the Home

Marrone, Margo, *The Organic Pharmacy*, Duncan Baird, 2009
Wong, James, *Grow your own drugs: Easy Recipes for Natural Remedies and Beauty Treats*, Collins, 2009

A great forum for all things domestic
  http://creativeliving.10.forumer.com

Arty Crafty Bits

Edwards, Lynne, *The Sampler Quilt Book*, David & Charles, 2002
Vaughan, Susie, *Handmade Baskets*, Search Press, 2006

Beautiful hand-carved wooden spoons
  www.crafty-owl.com/wooden-spoons.htm
Pyrography
  www.patrickfaleur.com/pyrography
Stylish sewing source
  www.burdastyle.com

Livestock, Meat Preparation and Basic Butchery

Ball, Ian, *Sea Fishing Properly Explained*, Right Way, 2008
Beattie, Rob, *101 Golden Rules of Fishing*, Ebury, 2007
Case, Andy, *Starting with Pigs*, Broad Leys, 2001
Fearnley-Whittingstall, Hugh, *The River Cottage Meat Book*, Hodder and Stoughton, 2008
Thear, Katie, *Starting with Chickens*, Broad Leys, 1999

The River Cottage website – a friendly forum with lots of information
  www.rivercottage.net
Smallholding suppliers, everything from a pig ark to a cheese press
  www.ascott.biz
  www.molevalleyfarmers.com

Smallholding and self-sufficiency experience days and courses with
    Debbie and Simon Dawson
    www.hiddenvalleypigs.co.uk/courses.html
Eglu and chicken houses
    www.CotswoldChickens.com

Curing and Preserving

Davies, Maynard, *Maynard: Adventures of a Bacon Curer*, Merlin
    Unwin, 2003
Erlandson, Keith, *Home Smoking and Curing*, Vermilion, 1994
Warren, Piers, *How to Store your Garden Produce: The Key to Self-
    Sufficiency*, Green Books, 2008

A complete sausage-making site
    www.sausagemaking.org
Sausage-making and kitchen equipment
    www.kenwood.co.uk
Stunning hot and cold home smokers
    www.bradleysmoker.co.uk
Pig processing, butchery and preserving courses with Debbie and
    Simon Dawson
    www.hiddenvalleypigs.co.uk/courses.html

Foraging

Fearnley-Whittingstall, Hugh, *A Cook on the Wild Side*, Boxtree, 1997
Mabey, Richard, *Food for Free*, Collins, 2007
Pegler, David, *The Easy Edible Mushroom Guide*, Aurum, 1999

Basic, but none the less informative introduction to mushrooms
http://academic.evergreen.edu/projects/mushrooms/introm/index.htm
Brilliant wild food site
    www.wildmanwildfood.com

Reduce, Reuse, Recycle

Scott, Nicky, *Reduce, Reuse, Recycle! An Easy Household Guide*, Green
Books, 2004

Online auctions
www.ebay.co.uk
A free 'give and take' site
www.freecycle.org

Harnessing Renewable Energy

Daniek, Michel, *Do It Yourself: 12 Volt Solar Power*, Permanent
Publications, 2007
Rosen, Nick, *How to Live Off-Grid*, Bantam, 2008
Strawbridge, Dick, *It's Not Easy Being Green: One Family's Journey
Towards Eco-Friendly Living*, Cheek, 2009
Yarrow, Joanna, *Eco-Logical: All the Facts and Figures, Pros and Cons
you Need to Make up your Mind*, Duncan Baird, 2009

Free advice about energy efficiency in the home, and local grants
www.energysavingtrust.org.uk
UK grant scheme supporting domestic and larger-scale renewable
energy systems
www.lowcarbonbuildings.org.uk
The Solar Trade Association can provide lists of suppliers and installers
of solar water-heating systems
www.solartradeassociation.org.uk
The Institute of Domestic Heating and Environmental Engineers
provides advice on the installation and maintenance of safe,
efficient central heating systems
www.idhee.org.uk
Details of suppliers and information on wood and wood-fuel heating
(including logs, pellets and wood chip)
www.logpile.co.uk and www.woodfuelwales.org.uk

Index